Layers of Learning Geography

People & Planet
A Family-Style Geography Program

Michelle Copher and Karen Loutzenhiser

Published by HooDoo Publishing
United States of America
© 2023 Layers of Learning

ISBN 978-1-7360624-7-0

(Grilled Cheese BTN Font) © Fontdiner - www.fontdiner.com

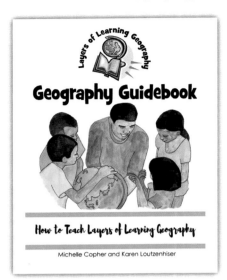

Geography Guidebook: How to Teach Layers of Learning Geography

Learn the philosophy behind Layers of Learning Geography, how to plan a unit, how to schedule your learning, and how to assess and grade.

This is a valuable and inexpensive PDF guide to using the curriculum effectively.

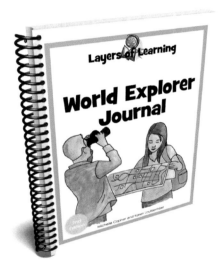

World Explorer Journal

The World Explorer Journal is a record of your learning about the world. You add maps, lists, paragraphs, illustrations, and foldables as you complete the Layers of Learning Geography courses.

Printable Packs

If you purchased this book directly from Layers of Learning, your Printable Packs were included on your receipt. If you purchased it elsewhere you can retrieve your free Printable Packs with the coupon code: FREEPACK.

Scan the QR code to visit the People & Planet Resources page.

How To Use This Course

People & Planet is a family-style program, which means your whole family, from ages six to eighteen and beyond, can use the program together. The activities are meant to be a family affair, with individual expectations being tailored to the ages and abilities of each child. We also encourage you to share completed individual work like reports, posters, and projects.

Like all of Layers of Learning, *People & Planet* is a pick-and-choose curriculum; you don't need to complete everything in the book. Instead, browse through and choose the library books, Explorations, and sidebars that appeal to you and are appropriate for your kids. Generally, you will choose one or two Explorations to do together each week.

Scheduling

Each unit within this book is designed to last about a month and then be repeated in subsequent years, but the exact schedule and timing are completely up to you. If your kids are engaged and enthusiastic about a topic, feel free to carry on for a little while longer.

In *People & Planet*, each Exploration is one complete lesson plan. The exact length of each one varies and depends on your needs, the ages of the students, and how absorbed in a lesson you get. However, you can generally plan on one hour per lesson. Geography should be a weekly part of your educational plan.

Sidebars

You will find sidebars throughout *People & Planet*. The sidebars are little snippets of information you can read aloud while children work, things you can touch on during a Morning Meeting, or springboards for lessons you create on your own. Do as many or as few as you like.

Printable Packs

This curriculum includes printables. For printing convenience and to keep your costs down, the printables are found in digital Printable Packs that you can retrieve from the Layers of Learning catalog. Find the product page for this book and scroll down to the link to download the Printable Pack. If you purchased this book directly from Layers of Learning, you will see a link to download the printables on your receipt. Otherwise, use the coupon code FREEPACK at checkout to get the Printable Packs for free.

Resources

Every unit comes with its own YouTube playlist of videos to use as enrichment or as video lectures to supplement lessons. The videos can be played during a lesson. Frequently, Explorations include instructions to watch a video. The videos are curated in these playlists.

On the Layers of Learning website, you can also find links to websites and resources that are especially useful when teaching each unit. The web links are located under "Resources" on the main menu.

At Layers of Learning, we believe learning is about exploring and we invite you to joyfully explore with us. In the words of Robert Louis Stevenson, "The world is so full of a number of things, I'm sure we should all be as happy as kings."

Table of Contents

Unit Overview

Key Concepts:
- The aims of geography include understanding mapping, the natural world, culture, and countries.
- A globe is a 3-D model of the earth that shows the correct shapes and relative sizes of the continents and oceans as well as their placement.
- A map is a diagram that gives lots of information about places. There are maps of the entire planet, countries, regions, states, cities, and even specific landmarks. They can help us navigate and can include lots of details.

Vocabulary:
- Geography
- Map
- Globe
- Equator
- Prime Meridian
- Hemisphere
- Hemi-
- Demi-
- Semi-
- Cardinal directions
- Compass rose
- Map key
- Map scale
- Continent
- Ocean

Important Places:
- North America
- South America
- Asia
- Africa
- Europe
- Australia
- Antarctica
- Pacific Ocean
- Indian Ocean
- Atlantic Ocean
- Arctic Ocean
- Southern Ocean

MAPS & GLOBES

Geography is the study of the planet Earth and the people who live on it. It includes the study of landscapes, continents, oceans, and environments, as well as cultures, governments, and the relationship between people and the planet. In short, geography encompasses everything about the earth as it is right now.

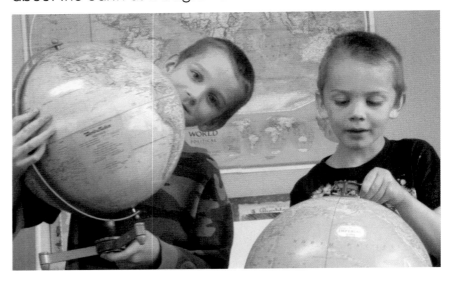

Maps are a big part of geography because they are how we conceptualize and organize much of the information about people's interactions with the land they live on. On a map, we can show locations, patterns, and demographics. With a map, we can see why people live where they live, why they go to war over the land, and how the land both supports and challenges the people.

Mapping skills include identifying landforms, showing time zones, interpreting latitude and longitude, understanding cardinal directions, and navigating. It also involves making and reading maps and atlases as well as memorizing countries, capitals, and other landmarks.

Step I: Library List

Choose books from your library that go with this topic. Here's a list of some favorites and also a list of search terms so you can utilize what your library offers. Read the books with your kids and/or assign them some to read independently. It is from these books your kids will learn most of the facts they need from this unit.

Search for: geography, maps, globes

☺ ☺ ☺*Geography of the World* by DK. Read "How to Use

This Book" and "The Physical World" on pages 8-11.

☺ ☺ ☻*Maps and Globes* by Jack Knowlton. A terrific picture book to read aloud and introduce this unit.

☺ ☺ ☻*My World and Globe* by Ira Wolf. A great overview of geography, maps, and globes. Comes with an inflatable globe and stickers you can add to the globe.

☺*Geography* by Ari Brennan. Explains what the study of geography is all about.

☺*Me on the Map* by Joan Sweeney. An introduction to maps for young kids.

☺*Henry's Map* by David Elliot. This is a picture book of a pig named Henry who believes everything has a place and makes a map to help the animals stay where they belong.

☺*Map My Room* by Jennifer Boothroyd. A boy is going on vacation and needs a friend to watch his hamster, so he makes a map of his room. Also check out *Map My Neighborhood* by the same author.

☺*Follow That Map!* by Scot Ritchie. Kids must search the pages of this picture book to find the clues. As they read, they learn about a compass rose, keys, scale, and more.

☺*Maps & Mapping* by Deborah Chancellor. A beginner's guide to maps and how to make them. Includes activities.

☺ ☻*Maps* by Aleksandra Mizielinska and Daniel Mizielinski. This is a book of hand-drawn and illustrated maps of places all over the world and all sorts of things. Have fun browsing.

☺ ☻*The Last Map* by John Newsom. A chapter book adventure of a boy and his cousin who go to summer camp, find a map, and must decipher clues to solve a mystery.

☺ ☻*How To Read Maps* by Arcturus Publishing. Full-color maps and images teach kids the basics of map reading. Includes a large fold-out map of the world.

☻*Atlas of the Invisible* by James Cheshire and Oliver Uberti. A book to get your kids excited about the potential of maps and how they can be used to tell a story. Want to see a map of the slave trade? Of happiness? An engrossing book to read cover to cover or just browse.

☻*How to Lie with Maps* by Mark Monmonier. Maps can be used as propaganda or to change perceptions. They can even be used unwittingly to deceive people about reality.

☻*Maphead: Charting the Wide, Weird World of*

On the Web

For videos, web pages, games, and more to add to this unit, visit the People & Planet Resources at Layers-of-Learning.com.

You will find a link to video play lists, web links, and more.

Bookworms

If you're looking for a family read-aloud, we'd like to suggest this one.

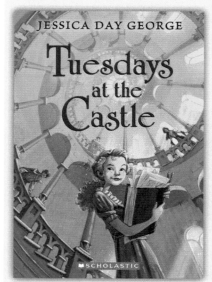

Tuesdays at the Castle by Jessica Day George includes a magical castle with moving hallways and disappearing rooms. The princess makes an atlas of the castle so the people who live there can find their way around.

Geography Wonks by Ken Jennings. If you think you know about maps, read this book for a map lover's feast of even more map lore.

Step 2: Explore

Choose a few hands-on Explorations from this section to work on as a family. They should be appealing activities that will create mental hooks so your kids remember the information in the unit. Save the rest of the Explorations for the next time you do this unit in four years when your kids are older. You can also read the sidebars together and explore some little rabbit trails.

This unit includes printables. See the introduction for instructions on retrieving your Printable Pack.

What Is Geography?

☺ ☺ ☺EXPLORATION: Building Your World Explorer Journal
For this activity, you will need:

- World Explorer Journal or a blank spiral notebook
- Card stock, any colors you like
- Colored pencils
- Colored markers
- School glue or craft clue
- Glue stick
- Foam brush
- Glitter, stickers, sequins, or other decorative craft items that you like (optional)
- Images printed from the internet (optional)
- Video about geography. You can find video recommendations in the YouTube Playlist for this unit.

As you learn about **geography,** you will color maps, make foldables, color or draw illustrations, and write information in your World Explorer Journal. It will take you four years to completely fill it in. When it is done, you will have written your own personal encyclopedia about the world, its people, and its countries.

You can purchase a World Explorer Journal from Layers of Learning or you can use a spiral bound notebook or art sketch pad with blank pages.

1. If you are making your own World Explorer Journal, label the first page "Table of Contents" and save three pages at the front for a table of contents. Then, at the top of the fourth page, write "Maps & Globes" and write

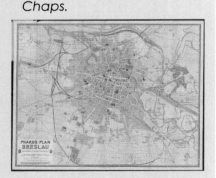

a number 4 down in the bottom left-hand corner. You will number your pages from 4, but you don't need to number them all right now; you can number them as you build the journal, day by day.

2. Put "Maps & Globes" and the page number in your table of contents. You will always use the title of each geography unit as the title in your World Explorer Journal and add it to your table of contents.

3. With either your purchased World Explorer Journal or your blank spiral notebook, you can design a cover if you'd like. Choose a color of card stock and add the title "World Explorer Journal." Use colored pens, stickers, pieces of paper cut into shapes, glitter, or other craft items to design your cover. While you work on your cover, watch a video about the subject of geography and what it is.

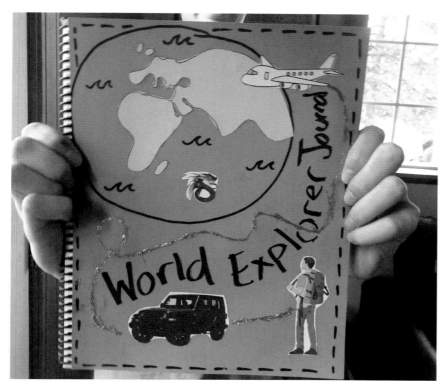

4. Once you have your cover design finished, spread school glue or craft glue on the cover of your World Explorer Notebook very thinly with a foam brush. Then carefully spread your paper cover over the cover of the notebook, making the paper nice and flat.

☺ ☺ ☺**EXPLORATION: Aims of Geography**
For this activity, you will need:

- "Aims of Geography" from the Printable Pack

Additional Layer

People build settlements and cities where there is good farmland and plenty of water, usually in the form of a river. Rivers begin in mountainous places where lots of rain and snow falls. They flow downhill, always in the lowest spot, until they reach the sea.

If you look at a map of the continent you live on, you will see that this is true.

Draw a map of an imaginary continent. Put mountains and rivers on your continent.

Where do you think the people on your continent would build the first city ever?

The first city ever is a cradle of civilization for your imaginary continent. You can learn more about cradles of civilization in *Ancient History: First Civilizations*.

Memorization Station

Geography: The study of planet Earth and the people who live on it

Map: A diagram representing a place and showing physical features like land, sea, and roads

Famous Folks

Ptolemy was an early Greek geographer, astronomer, and poet. He wrote *Geographia*, in which he compiled all that was known of the geography of the world in his day.

His maps weren't accurate, but were more complete than previous maps.

This is a world map that Ptolemy made in the second century and shows what the Greeks and Romans thought the world looked like.

Memorization Station

The aims of geography include understanding

- Mapping
- The natural world
- Culture
- Countries

- World Explorer Journal
- Scissors
- Glue stick
- Colored pencils or crayons
- Student atlas

The well-educated student of geography understands:

- **Mapping:** How to read maps and globes.
- **Natural World:** The physical characteristics of places and how humans are affected by and affect the natural world.
- **Culture:** The manners, customs, stories, rituals, dance, food, language, and dress of different people around the world.
- **Countries:** Human governments, countries, borders, population distributions, and economic systems.

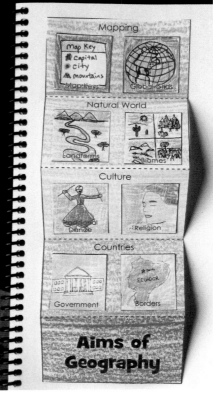

1. Discuss the aims of geography, as explained above.

2. Color the "Aims of Geography" printable.

3. Cut out the pieces on the solid lines.

4. Fold the large long rectangle accordion style. Glue the top box "Mapping" to the "Maps & Globes" page in your World Explorer Journal.

5. Decide which small picture boxes belong in each section of the accordion fold. Glue them into the correct spots in the gray dashed lines.

   - **Mapping: Global Grids, Map Keys**
   - **Natural World: Landforms, Biomes**
   - **Culture: Traditional Dance, Religion**
   - **Countries: Borders, Government**

6. Browse through a student atlas together and find examples of each of the aims of geography inside the student atlas.

☺ ☺ ☺**EXPLORATION: How To Color A Map**
For this activity, you will need:

- Black fine-tipped pen
- "How To Color A Map" from the Printable Pack or "How to Color a Map For Little Ones" if you have little ones who are not reading and writing well yet
- "Map Grading Rubric" from the Printable Pack
- Student atlas
- Colored pencils (or crayons for kids under 10)

Maps are a graphic tool used to convey information about places. Just like you can use a calendar and dating to talk about *when* things happened, maps are used to talk about *where* things happened. Maps are significantly more complicated than any dating system though. It is important that maps can be read by another person if you hope to convey any information.

When you complete maps in Layers of Learning, they should be neat, legible, and complete.

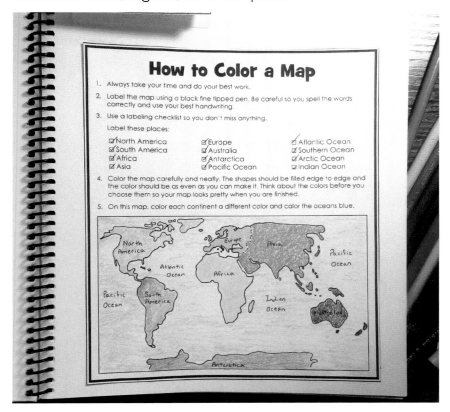

1. Read through the "Map Grading Rubric" together. This is how a map can be graded (when and if you choose to grade map work). Whether the map is actually graded or not, this rubric explains the standards you should expect.

2. Open a student atlas to a world map. Find each of the continent and ocean names. Observe how the words are easy to read, they don't overlap or crowd, and they

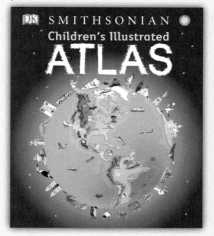
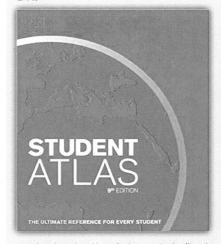

It is not necessary to grade every map your children complete, but if you want them to do their best work, announce that the map you are beginning will be graded and then give constructive feedback after it is finished.

Each child should be graded on his or her progress, not as compared to siblings, peers, or an abstract age level. If your child has done his best work ever, give the highest grade. If she has, for the first time, remembered to capitalize every place name, give the highest grade.

But if you have seen better work and you know your child was being lazy or hurried, then take points off.

When you do grade, these grades should be recorded and put into a grade book.

Additional Layer

Scientists use maps all the time. Astronomers map the stars. Geologists map rock formations or oil deposits. Biologists map ecosystems and species populations. Physicists map the curves of gravity and space. Meteorologists map weather patterns. Epidemiologists map outbreaks of disease.

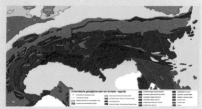

This is a geologic map of the Alps in Europe.

Can you think of other ways maps are used in science?

are spelled correctly. Evey place name begins with a capital letter.

3. Observe how the colors used on the map are pleasing and the color fills the shapes on the map neatly and completely.

4. ☻ ☻ Use the student atlas to label the "How To Color a Map" sheet. Read the instructions on the sheet and check off each item as you label it. Color it neatly.

   ☻ Young children who are not yet reading and writing can use the larger "How to Color a Map For Little Ones." Have them trace the letters, read them together, and then have them color the map as nicely as they can.

5. When you are finished labeling and coloring your map, cut it out around the heavy lines and glue it into your World Explorer Journal.

6. ☻ ☻ Grade the map using the "Map Grading Rubric" (for children 10 and up).

☻ ☻ ☻**EXPLORATION: Maps Are Useful**
For this activity, you will need:

- Blank paper and writing utensils
- Book or video about maps from the Library List or the YouTube playlist for this unit

1. In your mind, invent a place. It could be a park or a city block or an entire imaginary country. Draw a map of your place.

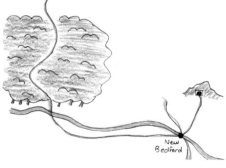

2. Write down directions, in words, of how to get from one place in your imaginary location to another. Give your description to another person, but do not let them see your map. As you read someone else's description, draw a map of what you picture in your mind based on what they wrote.

3. Compare the two maps, the one you drew and the one your reader drew. How important do you think maps are to understanding places?

4. Read a book or watch a video about maps.

😊 😊 😊 EXPLORATION: Roll-A-Culture

For this activity, you will need:

- Book or video about culture from the Library List or the YouTube playlist for this unit
- "Roll-A-Culture" from the Printable Pack
- Dice - one for each student
- World Explorer Journal
- Colored pencils or crayons

Culture includes all the things that make human societies different from each other. Religion, holidays, architectural styles, clothing, food, family structure, important values, and more make up culture. People in China place a high value on education and achievement while people in Mexico put an enormous value on family ties and spending lots of time together. These are aspects of each of these cultures that makes them unique. You will be learning about many cultures across the world in Layers of Learning Geography. Geography is more than just land and water; it also includes the people and other living things of our world.

1. Read a book or watch a video on culture.

2. Use the "Roll-A-Culture" from the Printable Pack to invent a unique culture for an imaginary people. First, roll a die to determine which kind of religion your people observe. Then roll for the biggest holiday of the year. Keep rolling until you have determined some major cultural aspects of your imaginary people.

3. In your World Explorer Journal, write down the definition of culture in your own words. Then, draw a picture of some imaginary people from your imaginary culture and make a list of the cultural details you rolled for them. You can add anything you rolled for and also add some of your own ideas.

Globes

😊 EXPLORATION: A Globe Is A Model

For this activity, you will need:

- Book or video about globes from this unit's Library List or YouTube playlist
- Toy cars, houses, people, planes, or trains
- Globe
- Wooden skewers
- Foam craft ball - between 6 and 8 inches (15 to 20 cm)
- Blue spray paint
- Green tempera paint and brushes

Fabulous Fact

Physical geography is the study of the earth itself, including plate tectonics, the structure of the earth, landforms, erosion, and the atmosphere. In this *People & Planet* course, you will learn physical geography as you learn about the continents and oceans.

Physical geography and earth science, which you can learn in the *Layers of Learning Science: Earth & Space* course, are close cousins. The difference is that in *Earth & Space* we will focus on the scientific processes, laws, and theories about Earth while in *People & Planet* we will learn how the way the Earth looks and functions right now affects people and how they live.

Teaching Tip

Reading a map requires abstract thinking, which kids typically develop between ages 7 and 9. Most younger kids won't yet understand that a map represents a real place, but they can still be introduced to maps and globes.

This is Unisphere. It was built for the 1964 World's Fair.

- Hook fasteners and school glue (if you want to hang the models from your ceiling)

Globes are round or spherical models of planet Earth. They show where the land and water are on the real planet.

1. Ahead of time, spray paint a foam ball blue for each child.

2. With toy cars, houses, people, and so on in front of you, explain the difference between the real thing and a toy model (a real car and a toy car, etc.). Discuss how a globe is a very tiny model of our very big planet.

3. Read a book or watch a video about globes.

4. Take time to explore your globe. Find the continents, oceans, North and South poles, and where you live.

5. Look out your window at the real world and explain that the real world is so big that we use models, called globes, to help us understand it. Compare where you live on the globe to what you see when you look outside of your window.

6. Poke a wooden skewer into a foam ball so the skewer can be used as a handle.

7. Using green paint, have the kids paint their own model of the earth on the foam balls. They can use the globe as a model, but don't worry about accuracy or precise borders and shapes.

8. Set the skewers in a vase or cup to let the paint dry.

9. Once it is dry, hang them from the ceiling. Dip a hook

fastener into paint, screw it into the foam, then let it dry. Hang it up with string or fishing line. Take it down at the end of the unit, or whenever you are ready.

☺ ☺ ☺EXPLORATION: Paper Maché Globe

For this activity, you will need:

- Round 11" (28 cm) balloon
- Newspaper strips
- Flour
- Water
- Large bowl
- Blue paint and brushes
- "Paper Maché Continents" from the Printable Pack (print this on green paper or have the kids color the continents)

Globes are models of the earth. They are too small to have much detail, but they do show the continents in their real relative sizes and shapes.

1. Blow up a balloon and tie it off. If you don't blow it up too much it will have a more rounded shape.

2. Make paper maché paste (1 c. boiling water, 1 c. flour, mixed well) and tear or cut newspapers into long strips.

3. Dip the paper into the paste and cover the whole balloon with the papers, criss-crossing each other. The more layers of paper you put on, the stronger it will be. Around three layers is about right. Let it dry for at least 24 hours.

Famous Folks

Eratosthenes was a Greek mathematician, astronomer, and poet who coined the term "geography" and was the first to make up the concept of latitude and longitude. He is considered the father of geography.

This is Eratosthenes teaching a student in Alexandria where he was the head librarian.

Bookworms

The Librarian Who Measured the Earth by Katherine Lasky is a picture book biography of Eratosthenes.

This book is aimed at ages 4 to 8, but read it to all of your kids. It combines history, geography, math, and libraries.

The analemma on a globe is a funny figure-8 shape, usually printed somewhere in the Pacific Ocean.

As the earth orbits the sun in an elliptical path, it gets closer and then further away, causing the speed of the earth to change slightly. The speed change makes the sun's position relative to the earth at midday change east to west slightly throughout the year. The analemma shows the side-to-side change as well as the seasonal change north to south.

You can see this change for yourself by pounding an upright stake into your yard. Every day for a year, at exactly the same time of day, mark the position of the end of the pole's shadow on the ground. At the end of the year you will have marked out a figure-8 pattern.

Writer's Workshop

If you could move the continents anywhere you wished in the world, where would they be? Would they all be connected? Would you put them all near to the equator or the poles? Would you have them more spread out or further away? Draw a sketch of your design and journal about your reasons.

4. Paint the whole globe blue. Let it dry.

5. Next, cut out the continents from the "Paper Maché Continents" and glue them on to your globe. If you'd like, you can paint the continents on instead of pasting them.

6. As a challenge for older kids, see if they can paint the continents without looking at a map. How well do they know the globe?

7. Hang your paper maché globes until this unit is over.

☺ ☺ ☺ **EXPLORATION: Draw Your Own Globe**
For this activity, you will need:

- Balloons - white or light blue
- Markers in various colors
- Cardboard - cut into 6" (15 cm) or larger squares.
- Knife or craft knife

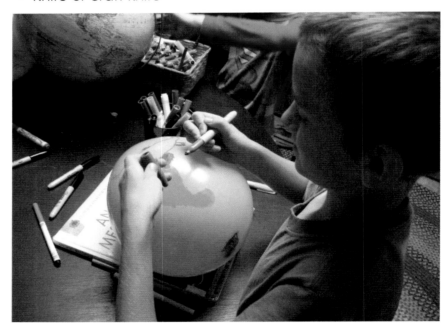

1. Read a book or watch a video about globes and how to use them.

2. Inflate a round balloon, one for each child and one for the mentor.

3. Make the balloon stand up by cutting an X in the middle of a piece of flat cardboard with a knife. Pull the tied spout of the balloon through the X so the balloon will stay in place on the cardboard.

4. Draw the continents on the balloon with a marker

5. Label continents and oceans.

6. Draw a mark for the North Pole and one for the South Pole.

7. Draw the **Equator**. Draw the **Prime Meridian**. Add other marks such as the Tropic of Cancer and the Tropic of Capricorn, the Arctic and Antarctic Circles, the International Dateline, and so on.

8. Find where your city is and mark it with a big star.

☺ ☺ ☺EXPLORATION: Globe Scavenger Hunt

For this activity you will need:

- Book or video about globes from the Library List or the YouTube playlist for this unit
- Globe
- "Globe Scavenger Hunt" from the Printable Pack

Globes don't just show the landmasses, oceans, and other features of Earth; they also include special marks that help us navigate the globe and organize it. These lines aren't visible on Earth, but we've added them to our globes to provide us with more information.

1. Read a book or watch a video about globes.

2. Fill in the "Globe Scavenger Hunt" printable with sketches of the things you find while searching a globe.

3. Take a few minutes to check answers and talk about the things you found.

4. You may also want to point out these features:

- Magnetic north versus true north
- The Arctic and Antarctic Circles have total darkness for part of the year.
- Tropic of Capricorn and Tropic of Cancer are the furthest south and furthest north the sun is ever directly overhead.
- The International Date Line and Prime Meridian are arbitrary lines used for dates and navigation.

Globe Scavenger Hunt

Find each of the items in the grid on a globe. Draw a sketch of each of the items in the boxes.

Continent	Ocean	Western Hemisphere
AFRICA	Indian Ocean	
South Pole	Equator	Tropic of Capricorn
	North Equator South	Tropic of Capricorn
Analemma	International Date Line	Key or Legend

Fabulous Fact

Magnetic north and true north are not the same thing.

Magnetic north is determined by Earth's magnetic field, which isn't exactly lined up with the poles.

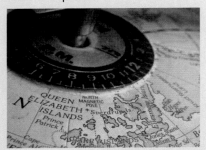

True north is determined by the axis around which the earth rotates. Look at the north or south of a globe. The true north or true south is right where the pole goes through the center of the globe. But nearby you should see a little mark, usually a + symbol labeled "north magnetic pole."

If you are at the latitudes that most people live in, the difference isn't enough to worry about, but near the poles, it is important.

Memorization Station

Hemisphere: half of a sphere

The prefixes hemi-, demi-, and semi- all mean half, but are used in different ways.

Hemi-: means one side or half, like a hemisphere on one side of the globe

Demi-: means less (or almost, but not quite); demigod means almost a god

Semi-: means partly, as in semi-civilized, meaning only partly civilized

- On one side of the International Date Line it is today and on the other side it is tomorrow. Which is which?
- Which direction does Earth spin in space?
- The grid on the globe can pinpoint any spot on earth.

☺ ☺ ☺ **EXPLORATION: Musical Globe Trotter**

For this activity, you will need:

- Globe
- Music
- Internet to look up places you see on the globe
- "Travel Brochure" from the Printable Pack.
- Colored pencils, markers, or crayons

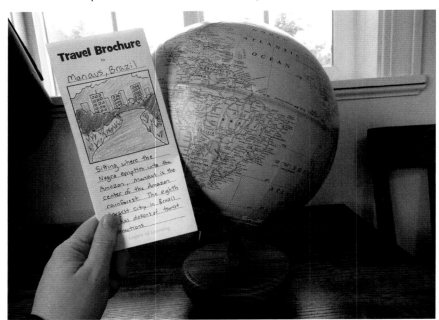

1. Pick some music to play while you play this game. Have one child spin the globe slowly while dragging a finger across the surface as the music plays.

2. When the music stops, stop the globe and take note of where your finger is pointing on the surface of the globe. Jot down the name of the place, then look it up online and find out a few facts about it.

3. Keep playing and looking up locations until you've found a number of fun locations to choose from.

4. Pick one of the places that intrigued you and create a "Travel Brochure" with facts and illustrations.

5. Fold the "Travel Brochure" accordion-style with the cover facing the front. Glue it into your World Explorer Journal.

☺ ☺ ☺ EXPLORATION: Hemispheres

For this activity, you will need:

- 2 apples (or more for snacking)
- Knife and cutting board
- Globe
- Video about the Prime Meridian and hemispheres from the YouTube playlist for this unit

"Hemi-" means half. A **hemisphere** is half of a sphere, or a ball shape. For convenience, people divide the earth into hemispheres in their imaginations. That way we can talk about the northern hemisphere or the eastern hemisphere and everyone knows what we mean.

1. On an apple, the stem and blossom scar on the opposite end can represent the poles of the earth. Cut one apple in half from pole to pole. You now have an east and west hemisphere.

2. On a globe find the Prime Meridian and the International Date Line. Notice that the Prime Meridian is assigned the number 0° longitude. If you travel west, the numbers climb from 0 to 180 on the opposite side of the globe.

   a. If you travel east, what happens to the numbers?

   b. Which continents are in the western hemisphere and which are in the east?

3. Cut the other apple in half along its "equator." This word comes from Latin and means equal.

4. Find the Equator on a globe. Above the Equator is the northern hemisphere. Below the Equator is the southern hemisphere.

5. Look at the numbers on the lines of latitude above and below the Equator. How are they counted and what is the highest number they get to?

6. Which continents are mostly in the northern hemisphere and which are mostly in the southern hemisphere? Which continents does the Equator cut through?

7. Could you cut an apple along any other axis besides the equator or through the poles? **(Yes, as a sphere you can cut it anywhere, but we use these lines to help us describe places on the globe.)**

8. Watch a video about the Prime Meridian and hemispheres while you finish eating your apple slices.

Additional Layer

Make planet Earth cookies during this unit.

First, make sugar cookie dough. Mix together these ingredients:

- 1 cup sugar
- 1 cup softened butter
- 1/2 cup milk
- 1 teaspoon vanilla extract
- 1 egg

Then stir in these ingredients:

- 1 teaspoon baking powder
- 1/4 teaspoon salt
- 3 1/2 cups flour

Divide the dough in half and add green food coloring to one half and blue food coloring to the other half.

Chill the dough for an hour.

Heat your oven to 350° F (180° C).

Take a little lump of green dough and a little lump of blue dough and smooth them together into a round shape to make oceans and continents. You can try to make the continents look like real ones or you can just let them be random.

Bake the cookies on a cookie sheet for 8 min.

Fabulous Fact

People make globes of the moon, other planets besides Earth, and the celestial sphere, or the stars in the night sky as they look from Earth.

This is a lunar globe, showing the surface of the moon.

Writer's Workshop

Imagine you are lost and stranded in the wilderness. Write about how you will get back.

Before you start writing decide on your setting, characters (this could include animals you encounter), and basic storyline.

Mapping your basic storyline could include determining how you got into your predicament, what challenges you will encounter along the way, and how you will finally solve the problem. Now craft a catchy opening sentence and see where it takes you.

"The sun was just coming up over the mountains when the ground started to rumble. . . shake. . . crack. . . I barely escaped . . ."

For help on crafting a story check out *Writer's Workshop: Fanciful Stories.*

☺ ☺ EXPLORATION: Where Is Earth In Space?

For this activity, you will need:

- Video or book about the location of Earth in the solar system from the Library List or the YouTube playlist for this unit (Atlases often have information about the location of Earth in space in the introductory pages at the front.)
- "Where Is Earth In Space?" from the Printable Pack
- Scissors
- Glue stick
- Colored pencils or crayons
- World Explorer Journal

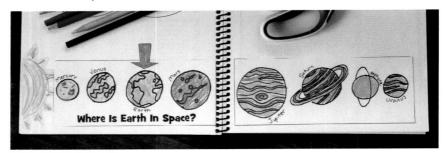

1. Read a book or watch a video about the location of Earth in the solar system.

2. Color the planets on the "Where Is Earth In Space?" printable. Color the arrow as well.

3. Name the planets and write the names next to each one.

4. On the bottom left hand side of the two-page spread in your World Explorer Journal, draw a partial sun peeking out from the side of the page. Make it nice and big.

5. Cut out the rectangles with the planet and the arrow. Glue the top rectangle with the title next to the sun and the second rectangle on the facing page to make a long row of planets. Glue the arrow so it is pointing at Earth.

☺ EXPLORATION: Where I Live

For this activity, you will need:

- Video or book about levels of location (house, city, state, nation, and so on) from the Library List or the YouTube playlist for this unit
- "Where I Live" from the Printable Pack (5 pages)
- Scissors
- Crayons or colored pencils
- Stapler

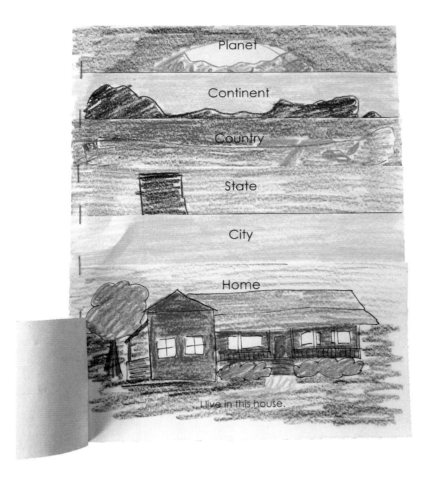

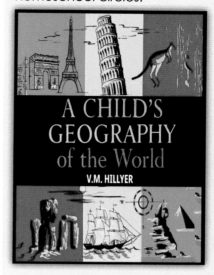
1. Read a book or watch a video about levels of location.

2. Cut apart the "Where I Live" book on the solid lines.

3. Arrange the pages so that the tallest sheet is in back and the shortest in front. Staple the pages together along the left side to make a book.

4. Read and color the pages one by one, filling it in with information about where you live. Talk about where you live in all of these places.

Maps

☺ ☺ ☺EXPLORATION: Sphere to Flat

For this activity, you will need:

- Orange for each student
- Markers
- Book or video about map projections from the Library List or this unit's YouTube playlist

It's not easy depicting a sphere on a flat surface. All flat maps of Earth are distorted for this reason.

Archaeologists have to learn mapmaking skills in order to do their jobs. They map their dig sites to show exactly how the ruins and artifacts were placed as they were found. They also map a region of archaeological sites in relation to one another.

Maps of a dig show how the artifacts and landscape were related.

All archaeologists can make a map of a dig site with a compass, pencil, and tape measure. But they also use laser theodolites, a tool used to measure angles and distances, and computers with mapping software, if they can afford these expensive pieces of equipment.

This is a map of the ruins of an ancient Byzantine Christian site that was dug up in the mid-1800s in Bosnia.

Teaching Tip

As you walk or drive around town, practice the cardinal directions with your kids.

"Which way are we driving now?"

"If I turn left at the next street which way will be facing?"

"Tell me which way to turn so we can get to the library."

1. Draw your own imaginary continents on your orange globe with a marker.

2. Peel an orange so the peel is in as few pieces as possible.

3. Try to flatten the orange peel on a surface. How well does the sphere shape translate into a flat shape? How did flattening the orange distort your continents?

4. Read a book or watch a video about map projections.

5. Eat orange slices while you learn.

☺ ☺ EXPLORATION: Map Projections

For this activity, you will need:

- Book or video about map projections from the Library List or YouTube playlist for this unit
- Transparent inflatable ball, balloon, or globe
- Permanent marker (optional)
- Light source, like a lamp
- Oversized sheet of paper

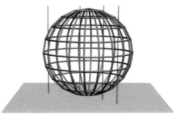

Conical   Cylindrical   Azimuthal

A map projection is a compromised way to show the round world on a flat map. There are three major types of map projections: conical, cylindrical, and azimuthal.

If you imagine a light inside of a globe shining outward and projecting the image of the map onto a surface, you get the idea of what a map projection is and why it would distort the globe's continents.

1. Read a book or watch a video about map projections. Discuss together which one you prefer or think is the most accurate picture of the globe.

2. Blow up a transparent ball. If it is blank, draw some continents on it with a permanent marker. In a darkened room, set the light next to the ball and shining toward it.

3. Hold a piece of paper on the opposite side of the ball from the light. Move the ball and the paper back and forth, nearer to and further from the light, until you get a sharp image of the continents on the paper. Observe the shapes projected on the paper. Are they distorted?

4. Change the shape of the paper by giving it a curve or making it into a cone shape. How are the continents distorted in each projection? No matter how hard we try, if we are drawing the round globe on a flat surface, there will be areas that are distorted in some way.

5. Draw a sketch of each type of projection (conical, cylindrical, and azimuthal) in your World Explorer Journal, label them, and write a caption about map projections and why flat maps can't perfectly show the round globe.

Deep Thoughts

If a continent or country is skewed on a map so it looks larger or smaller than it really is, do you think the depiction actually changes how people see that country or continent?

This is a map showing India in its actual position. When shifted up along the projection, you can see how much larger it appears. Can you imagine how much larger Greenland seems on a map than it actually is?

Do you think we sometimes equate the sizes we see with importance? For example, since India looks smaller on maps because of its proximity to the equator, do you think that makes people think it has less significance as well? Why or why not? Give examples.

Famous Folks

Al Idrisi was a famous 12th century cartographer who created a map of Eurasia and North Africa, including detailed descriptions of geographical features and cultural information.

Famous Folks

The Mercator projection is named after Flemish cartographer Gerardus Mercator.

In 1569, he invented a world map that made navigation easier by making the grid lines on the globe into perfect rectangles. His projection is still used in nautical charts.

But it has the side effect of massive distortion near the poles. Compare a Mercator projection of Greenland to how Greenland looks on your globe.

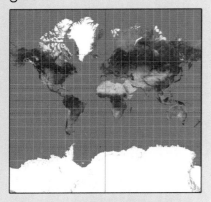

On the Mercator projection Greenland looks like it is bigger than Africa!

Antarctica looks absolutely huge because as you reach the poles the space needed is infinite.

☺ ☻ EXPLORATION: Globes Versus Maps

For this activity, you will need:

- Book or video about "globes" and one about "maps" from the Library List or this unit's YouTube playlist
- Globe
- World map
- World Explorer Journal

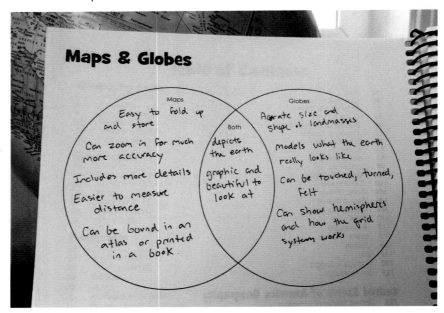

1. Read a book or watch a video about globes and then one about maps.

2. Point out the globe and the world map and that they represent the same planet, our Earth.

3. Find North America on the globe. Then find North America on the map. Emphasize that these are the same places. Repeat for the rest of the continents and the oceans.

4. Fill out the maps and globes Venn diagram in your World Explorer Journal. Under each heading write down the advantages or specifics of each one. Where they overlap, write down some things both maps and globes have in common.

☺ ☺ ☻ EXPLORATION: An Atlas Is A Book of Maps

For this activity, you will need:

- Student Atlas

1. Browse through a student atlas as a group.

   - Notice the introductory pages at the beginning and what they teach.

- Find the table of contents and demonstrate how to use it. How is your atlas organized?
- Notice the maps. Find the key. Find the scale. Find the title of the map.
- Find the coordinates on the map (the A, B, Cs along the top edge and the 1, 2, 3s down the side of the map). Show how the coordinates are used.
- What other things do the pages include besides just maps?
- Find the index or gazetteer at the back of the atlas. Demonstrate how to look up a place in the index. For example, Mumbai. The entries are arranged alphabetically. Once you find the entry, the first number is the page number in the atlas. Next you see a letter and number together. This is the coordinate on the map where Mumbai can be found. Go find it in your atlas.

2. Let each person take turns looking through the atlas to find a city, then challenge the others to locate the city using the index and the atlas.

☺ ☺ ☺ **EXPLORATION: My Own Map**
For this activity, you will need:

- Book or video about how maps are made from the Library List or the YouTube playlist for this unit
- Sheet of paper
- Colored pencils or crayons
- Tape measure

1. Read a book or watch a video about how maps are made.

2. Draw a map of your house and yard. You can also just map the inside of your house if you don't have a yard or if the weather isn't cooperating. You may need to measure distances or pace them off to make your map more accurate.

3. Include important landmarks like a tree fort, flower garden, sidewalk, or fire pit.

☺ ☺ ☺ **EXPLORATION: Cardinal Directions & the Compass**
For this activity, you will need:

- Book or video about cardinal directions or using a compass from the Library List or YouTube playlist for this unit
- Several maps or atlases
- "Compass Rose" from the Printable Pack

Fabulous Fact

There were two mythical figures named Atlas that have been associated with books of maps. The first was King Atlas who supposedly made the first celestial globe.

The second was a Greek mythological figure who was punished by Zeus and told he would forever have to hold the weight of the heavens on his back.

He was said to live in the west and the Atlas Mountains and Atlantic Ocean were both named after him.

Additional Layer

You might be interested in the mapping activities about ancient cities in Layers of Learning *Ancient History: First Civilizations*.

People & Planet

Teaching Tip

The mnemonic DOGS TAILS can help you remember the elements that every completely finished map should have:

Date
Orientation
Grid
Scale

Title
Author
Index
Legend
Sources

Memorization Station

Cardinal directions: the four main compass points - north, south, east, and west

Compass rose: a circle that is printed on a map that shows the points of a compass, or cardinal directions, in relation to the map

Additional Layer

A compass rose can be a work of art as can a map.

Decorate the compass rose you labeled to make it not only functional, but beautiful.

- "Boxing the Compass" and "Boxing the Compass Answers" from the Printable Pack (for older kids who are ready to move past the basic compass rose)
- Compass - handheld analog or an app on your phone
- Open grassy area, like a park or yard

Cardinal directions are north, south, east, and west. Unlike right and left, cardinal directions are absolutes. If you tell someone to turn left, they could be facing any direction. What is to your left may not be to their left. But if you tell them to turn to the west, then they can only be facing in one direction. Maps use a **compass rose** to show you which way each of the cardinal directions is in relation to the map.

1. Read a book or watch a video about cardinal directions or the compass rose.

2. Using a handheld compass, find out which way is north. The needle always points north.

3. Notice the numbers around the outside of the compass. Those are degree marks, the same as the degrees of a circle. One quarter of the way around a circle is 90 degrees. Halfway around is 180 degrees. Three quarters of the way around is 270 degrees. And all of the way around a circle is 360 degrees.

4. Practice facing north, south, east, and west. Once the kids have that down, practice facing northwest, northeast, southwest, and southeast.

5. Play Simon Says with the cardinal directions: "Simon says face north." "Simon says point to the southwest." Let different people be Simon a few times. Don't forget to catch people out by not saying "Simon says." If they move when Simon didn't say to, they are out for that round.

6. Find the compass rose on several different maps.

7. 😊 😊Write in the cardinal directions on the "Compass Rose" printable. Color it and add decorations if you like.

   😊 😊Older kids can "box the compass" by naming all 32 points of the compass rose.

   - Cardinal points: N, E, S, W
   - Inter-cardinal points: NE, SE, SW, NW
   - Half Points: NNE, ENE, ESE, SSE, SSW, WSW, WNW, NNW
   - Quarter points: NxE (read this "north by east"), NExN, NExE, ExN, ExS, SExE, SxE, SxW, SWxS, SWxW, WxS, WxN, NWxW, NWxN, NxW

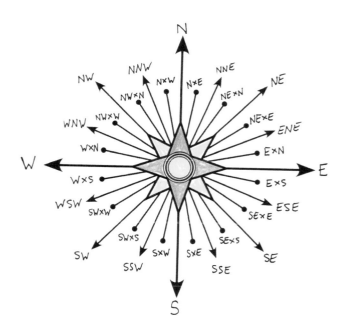

Teaching Tip

To help kids remember how to label a compass rose, teach them that the letters spell out "NEWS." North and South are up and down. West and East spells "we."

8. ☺ ☻Go outside in a large open space. Start in the southwest corner of the space.

9. Hold your compass flat in your hand. Orient your compass so the needle is lined up with north. Looking north from your current position, find a landmark in the distance; it should be something like a tree or a power pole. Walk 100 paces toward your landmark. (If you have a small space, you can cut down the number of paces, but all three times you walk paces it should be the same number.)

Expedition

For a challenge, get a topographical map of your area and do a real orienteering course.

Take the map, a compass, water, snacks, a cell phone, a first aid kit, and an experienced orienteering expert. Outdoorsy people, scouts, and military folks usually have orienteering training.

When orienteering, you must navigate using a map and compass from your starting point to a goal point. Some orienteering courses will have several check in points you have to pass along the way to the goal.

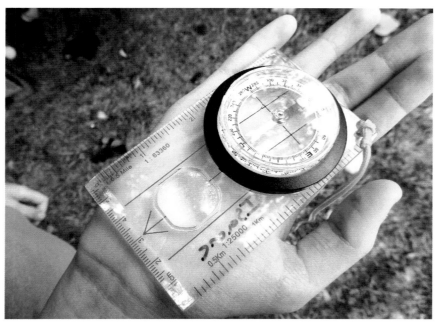

10. Line the compass needle up to the north, turn clockwise

Deep Thoughts

We now rely heavily on GPS (global positioning systems) more than we do on compasses. A compass uses magnetic fields. What does GPS use?

Should we throw away our compasses now that we have GPS or are there still some benefits to the tried-and-true map and compass methods of navigating?

What limits are there to GPS?

What limits are there to a compass?

Additional Layer

Think about the course you walked during the "Cardinal Directions & the Compass" Exploration. Which geometric shape did your path follow? What is the perimeter of your path? Can you determine the area of the shape you walked?

Deep Thoughts

A key is usually something that opens a lock or door. Can you think of any similarities between a key to a lock and a map key?

until you are facing 120 degrees on your compass. Which cardinal direction is that? Look for another landmark in the distance. Walk 100 paces toward your landmark.

11. With the compass needle lined up with north, turn clockwise until you are facing 240 degrees. Which cardinal direction is that? Find a landmark in the distance. Walk 100 paces toward your landmark.

12. You should be very close to where you started. How did you do?

☺ ☺ EXPLORATION: Map Key Scavenger Hunt

For this activity, you will need:

- Book or video about continents and oceans from this unit's Library List or YouTube playlist
- Map (any map, but bigger maps are easier to use as a group)
- Rewards - crackers, small candies, apple slices, or stickers

1. Read a book or watch a video about **map keys**.

2. Find the key on a map. What do the symbols mean? Together, as a group, find an example of each symbol on the map.

3. Next, the mentor calls out a symbol from the map and each child must find an example from the map. It cannot have been used before.

4. As each correct answer is given, give a reward. It could be a cracker, an apple slice, a small candy, or a sticker.

5. Repeat, calling out various symbols and practicing finding them.

☺ ☺ EXPLORATION: City Map

For this activity, you will need:

- Book or video about maps from the Library List or YouTube playlist for this unit
- "Map of ___ City" from the Printable Pack
- Colored pencils or crayons

1. Using the "Map of ___ City" printable, name your city and your roads. Everyone can have individual road names or you can all decide on the road names together as a group.

2. Fill in the compass rose in the key using cardinal directions (North, South, East, West).

3. Draw your own buildings on the map. If you'd like, you can use this activity to practice following directions, both "do as you are told" and cardinal directions. Say something like: "Put a store on the northwest corner of (intersection between roads)."

4. Make a key and add symbols to the map.

5. Color your map.

6. Practice giving directions to someone else as they drag their finger over the map. "Start at the school. Go west on Oak Street, then turn left on River Road."

☺ ☺ EXPLORATION: Pirate Island Map

For this activity, you will need:

- Book or video about map keys, symbols, and the compass rose from the Library List or YouTube playlist for this unit
- "Pirate Island" from the Printable Pack.
- Colored pencils or crayons

1. Read a book or watch a video about map keys, symbols, and the compass rose.

2. Come up with a fun name for an imaginary island, then fill in the name of your pirate island on the flag at the

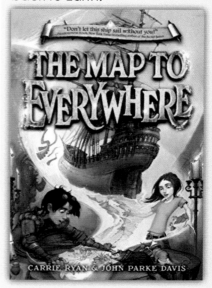
Memorization Station

Map key: the section on a map that explains the symbols, colors, or other markings; map keys can also be called legends

Map scale: a symbol on a map that shows a ratio of the distance on the map to the actual distance of the ground

Just like a globe and a map are small things that stand for something in the real world, the symbols on a map are also small things that stand for something real. A tiny triangle on a map may represent a very large mountain, for example.

Bookworms

City by David Macaulay is about how the Romans planned and built their cities.

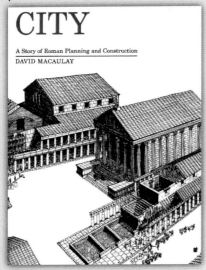

CITY

A Story of Roman Planning and Construction

DAVID MACAULAY

This book includes mapping, planning, and architecture.

This book will appeal to ages 8 and up.

Fabulous Fact

Treasure maps are popular in fictional stories, but there haven't been many actual instances of buried treasure being located by maps.

Captain Kidd was one pirate who famously buried treasure on Long Island in New York. He was arrested and killed before he could ever retrieve it though.

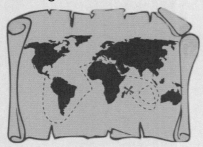

bottom of the "Pirate Island" map.

3. Color the symbols in the key. Label the compass rose.

4. Draw each of the symbols from the key at least once on your map.

5. Color the rest of your map any way you like.

6. Write directions on the back of your map so that the treasure can be found.

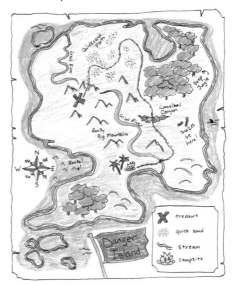

☺ ☻ EXPLORATION: Map Scales

For this activity, you will need:

- Book or video about map scales from the Library List or YouTube playlist for this unit
- 3-4 maps or atlases
- Ruler
- "Map of My Room" from the Printable Pack
- Tape measure

Maps always use a **map scale** to show how the map relates to actual distances. There are three ways a map can show a scale. Sometimes a map will have more than one of these. They are:

- Verbal method: 1 inch represents 1 mile
- Fractional method: 1: 1,000,000 (1 unit on the map equals 1 million units on the ground)
- Graphic method:

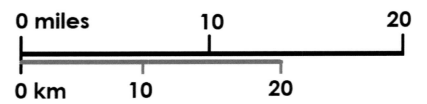

1. Read a book or watch a video about map scale.

2. Find the scale on several different maps or atlases.

3. Use a ruler to measure the distance between two cities or landmarks on a map. Using the map scale figure out how many miles (km) that would be on the ground.

4. Take careful measurements of the size of your bedroom.

5. Draw a map of your bedroom on the "Map of My Room" graph paper page. How many squares on the graph paper will equal 1 foot (1 meter) in your real-life bedroom?

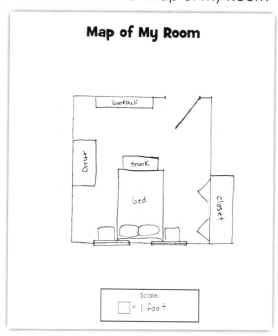

Map of My Room

6. Measure the placement of your door and window and put them on the map in the right places and at the right size.

7. Add in your bedroom furniture, making it to scale.

Continents & Oceans

Continents are large masses of land with ocean at least mostly surrounding them with borders that are generally agreed upon. In the English-speaking world, most people agree there are seven continents: Africa, Asia, Europe, Australia, North America, and South America. **Oceans** are massive bodies of saltwater that fill much of the planet. In most of the English-speaking world, there are five defined oceans: Atlantic, Indian, Southern, Pacific, and Arctic.

☺ ☺**EXPLORATION: Continents & Oceans Puzzle**
For this activity, you will need:

• Book or video about continents and oceans from this unit's Library List or YouTube playlist
• "The World" from the Printable Pack
• Scissors
• Colored pencils or crayons
• Glue stick

Begin to memorize the continents and oceans. Young children will need lots of practice before they have this down.

Additional Layer

The mathematical principle used to make map scales is proportion. If maps weren't made proportionally to the distances of the real places they represent, they would be completely useless in determining distances or finding your way.

Proportion is also an important concept in art and architecture. You can learn more about it in *Layers of Learning Art Beginnings: Principles of Design*.

Additional Layer

Architects, interior designers, and landscape designers all create scaled maps of their designs to show to customers and to be approved before any construction can happen. Find out what kind of an education you need if you want to go into one of these careers.

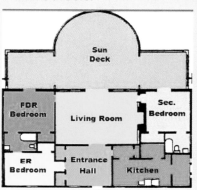

Memorization Station

Continent: large masses of land, mostly surrounded by water

Ocean: a continuous body of saltwater that is contained in an enormous basin on Earth's surface

On the Web

Sometimes we aren't very sure about the true sizes of things on our planet. You can go visit a website where you can select locations and compare them to other locations on Earth. For example, did you know that Australia is about the same size as the United States?

You'll find the link to this cool comparison website on the People and Planet Resources Page on Layers-of-Learning.com.

Additional Layer

Some scientists hypothesize that long ago all of the continents were once connected into one giant mass of land called Pangaea. We can see that our continents drift as the geologic plates shift. Learn more about Pangaea.

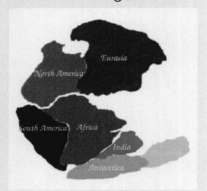

Pangaea, shared by Markko under CC BY-SA 3.0 license.

1. Read a book or watch a video about the continents and oceans.

2. Color "The World," making each continent a different color and the oceans all light blue.

3. Cut out the tags at the bottom of the printable and glue them in the correct locations.

4. Cut apart the map into six large puzzle pieces. Mix them up and put them back together to practice.

5. Name the continents and oceans several times during the activity as you color, cut, paste, and play with the puzzle.

☺ ☺ ☻**EXPLORATION: Pin The Continents On The World**

For this activity, you will need:

- Book or video about continents and oceans from the Library List or YouTube playlist for this unit
- World Map that you don't mind cutting up or the full-page continent printables from the Printable Pack
- Scissors
- Masking tape
- Large sheet of paper or poster board
- A blindfold

1. Read a book or watch a video about the continents and oceans.

2. Cut your world map up so each continent is apart from the others, or color and then cut out around the full-page continents pieces from the Printable Pack.

3. Draw a large oval on a big sheet of paper or poster board to represent the globe. Draw an Equator line

and a Prime Meridian line for reference in placing the continents.

4. Pick one continent and tape it on the globe in the right place. For older kids, make this a challenge by blindfolding them first. Take turns pinning each of the continents to the globe. You can peel the continents off and repeat as many times as you like.

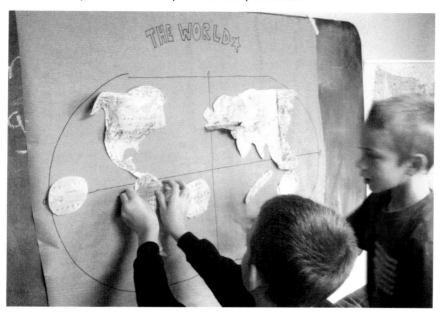

☺ ☺ EXPLORATION: Which Continent?

For this activity, you will need:

- Book or video about "globes" and one about "maps" from the Library List or YouTube playlist for this unit
- Full-page continent outlines from the Printable Pack
- Picture squares of things from each continent and the following page of descriptions, both from the Printable Pack (Print the two pages back to back, to put the descriptions of the images right on the back of the picture cards.)
- Scissors
- Colored pencils or crayons
- Glue stick

1. Color and then cut out each continent on the dashed line.

2. Once the continents are cut out, name them from memory as you place them on a table in their relative positions.

3. Cut apart the picture squares. One at a time, try to identify which continent each image comes from. The short descriptions and continent answers are on the

On the Web

There are lots more websites and learning links on the People and Planet Resources page on Layers-of-Learning. com. You'll find quiz games, articles, printables, and more.

Deep Thoughts

How do you think our world would be different if the continents were connected and there was just one ocean?

Would we be less diverse? Is less diversity good or bad?

Would we communicate differently?

Would our vacations and travel be different?

Would anyone sail across the whole ocean?

What role do you think air travel and the internet have played in how connected our world is?

On the Web

There are songs on YouTube to help you memorize the names of the continents and the oceans. Look some up and sing along as you point to the continents and memorize.

Unit Trivia Questions

1. Which part of a map shows symbols and what they mean?

   Map key (or legend)

2. If we divide the globe in half along the equator, what do we call each of the halves?

   The Northern hemisphere and the Southern hemisphere

3. Which imaginary line divides Earth into eastern and western hemispheres?

   The Prime Meridian

4. The circular symbol that shows directions on a map is called the _____ _____.

   Compass rose

5. Which of these are not cardinal directions? North, West, Left, Right

   Left, right

6. Name the seven continents.

   North America, South America, Europe, Asia, Africa, Australia, Antarctica

7. How many oceans are there on the earth? (Bonus points if you can name them!)

   Five - Pacific, Atlantic, Indian, Arctic, Southern

8. The physical features of the earth are more accurately shown on a _____ while a _____ is better for showing closer details and measuring distances.

   Globe, map

9. This compares the distance on a map to the actual distance on Earth.

   Map scale

back of the cards if you printed the pages double sided.

4. You can glue the cards to the continents or you can save them to review and practice again later.

Step 3: Show What You Know

During this unit, choose one of the assignments below to show what you have learned during the unit. Add this work to your Layers of Learning Notebook. You can also use this assignment to show your supervising teacher or your charter school as a sample of what you've been working on in your homeschool, if needed.

There are more ideas for writing assignments in the "Writer's Workshop" sidebars.

☺ ☺ Coloring or Narration Page

For this activity, you will need:

- "Maps & Globes" printable from the Printable Pack
- Crayons, or colored pencils

1. Depending on the age and ability of the child, choose either the "Maps & Globes" coloring sheet or the "Maps & Globes" narration page from the Printable Pack.

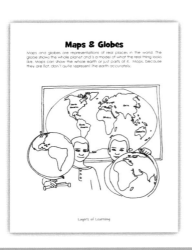

2. Younger kids can color the coloring sheet as you review some of the things you learned about during this unit. You might talk about the differences between maps and globes; map keys, map scales, and the compass rose; or list the continents and oceans. On the bottom of the coloring page, kids can write a sentence about what they learned. Very young children can explain their ideas orally while a parent writes for them.

3. Older kids can write about some of the concepts you learned on the narration page and color the picture as well.

4. Add this to the Geography section of your Layers of Learning Notebook.

☺ ☺ ☺ Map & Globe Challenge Game

For this activity, you will need:

- A big world map
- A globe

1. Call out the names of places and concepts you've learned during this unit and have kids race to be the first to touch them on either the map or the globe. You can include the continents, oceans, specific hemispheres, a map key, the Equator, and more.

☺ ☺ ☺ Big Book of Knowledge

For this activity, you will need:

- "Big Book of Knowledge: Maps & Globes" printable from the Printable Pack, printed on card stock
- Markers
- Big Book of Knowledge

1. Color, draw on, or write on the Big Book of Knowledge page. Record concepts, definitions, and facts you learned during this unit. It's a record of the things you learned and hope to remember. Add the page to your Big Book of Knowledge.

2. Use your Big Book of Knowledge regularly to help you review, quiz, or create games that will help you commit the things you've learned to memory.

Big Book of Knowledge

The Big Book of Knowledge is a book for you, the mentor, to use as a constant review of all of the things you're learning about. You can use it to quiz your kids or prepare tests or review games. Whenever you learn something in Layers of Learning that you want your kids to remember, add it to your Big Book of Knowledge.

Assemble your Big Book of Knowledge in a binder or with binder rings. Divide it into sections for each subject.

In the Printable Pack for this unit you will find a "Big Book of Knowledge" sheet. You can add this sheet to others you collect or create yourself as you progress through the Layers of Learning curriculum. Customize the Big Book of Knowledge to your family by adding facts and topics that you enjoyed exploring as you were learning.

Visit Layers of Learning online to find more information on how to assemble and use your own Big Book of Knowledge.

You will also find cover and section pages to print along with creative games to play with your Big Book of Knowledge to keep school, even the tests, fun!

Unit Overview

Key Concepts:
- Landforms are the physical features of earth shaped by wind, water, volcanism, and earthquakes. They include things like mountains, caves, waterfalls, bays, and islands.
- Africa is the second largest continent and has diverse landscapes and peoples.
- The world's largest desert, the Sahara, is in northern Africa.
- The Nile River is the longest river within Africa.
- Victoria Falls is a giant waterfall that is one of the world's seven natural wonders.
- Mt. Kilimanjaro is the highest peak in Africa.

Vocabulary:
- Landforms
- Erosion
- Physical map
- Safari
- Endemic
- Savanna
- Rainforest
- Desert
- Wetland
- Thematic map

Important Places:
- Nile River
- Great Rift Valley
- Mt. Kilimanjaro
- Sahara Desert
- Congo Basin
- Horn of Africa
- Cape of Good Hope
- Victoria Falls
- Strait of Gibraltar
- Red Sea

AFRICA

Africa, the second largest continent, lies across the equator and has diverse landscapes, from deserts and jungles to grassland plains and rugged mountains.

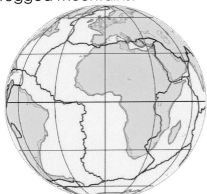

Most of Africa is on the African tectonic plate which extends halfway across the Atlantic Ocean. However, the eastern side of Africa lies on the Somali Plate. Where the two plates diverge, Africa is splitting; deep rift valleys, a series of lakes, and Africa's highest mountains have formed in that zone.

The world's largest desert, the Sahara, is in the northern part of Africa. The Sahara lies straddling the 30th parallel, a dry zone across the entire planet. On top of that, the Atlas Mountains in the west create a rain shadow, blocking what rain does travel inland from the Atlantic Ocean. Another desert zone, along the 30th southern parallel, includes the Kalahari, Karoo, and Namib deserts of Angola, Namibia, and South Africa.

The region of Africa that lies across the equator is much wetter and supports a dense rainforest and unique wildlife, including gorillas, elephants, giraffes, and okapi. In addition, the equatorial zone and areas to the north and south of it have vast grasslands that support many animals and human societies.

Africa is connected to the Eurasian landmasses, but only with a narrow piece of land across a forbidding desert. This means that much of the wildlife of Africa, as well as the human history and cultures of Africa, are unique to the continent. The people range from big city dwellers in places like Cairo and Kinshasa to tribal communities like the Hamar of Ethiopia and the Maasai of Kenya and Tanzania. Africa is a continent of diverse landscapes, wildlife, and peoples.

Step I: Library List

Choose books from your library that go with this topic. Here's a list of some favorites and also a list of search terms so you can utilize what your library offers. Read the books with your kids and/or assign them some to read independently. It is from these books your kids will learn most of the facts they need from this unit.

Search for: Africa, African folk tales, savanna, Sahara, African animals, African cuisine, landforms, latitude and longitude

☺ ☺ ☺*Geography of the World* by DK. Read "Africa" and "Peoples of Africa" on pages 204-207.

☺ ☺ ☺*Smithsonian Earth* by DK. More than 500 pages of gorgeous photographs and descriptions of Earth, including landforms and how they came to be.

☺*Goodnight Africa* by Marquez Rey Ramirez. Full-page illustrations highlight African animals as the sun goes down and they all say good night.

☺*Over In the Grasslands: On An African Savanna* by Marianne Berkes. Told in the same sing-song rhythm as "Over In the Meadow," this picture book takes the little reader on a counting adventure of African grasslands.

☺*The Seven Continents: Africa* by Zukiswa Wanner. This is a simple, but thorough, non-fiction book that introduces young children to African climates, plants, animals, history, and people living there today.

☺*My Africa Vacation* by Ozi Okaro. Little Arinze goes on vacation with his family, visiting ten different African countries along the way.

☺*Ashanti to Zulu* by Margaret Musgrove. An ABC book of cultures and ethnic groups of Africa. This book is a Caldecott Medal winner.

☺*U.S. Landforms* by Dana Meachan Rau. Readers take a tour though different regions of the United States and see deserts, mountains, geysers, and more.

☺*Landforms* by William B. Rice. An easy reader for young kids. Learn about canyons, climate, ridges, peaks, trenches, and more with full-color photographs and activities.

☺*Water Land: Land and Water Forms Around the World* by Christy Hale. A very simple book. Most pages have just one word. The pages are designed to contrast and coordinate. Lake, island. Bay, cape.

Family School Levels

The colored smilies in this unit help you choose the correct levels of books and activities for your child.

☺ = Ages 6-9
☺ = Ages 10-13
☺ = Ages 14-18

On the Web

For videos, web pages, games, and more to add to this unit, visit the People & Planet Resources at Layers-of-Learning.com.

You will find a link to video playlists, web links, and more.

Bookworms

If you're looking for a family read-aloud, we'd like to suggest this one.

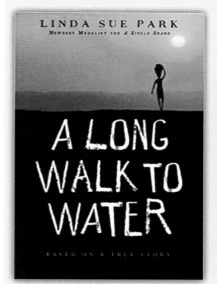

A Long Walk To Water by Linda Sue Park is about two children, Nya who must walk hours to a pond to fetch clean water and Salva who is displaced by war. This is a novel based on a true story.

Africa is the second largest continent and is home to 52 countries, 1,000 or so different languages, and about 800 million people. 10% of the world's population lives there.

Teaching Tip

African nations rely heavily on the land's physical characteristics. Within this unit, you'll be learning about landforms as well as studying the continent of Africa. Pay attention to the specific landforms you learn about and then find those landforms within Africa as you learn about them together.

Memorization Station

Begin to memorize the countries of Africa. It's not absolutely necessary to have every country down perfectly, but a great deal of familiarity is desired. When a person hears "Kenya" or "Sierra Leon," he or she should at least recognize that those countries are in Africa.

Geography songs are really helpful in memorization, as are quizzes and games. You can start each geography lesson by calling out a series of countries and having the kids race to find them on a map or globe for practice.

☺ ☺ *Geography From A to Z* by Jack Knowlton. Every letter of the alphabet is accompanied by a different type of landform. "G is for gulch." The illustrations are charming.

☺ ☺ *Geography: An Illustrated A-Z Glossary* by B.C. Lester Books. Similar to *Geography From A to Z*, each page is an illustration of a different landform. This book has slightly more information and explanations.

☺ ☺ *What Shapes the Land?* by Bobbie Kalman. Describes how landforms are made and change over time.

☺ ☺ *A Is For Africa* by Ifeoma Onyefulu. The author of this book is an African from the Igbo people. It's an alphabet book with neat descriptions and full-color photographs.

☺ ☺ *Africa: Amazing Africa Country by Country* by Atinuke. Full of facts and colorful illustrations, this book is a tour of Africa, taking all 55 countries in turn.

☺ ☺ *Africa Is Not a Country* by Anne Sibley O'Brien. Colorful illustrations are paired with paragraphs of text on each page, describing the daily lives of children across Africa in many different countries.

☺ ☺ *Amazing Africa Projects You Can Build Yourself* by Carla Mooney. If you have crafty kids, they will love this book of projects. This book is also packed with information about the continent.

☺ ☺ *Ultimate Book of African Animals* by Dereck and Beverly Joubert. All sorts of animals from snakes to monkeys to insects are examined in this book full of photographs.

☺ ☺ *Draw Africa* by Kristin J. Draeger. This is a book that teaches kids to draw Africa from memory step-by-step.

☺ ☺ *The Official Wakanda Cookbook* by Nyanyika Banda. Includes real African-inspired recipes of the mythical Marvel kingdom of Wakanda.

☺ ☺ *Flavors of Africa* by Evi Aki. A cookbook featuring authentic African recipes from many different countries across the continent. The author is from Africa.

☺ ☺ *Aerial Geology* by Mary Caperton Morton. This book is a tour of North American landforms. It describes landforms and how each was formed. Includes full-page, full-color photos. Excellent for browsing.

☺ *Target Africa: Ideological Neo-Colonialism of the Twenty-first Century* by Obianuju Ekeocha. Written by a native African, this book describes how the modern practice of "helping" Africa is tied inextricably to the values and priorities of the rich western nations and individuals who give aid. Africa is hostage to these interests and, once again, their cultures are under attack. Discusses AIDS, birth control, abortion, child marriage, and other adult topics.

😊*The Looting Machine: Warlords, Oligarchs, Corporations, Smugglers, and the Theft of Africa's Wealth* by Tom Burgis. Taking a look at different African countries in turn, the author traces Africa's poverty to corruption in government and exploitation in big businesses of the wealthy west.

😊*The Bright Continent: Breaking Rules and Making Change In Modern Africa* by Dayo Olopade. The author, desiring to know the things about Africa that the media never shows, went on a tour interviewing Africans. She found optimism, an entrepreneurial spirit, innovation, and a bright future for Africa among its ordinary people.

Step 2: Explore

Choose a few hands-on Explorations from this section to work on as a family. They should be appealing activities that will create mental hooks so your kids remember the information in the unit. Save the rest of the Explorations for the next time you do this unit in four years when your kids are older. You can also read the sidebars together and explore some little rabbit trails.

This unit includes printables. See the introduction for instructions on retrieving your Printable Pack.

Landforms

Landforms are the physical features of earth shaped by wind, water, volcanism, and earthquakes. They include things like mountains, caves, waterfalls, bays, and islands.

😊 😊 😊**EXPLORATION: Living Room Landscape**
For this activity, you will need:

- Book or video about landforms from the Library List or YouTube playlist
- Blankets, pillows, chairs, and other household items
- Camera and printer
- Glue stick
- World Explorer Journal

1. Read a book or watch a video about landforms.

2. Using blankets, chairs, pillows, and other things from around your house, build a landscape in your living room with as many landforms as you can fit.

Memorization Station

Landforms: naturally-formed features of the earth's surface

You may want to memorize some common landforms and what they look like as well. Here are some to choose from:

- Mountains
- Hills
- Islands
- Canyons
- Rivers
- Oceans
- Deserts
- Marshes
- Waterfalls
- Plains
- Canyons
- Beaches
- Peninsulas
- Lakes
- Volcanoes
- Plateaus
- Inlets
- Straits
- Archipelagos
- Valleys
- Caves
- Cliffs
- Deltas
- Dunes
- Ponds
- Cascades
- Buttes
- Glaciers
- Basins
- Mountain ranges
- Mesas
- Reefs
- Geysers
- Knolls
- Bays
- Capes
- Tundras
- Icebergs
- Lagoons
- Seas
- Fjords
- Hoodoos

Fabulous Fact

A sea is a smaller part of an ocean that is typically surrounded, at least partially, by land.

The Red Sea is along the eastern coastline of northern Africa. It contains some of the hottest and saltiest seawater in the world. It is also one of the most traveled waterways because the Suez Canal connects it to the Mediterranean Sea. It gets its name because there are frequent algae blooms within it that turn the sea reddish at times, although it's normally bluish-green in color.

Additional Layer

The Cape Verde Islands are one archipelago off the coast of Senegal. It is a group of ten islands and five islets (small islands). They are volcanic and have peaks that reach over 6,500 feet (2,000 meters) high. They are home to a variety of birds, lizards, and other wildlife that are endemic to the islands and only live there.

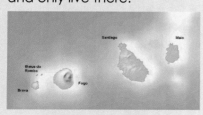

Learn more about some of the islands of Africa.

3. Take a picture of you in your landscape. Print the picture and glue it into your World Explorer Journal. Write a caption that explains which landforms are in your picture.

☺ ☺ ☺ **EXPLORATION: Landforms Book**
For this activity, you will need:

- Book or video about landforms from the Library List or YouTube playlist
- "Landforms" booklet from the Printable Pack (2 pages, print double-sided)
- Stapler
- Colored pencils or crayons
- Glue stick
- World Explorer Journal

1. Read a book or watch a video about landforms.

2. Cut apart the pages of the "Landforms" booklet. Staple the pages of the book together along the edge with the title page on the front and the page that says "glue" on the back. Illustrate the landform listed on each page. If you don't know a landform, look it up.

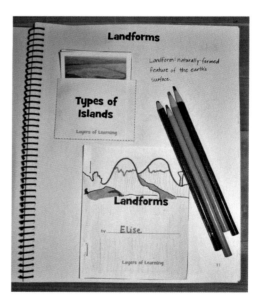

3. Glue the back of the book into your World Explorer Journal.

☺ ☺ ☺ **EXPLORATION: Jello Archipelago**
For this activity, you will need:

- "Types of Islands" from the Printable Pack
- Blue gelatin dessert
- Cereal or soup bowls
- Graham crackers or chocolate cookies
- Strawberries, grapes, and/or blueberries
- Chocolate chips or mini-marshmallows
- Scissors
- Glue stick
- World Explorer Journal

1. Ahead of time, prepare the jello and pour into bowls, one for each child, and let it set up in the refrigerator.

2. Cut apart the "Types of Islands." Read the descriptions on each card.

3. Craft islands on your gelatin sea using crumbled cookies or graham crackers, fruit, and mini-marshmallows or chocolate chips. Use at least three of the types of islands in your island diorama.

4. Explain your island types to your group. Then you can eat your treat.

5. Make a pocket out of the "Types of Islands" title by cutting around the solid lines, folding on the dashed lines, and then gluing the flaps down into your World Explorer Journal.

☺ ☺ EXPLORATION: Erosion

For this activity, you will need:

- Book or video about erosion from the Library List or YouTube playlist
- Outdoor area with sand or soil
- Leaf blower or electric fan
- Bucket or watering can and water

Many landforms are caused by **erosion**, the wearing away of earth and rock by wind, water, and chemicals. Waves on the seashore, frozen glaciers of ice, rain, and rivers of water all shape the landscapes we see around us.

1. Read a book or watch a video about erosion.

2. Outside, make a mound of dirt or sand. A sandbox is a great place to try this if you have one.

3. Blow air across the dirt with a fan or leaf blower. Observe what happens to the dirt.

4. Next, use a bucket or watering can to pour water over the earth mound, creating little rivers of water through the sand. Observe what happens to the earth as water washes over it. Observe how the earth washes away and the shapes it leaves behind.

Memorization Station

Erosion: when earthen materials are worn away and transported by natural forces like wind or water

Fabulous Fact

Victoria Falls isn't the highest waterfall in the world nor is it the widest. However, it is considered the largest waterfall in the world because it is the world's largest sheet of falling water. Some daring tourists sit in the pool at the top called Devil's Pool.

Famous Folks

David Livingstone was a Scottish missionary, explorer, and activist who devoted his life to Africa. He is both admired and hated. Learn about his life and legacy.

People & Planet

Writer's Workshop

Make up some landform riddles and write them in your Writer's Notebook.

I have roots but no branches. I have heights but no depths and am stronger than fire but weaker than water.

What am I?

A mountain

Additional Layer

Use fine art landscape paintings to review landforms. This painting, *Tropical Landscape with Fishing Boats* by Albert Bierstadt, shows a forested coastal plain, a bay, a rocky coast, and the sea.

Expedition

Research the landforms of the place you live. Place them on a blank map of your area. Attach images of the places to the map. Visit a few of the landforms that are near you.

☺ ☺ ☻EXPLORATION: Landforms Memory Game

For this activity, you will need:

- Book or video about landforms from the Library List or the YouTube playlist for this unit
- "Landforms Memory Cards" from the Printable Pack, printed onto card stock (3 pages)
- Scissors

1. Read a book or watch a video about landforms.

2. Cut apart the "Landforms Memory Cards." Shuffle them, then lay them face down on a tabletop.

3. Take turns turning over two cards at a time. If the picture card matches a word card, then you get to keep the match. For an extra challenge for teens, you can have them also name a specific place on Earth where the landform is found in order to collect the match.

   The printable is a key, with the picture cards and words matched up on each page in the Printable Pack.

4. Keep playing until all the cards are matched. The player with the most matches wins.

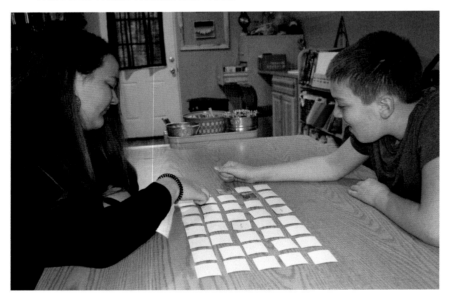

☺ ☻EXPLORATION: Crispy Treat Landscape

For this activity, you will need:

- Book or video about landforms from this unit's Library List or YouTube playlist
- 6 cups crispy rice cereal
- 1/2 cup butter
- 10 ounce bag marshmallows
- Large saucepan
- Mixing spoon
- Paper plates

1. Read a book or watch a video about landforms.

2. The crispy treat recipe makes enough for four children to each build a landscape. Melt 1/2 cup of butter in a saucepan over medium heat.

3. Add 10 ounces of marshmallows and cook and stir until melted completely.

4. Remove from heat. Then stir in 6 cups crispy rice cereal.

5. Let it cool just enough that you can touch it. Then dump a portion onto each of four paper plates.

6. Butter clean hands and then sculpt the crispy treats into at least four different landforms.

7. Let it cool and harden, then show and describe your landforms to someone before you eat it.

😊 😊 😊 **EXPLORATION: Landscape Pop-up Card**

For this activity, you will need:

- Book or video about landforms from the Library List or YouTube playlist
- Colored paper
- Markers or crayons
- Scissors
- Glue stick
- World Explorer Journal

1. Read a book or watch a video about landforms.

2. Use a sheet of blue for the background of your pop-up card. Fold it in half the short way, hamburger-style.

Fabulous Fact

Mt. Kilimanjaro is the highest mountain peak in Africa. It is covered with snow even though it's near the Equator. It is actually a dormant stratovolcano that was formed with alternating layers of lava and ash. Its icecap and glaciers are shrinking, so scientists are studying it to try to discover why.

Additional Layer

Traditional legends often seek to explain certain landforms. There is a legend from the Chagga people around Mt. Kilimanjaro that describes that the crater in the mountain is full of the graves of elephants with their treasured ivory tusks. They say that elephants go there to die, jumping from the rim of the crater, so greedy poachers can never find their ivory. Anyone who tries to climb down into the crater will never escape.

Read more legends from Africa.

Additional Layer

The Sahara Desert is the largest desert in the world. It stretches from the Atlantic Ocean all of the way to the Red Sea and spans eleven African countries. It covers almost a third of the continent.

Go find out which countries lie within the Sahara Desert.

Fabulous Fact

The Strait of Gibraltar is the narrow waterway (8 miles across) that connects the Atlantic Ocean to the Mediterranean Sea and divides Africa from Europe.

Memorization Station

Learn these different regions within Africa. Find out where each of these are located on a map or globe and practice pointing to them as they are called out.

- Sahara
- Sahel
- Savannas
- Tropical rainforests
- Ethiopian Highlands
- Southern Africa

3. Decide what kind of landscape you are going to make. Will it have mountains, cliffs, waterfalls, canyons, sand dunes? Then design the pieces you want to include with more colored paper.

4. Glue the pieces together.

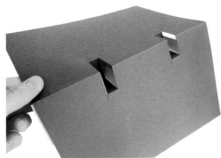

Some of the background pieces can pop off the back by cutting two notches in the fold of the card and then inverting the notches and gluing your background pieces to the notches of paper.

You can also make paper tabs for smaller foreground pieces so they can pop up as well.

5. Label the landforms on your card.

6. Glue your card into your World Explorer Journal.

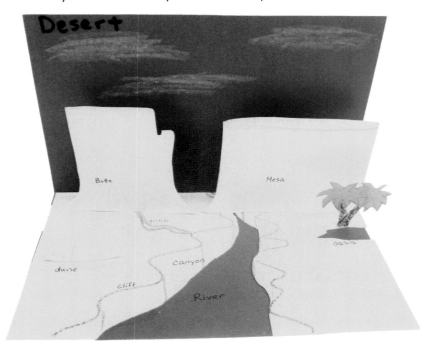

☺ ☺ ☺**EXPLORATION: Landform Collage**

For this activity, you will need:

- Book or video about landforms from the Library List or YouTube playlist
- Fat quarter fabric swatches in several colors, especially greens, yellows, browns, and blues.
- Colored paper
- Oversized sheet of paper or poster board

- Scissors
- Craft glue or school glue
- Paints and brushes
- Crayons or markers
- Other craft supplies as desired(beads, cotton balls, glitter, foil, felt scraps, sand paper, etc.)
- "Landform Labels" from the Printable Pack

1. Read a book or watch a video about landforms.

2. Design a landscape with as many landforms as you can. See how many of the "Landform Labels" you can use up.

3. Use colored cloth, paper, paints, markers, and any other craft supplies you like to make your scene.

4. Glue the "Landform Labels" to the scene you have made.

5. Show your poster to a family member or friend. Explain all of the landforms.

African Landscapes

😊 😊 😊 **EXPLORATION: Cookie Dough Map of Africa**
For this activity, you will need:

- Book or video about Africa from this unit's Library List or YouTube playlist
- Sugar cookie dough - one batch per child
- Cardboard sheets
- Aluminum foil
- Frosting - green, yellow, brown, blue
- Coconut - dye it green by putting in a zipper bag with a drop or two of green food coloring
- Sugar - dye it yellow by putting it in a bag with a drop or

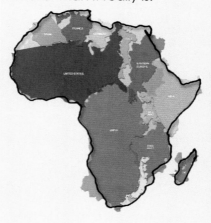

Additional Layer

Make sure you look at Africa on a globe and not just a world map. Because Africa straddles the equator, it has little distortion on a flat map, but the land nearer the poles is massively distorted, meaning that Africa looks smaller than it really is.

Bookworms

Nelson Mandela's Favorite African Folktales is a great book to read aloud to your family as they work on maps or projects during this unit. You can also get the audio version so it can play as you're all working. It includes lots of different readers and music as well.

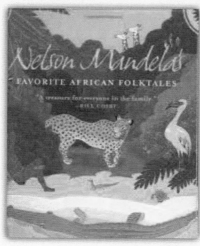

Deep Thoughts

Slavery and colonialism have had a massive negative impact on Africa that persists today.

- African cultures were dismantled.
- African traditional governments were dismantled.
- Africans were made to feel that their culture and themselves were inferior to Europeans.
- European power structures were superimposed on a people not prepared to navigate them.
- Europeans and Americans still interfere in Africa via diplomacy and aid programs that are often counterproductive.
- Africa's economic resources are still primarily controlled by foreigners.
- African people were purposely kept uneducated and outside the system that, with the end of colonialism, they were suddenly expected to run.
- Borders were drawn without regard to tribes, languages, ethnicities, or natural alliances.

Discuss how the practices of slavery and colonialism have left Africa vulnerable and poor,

two of yellow food coloring.
- Chocolate chips or other candies, as desired
- Student atlas or map of Africa

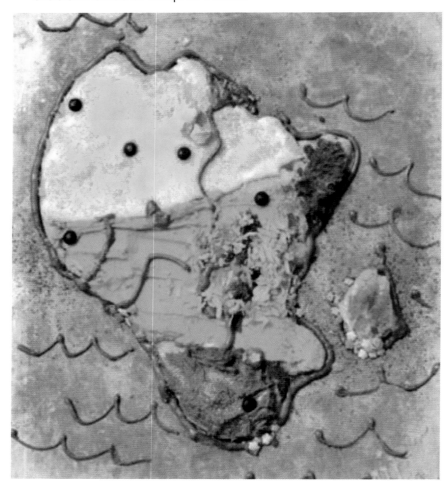

1. Shape raw sugar cookie dough into the shape of Africa, on a large sheet of cardboard covered in foil, using a map as a guide. Each child should make his or her own.

2. Bake the cookies at 350° F (180° C) for 12 minutes or until the edges are golden. Let the cookies cool completely.

3. Read a book or watch a video about Africa.

4. Use frosting, dyed coconut, dyed sugar, and chocolate chips to make jungles, deserts, grasslands, mountains, and rivers in Africa. Again, use a map of Africa as a guide and learn a bit about each region as you go.

☺ ☺ ☻**EXPLORATION: African Landscapes**

For this activity, you will need:

- Book or video about the physical geography of Africa from the Library List, an illustrated atlas, or the YouTube playlist for this unit

- Student atlas
- "African Landscapes" from the Printable Pack
- Colored pencils or crayons
- Ruler

A map that shows the natural features of a place is called a **physical map.** The physical map of Africa helps us understand why people live where they do, the history of Africa, and the natural resources and diversity of the continent.

🙂You can simplify this activity for younger children by having them color, but not label, the map as you talk through it. If they get tired, put it away to finish later in the day or week.

African Landscapes

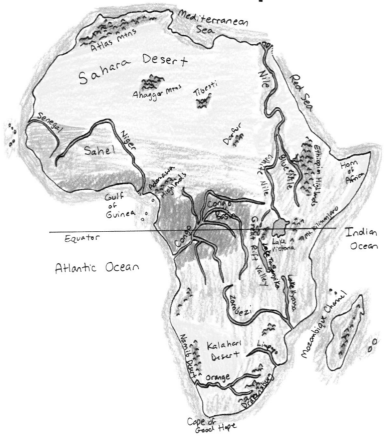

1. Use a student atlas. Label these rivers of Africa and color them blue: Nile, Blue Nile, White Nile, Niger, Senegal, Congo, Zambezi, Limpopo, and Orange.

2. Label Lake Victoria, Lake Tanganyika, and Lake Nyassa. Color them blue.

3. The valley these lakes sit in is a rift valley, where the

Deep Thoughts

Africa is ripe with natural resources like diamonds, copper, gold, oil, rare earth elements, timber, salt, coal, coffee, cotton, rubber, spices, and more. Yet Africa is also poor.

Here are some possible reasons for poverty amid plenty. Discuss how each of these problems contributes to poverty.

- The governments are corrupt, and powerful people steal much of the wealth.
- Foreign nations and corporations own most of the mines, factories, and productive land in Africa.
- Foreigners who do business in Africa underpay taxes and fail to safeguard the environment.
- People are taxed, but their money does not go to schools, healthcare, or infrastructure. Instead, bureaucrats steal the wealth.
- The education system is so poor that most people have little opportunity to learn to read or better themselves so they can be in a position to compete in a modern economy.
- Africans have few skills to make finished products or run factories which means most finished goods are expensive imports.
- Governments violate their citizens' rights routinely, failing to establish a rule of law, a safe environment, or stable conditions where individuals can flourish.
- Civil unrest and war between groups is common.

Additional Layer

Traditional African music with its strong beats and make-me-want-to-dance rhythms was the basis for western music genres such as reggae, blues, jazz, hip hop, rock 'n roll, and samba.

These young men are playing drums in a Ghana.

Additional Layer

Africa is mostly Christian in the south and mostly Muslim in the north.

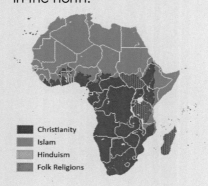

Christianity
Islam
Hinduism
Folk Religions

Throughout Africa, native religions are still practiced, sometimes right alongside the dominant Christianity or Islam.

Fabulous Fact

Football (soccer) is the most popular sport in Africa.

African and Somali plates are pulling apart. It is a region with lakes, cliffs, mountains, and beautiful landscapes. Label the area "Great Rift Valley."

4. Label the Atlantic Ocean, Gulf of Guinea, Mediterranean Sea, Red Sea, Indian Ocean, and Mozambique Channel. Color the seas blue.

5. Label the Atlas, Ahaggar, Tibesti, and Drakensburg mountains. Then label the Adamawa, Ethiopian, and Darfur highlands. Color all these brown. Label Mount Kilimanjaro, the highest mountain in Africa. Color it and it's neighboring mountains in the Great Rift Valley brown.

6. Label the Congo Basin. Color it dark green. This is an area of heavy, thick jungles. The Congo Basin is a low-lying flat area of land inland and surrounding the Congo River and its tributaries. The thick rainforest extends clear to the coast and along the Gulf of Guinea coast, clear to the western edge of Africa. Color all of this area dark green as well.

7. The equator runs right through the Congo Basin and through the middle of Lake Victoria. Draw it onto your map with a ruler. Label it. All over the world there are rainforests in the land surrounding the equator.

8. Label the Sahara, Namib, and Kalahari deserts. Color them yellow. Label the Horn of Africa. Color the coast yellow as it is also a dry desert region.

9. Label the Sahel, an area of dry grassland between the Sahara desert and the rainforest coast in West Africa. Color it light green.

10. Label the Cape of Good Hope, the southernmost point in Africa.

11. Color the remaining land light green. These areas are dry forests or grasslands.

12. Read a book or watch a video about the physical geography of Africa.

13. Put your map of Africa in the Geography section of your Layers of Learning notebook.

☺ ☺ ☺**EXPEDITION: Backyard Safari**

For this activity, you will need:

- Book or video about African animals from the Library List or YouTube playlist
- Five pages of "Safari Animals" from the Printable Pack
- Scissors

- Outdoor space, like a yard or park

Safari is a Swahili word from the east coast of Africa that means "journey." People travel to Africa to go on safari in one of the national parks or nature preserves. They are hoping to see the magnificent African animals, like giraffes, lions, zebras, and elephants. Africa has lots of animals that are **endemic** to their areas, meaning they only live within that one part of the globe.

1. Ahead of time, cut apart the "Safari Animals" cards. Hide them in plain sight along a path in a park or in your back yard. You can do this indoors too, if the weather is bad or you don't have a good outdoor spot for an excursion.

2. Read a book or watch a video about African animals.

3. Go outside on safari and look for the African animals cards. Once you spot one, stop a moment and see which facts from the book or video you can remember about that animal.

4. Continue until you have found each of the ten animals on your safari.

5. Choose one of the animals to paste into your World Explorer Journal. Glue only the top edge so under the flap you can write some things you learned about that animal.

☺ ☺ ☺ **EXPLORATION: African Animal Diorama**
For this activity, you will need:

- Card stock
- Drawing utensils
- Internet, to look up facts about your animal and a "how-

Memorization Station

Safari: Swahili for "journey," this is usually a trip to watch, photograph, or hunt wild animals in their natural environment

Endemic: a species that is native and only lives in one place on earth

Additional Layer

DiceAFARI is a fun photo safari board game your family will enjoy.

Writer's Workshop

Africa is home to over one million different species of animals. Choose an African animal to learn about, then make a poster or report on it. *Writer's Workshop Reports and Essays* has lots of resources to help you get started.

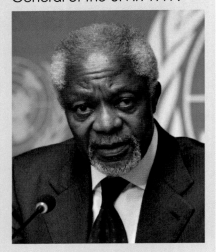
to-draw" tutorial for your animal
- Colored paper
- School glue or craft glue
- Paint and brushes
- Other craft supplies to create a diorama
- Medium cardboard box, like a shoe box

1. Choose an African animal to focus on. Here is a chart with some ideas of animals from different African habitats - **savanna**, **rainforest**, **desert**, and **wetland**. Some of them actually live in more than one habitat.

Savanna	Rainforest
Baboon	African forest elephant
Giraffe	Porcupine
Lion	Mountain gorilla
Black mamba snake	Chimpanzee
Impala	Okapi
Desert	**Wetland**
Desert warthog	Hippopotamus
Fennec fox	Crocodile
Springbok antelope	Flamingo
African wildcat	African buffalo
Dromedary camel	Nile monitor lizard

2. Use a "How to draw . . . " tutorial from the internet to draw your animal on a piece of card stock. If you can't find a how-to-draw tutorial for your animal, just choose a picture to use as reference. Color the animal, then cut it out.

3. Find out what the habitat is like where your animal lives. Is it dry, wet, hot, cold? What are some of the important plants where your animal lives?

4. Paint a background for the animal on the inside of a cardboard box. Draw some of the plants on card stock and on the background of a cardboard box as well.

5. Glue your animal into the African habitat you have made for it.

6. On a map in a student atlas, find the region of Africa where your animal lives.

7. Use your diorama to present some facts about your African animal and its habitat to an audience.

☺ ☺ ☺EXPEDITION: Africa At Your Local Zoo

For this activity, you will need:

- Book or video about African animals or a specific African animal from the Library List or YouTube playlist
- Zoo near you
- Camera
- World Explorer Journal

Most zoos are full of animals from Africa like monkeys, zebras, lions, giraffes, rhinoceros, and more. These animals are exotic for those of us who don't live in Africa, which makes them exciting to watch and learn about. Africa is also home to many big, powerful animals, which is also exciting. Seeing these animals in person is worth it if you have a zoo nearby.

1. Read a book or watch a video about African animals or your favorite African animal.

2. Take a trip to a zoo. Get a zoo map to help you navigate while you are there.

3. Identify the animals that come from Africa. Your zoo should have signs that will tell you where each animal's native home is.

4. Take pictures while at the zoo.

5. Print out your favorite picture and paste it into

Bookworms

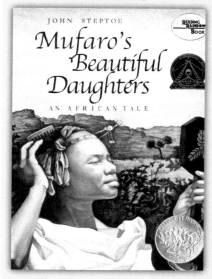

Mufaro's Beautiful Daughters by John Steptoe is an old African folk tale of two beautiful sisters, one kind and the other selfish. Which one will become the next queen?

Writer's Workshop

Write a persuasive argument about your position on zoos. Are zoos good or bad for animals, the environment, and people?

Use the *Writer's Workshop: Persuasive Writing* unit to help with learning to write a good persuasive argument.

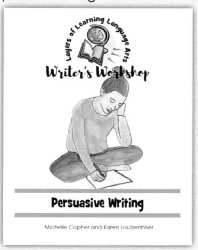

your World Explorer Journal with a caption about what you saw and what you learned about that animal.

☺ ☺ ☺EXPLORATION: Poster Map of Africa

For this activity, you will need:

- Book or video about Africa from the Library List or YouTube playlist for this unit
- "Africa" from the Printable Pack (This is a simple outline of the continent. Print it onto 9 sheets of paper, a 3x3 grid. Your printer should have settings for "multi-page" or "poster" printing.)
- Tape
- Student atlas
- Colored crayons, pens, or pencils
- Glitter and school glue or glitter glue
- Colored paper
- Scissors
- Glue stick
- Oil pastels (optional)
- Paints and brushes (optional)

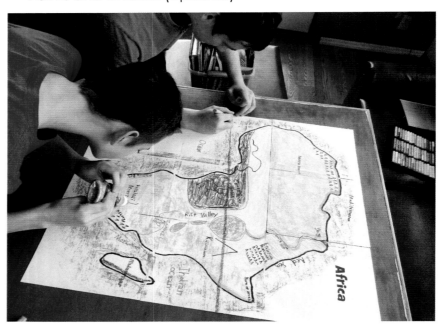

1. Read a book or watch a video about Africa.

2. Tape the large Africa map together into one large map. Put the tape on the back of the sheets of paper so it won't get in the way of coloring and crafting.

3. Use a student atlas and your craft supplies to add the features to Africa that you want. Add rivers like the Nile, Congo, and Niger. Add mountains like Atlas and Drakensburg. Add the tallest mountain: Mount

Famous Folks

Jane Goodall spent a great deal of time in Africa, observing and researching chimpanzees within Tanzania. She named the animals she was studying and noticed all kinds of human-like behaviors in them. She bonded with them and actually became a part of their society. She has spent her life protecting chimpanzees and their habitats through conservation and education programs.

Additional Layer

In addition to adding rivers, mountains, regions, and cities to your poster map, you could also add landmarks like the pyramids at Giza, the Rock-Hewn Churches of Ethiopia, Djingareyber Mosque in Timbuktu, the avenue of 2800-year-old Baobab tress in Madagascar, and Serengeti National Park.

Kilimanjaro. Add the Equator. Add the Congo Basin Rainforest. Add Victoria Falls. Include cities like Cairo, Johannesburg, Lagos, and Kinshasa.

4. Put your completed map of Africa on the wall until the end of this unit. Review the landmarks you added regularly to memorize the important places within Africa and where they are located.

People of Africa

☺ ☺ ☺ EXPLORATION: African Populations

For this activity, you will need:

- Book about Africa from the Library List and a video about population density from the YouTube playlist for this unit
- "Population Map of Africa" from the Printable Pack
- Colored pencils or crayons

Population Map of Africa

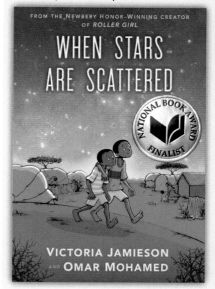

People per square mile

1 Less than 25

2 25 - 70

3 70 - 200

4 More than 200

1.1 billion people live in Africa. We'll make a map to explore the population. Maps can be used to show things like where people live or the amount of rainfall in different

Fabulous Fact

Madagascar is the largest island in Africa. Most of the wildlife there, including this red-ruffed lemur, isn't found anywhere else in the world. They are endemic to Madagascar.

Memorization Station

Thematic maps: maps that display one specific topic or theme

Some examples of thematic maps include weather maps, population density maps, geology maps, or even maps that show the location of a specific fast food chain restaurant. This thematic map shows the prevalent religions within Africa.

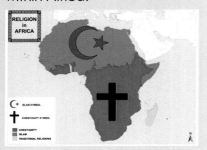

Additional Layer

Much of the population of Africa lives within permanent homes, towns, and cities, but there are some African peoples who are nomads, moving from place to place without permanent homes.

Discuss how your life and possessions would be different if you didn't have a permanent home.

Teaching Tip

In other years of *Layers of Learning Geography*, we will study each of these four regions in greater depth.

---

areas. These types of maps are known as **thematic maps**, because they are about one theme, or topic. A population map shows where people live. If you know where people live, you can ask why. You can also ask how the population affects the natural world and how resources should be distributed.

1. Read a book or watch a video about Africa.

2. Use the "Population of Africa" map. Color the key, and then, color the map according to the key.

   Choose four colors in the same color family like all yellows, oranges, and reds or all blues and greens. The darkest color should be the heaviest populated areas.

3. Watch a video about population density.

4. Based on what you learned from the video and from the population map of Africa, discuss the populations of Africa.

   a. What do you think has attracted people to highly populated areas?

   b. People often move from rural, or low population places, to cities, or high population areas. Why do you think they do this?

   c. If you were going to invest in more power production in Africa, where would you build more plants? Which areas need it the most? Why?

☺ ☺ ☺ **EXPLORATION: African Countries**
For this activity, you will need:

- Book or video about Africa from the Library List or YouTube playlist
- "African Nations" from the Printable Pack
- Colored pencils or crayons

Africa is composed of 54 countries and one disputed, but de facto, country (Western Sahara). For convenience, we have divided Africa into four regions - Saharan Africa, West Africa, Southern Africa, and the Swahili Coast. Regions are useful for discussing areas of the world that encompass more than one country. Regions are arbitrary; there are no accepted geographical regions that everyone agrees on.

1. Read a book or watch a video about African countries.

2. Color the "African Countries" map by region. Use this map to help you.

Africa

Saharan Africa	West Africa	Southern Africa	Swahili Coast
• Western Sahara • Morocco • Mauritania • Mali • Algeria • Tunisia • Niger • Libya • Chad • Egypt • Sudan • South Sudan • Ethiopia	• Cape Verde • Senegal • Gambia • Guinea-Bisseau • Guinea • Sierra Leon • Liberia • Ivory Coast • Burkina Faso • Ghana • Togo • Benin • Nigeria • Cameroon • Central African Republic	• Equatorial Guinea • Sao Tome and Principe • Gabon • Congo • Democratic Republic of the Congo • Angola • Zambia • Namibia • Zimbabwe • Botswana • South Africa • Lesotho • Swaziland	• Eritrea • Djibouti • Somalia • Kenya • Uganda • Rwanda • Burundi • Tanzania • Malawi • Mozambique • Madagascar • Comoros • Seychelles • Mauritius

3. Put the map in your Layers of Learning notebook in the Geography section.

Bookworms

Read *Who Is The Black Panther?* by Jesse J. Holland. Set in the imaginary modern African kingdom of Wakanda, this is a superhero story from Marvel.

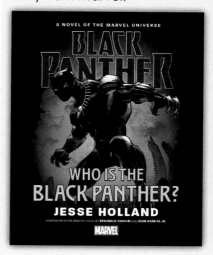

Famous Folks

Nelson Mandela was a South African leader who fought against apartheid, the legalized segregation of society in South Africa.

He spent 27 years in prison because of his struggle against the government. Then, in 1994, he was elected president of South Africa and spent his presidency dismantling apartheid policies in the country.

Bookworms

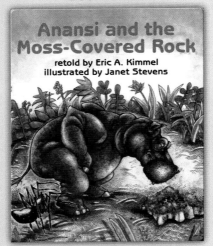

Anansi and the Moss-Covered Rock by Eric A. Kimmel is our favorite of the Anansi stories. You can find lots of fun Anansi stories to read to your kids. They will fall in love with the little trickster.

Fabulous Fact

Capetown is the southernmost city in Africa. It is about 31 miles (50 km) north of the Cape of Good Hope, which is at the southern tip of Cape Peninsula. The Cape of Good Hope is a rocky promontory that is known for its stormy weather. Currents in that area make it dangerous for sailing. There is a rumor that it was initially named the Cape of Storms by the explorer, Bartolomeu Dias. Some say it was renamed so sailors wouldn't be so scared to sail around it.

☺ ☺ ☺ EXPLORATION: Trip To Africa

For this activity, you will need:

- Video about Africa from the YouTube playlist
- "Boarding Pass" from the Printable Pack
- "My Trip To Africa" from the Printable Pack (Cut this apart on the solid line to make two copies.)
- Snacks to eat while on the "plane"
- Television and comfy seating
- Colored pencils or crayons
- Scissors
- Glue stick
- World Explorer Journal

1. Ahead of time, prepare some snacks and cut out the "Boarding Passes" and "My Trip to Africa" printables. Choose a video from the YouTube playlist for this unit. We recommend choosing a longer documentary or tour video that is at least 30 minutes.

2. Give each child a boarding pass and board the plane to Africa in your living room.

3. As you watch a travel documentary about Africa, take a "photo" of two things you see on your trip, by drawing on the Polaroid photos on the "My Trip To Africa" sheets.

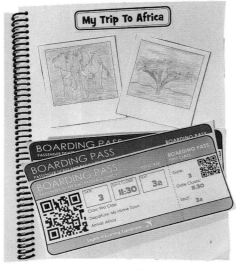

4. Pass out snacks during the trip.

5. When you are finished watching, cut out the two "photos" you took along with the title heading. Glue them into your World Explorer Journal. You can also glue in the stub of your boarding pass to remember your trip. Feel free to add captions or a written narration about what you learned.

☺ ☺ ☺ EXPLORATION: African Cuisine

For this activity, you will need:

- Book or video about Africa from the Library List or YouTube playlist for this unit
- "North African Couscous" and other recipes from the Printable Pack

- Ingredients from the recipes you choose to make
- Cooking utensils and a kitchen
- World Explorer Journal
- Camera/phone
- Scissors
- Glue stick

Crops that are grown in Africa have to be able to stand heat and, in most places, drought. Most of Africa also has poor soils, which means many crops that are grown in Europe or North America won't thrive there. The main staples of African cooking are cassava root, yams, green bananas and plantains, ground nuts, sorghum, millet, rice, barley, and lentils. Africans also consume a lot of fruits like oranges, coconut, papaya, and watermelon. Meats like chicken, beef, and fish are also common. Africa is known for its spices like cinnamon, vanilla beans, pepper, cloves, coriander, cumin, garlic, and ginger.

1. Choose one or more of the recipes from the Printable Pack to cook together.

2. During a lull in the cooking, when something is baking or simmering, read a book or watch a video about Africa.

3. Eat your African food! Make sure to take a picture. Either print the picture and glue it into your World Explorer Journal with a caption or make a quick sketch of your meal. Give it a rating. Did you enjoy the flavors?

☺ ☺ ☺ **EXPLORATION: Ethnicities & Diversity in Africa**
For this activity, you will need:

Writer's Workshop

Choose several African animals from this list and write a dialogue between them as they are sitting at a watering hole. Make sure you add quotation marks and proper punctuation as they speak back and forth.

- Zebra
- Elephant
- Mongoose
- Giraffe
- Hippo
- Gazelle
- Crocodile
- Lion

The Resources page for this unit also links to a live webcam at a watering hole.

Fabulous Facts

There are lots of languages spoken within the continent of Africa, but the most common is Arabic.

The largest country by area in Africa is Algeria.

Nigeria has the biggest population of all of the African countries. There are over 190 million people who live there.

The world's tallest land animal, the giraffe, comes from Africa.

The world's heaviest land animal, the African elephant, also comes from Africa.

Ethiopia is the world's hottest place.

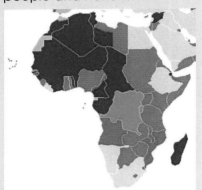

Colonialism in 1945

Writer's Workshop

🙂 Here are a few essay topics about Africa for high schoolers:

- Effects of colonialism
- Effects of the slave trade
- Misinterpretations about Africa
- Diseases in Africa
- Apartheid in South Africa
- Legacy of ancient beliefs and artwork in Egypt
- Trade through the Suez Canal
- African contributions to Western nations
- The Salt Road
- Islam and Christianity within Africa
- Art and music of Africa

- Book or video about African people and diversity from the Library List or YouTube playlist
- "Ethnicities in Africa" from the Printable Pack (2 pages)
- Colored pencils or crayons
- Scissors
- Glue stick
- World Explorer Journal

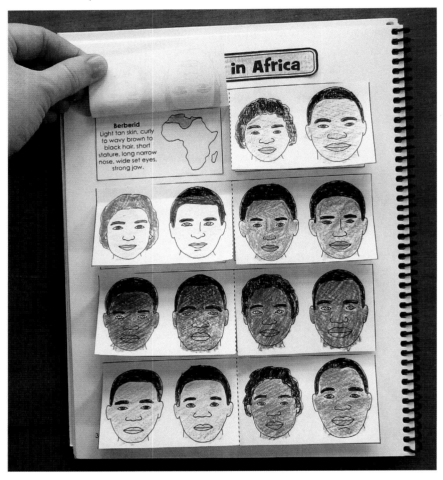

There are thousands of different ethnic groups within Africa. These groups have different language families, cultural traditions, and phenotypes (physical features). Skin colors range from light tan to deep brown or almost black. Some ethnicities tend to be tall and thin, while others are of medium height and muscular. Some have curly or wavy hair while others have kinky hair. Noses range from wide and flat to thin and hawk-like.

1. Watch a video about people of Africa.

2. Color the faces of the people from the "Ethnicities of Africa" printable. Use the description cards of each group as your guide in coloring. The grid of faces matches up with the grid of descriptions.

Highlight that Africans are diverse with thousands of ethnicities and cultures and phenotypes.

3. Color the title and the marked zones of the map on the description cards.

4. Cut apart the face cards and the description cards. Cut out the title.

5. Glue the title and the top edge of the face cards to a page in your World Explorer Journal.

6. Under the flap of each set of faces, glue the description cards that match.

☺ ☺ ☺ EXPLORATION: Cities of Africa

For this activity, you will need:

- Video about African cities from this unit's YouTube playlist
- Poster board or oversized sheet of paper
- "Cities in Africa" from the Printable Pack (3 pages)
- Internet (optional)
- Colored pens, crayons, or pencils
- Other craft supplies as desired
- Student atlas
- Scissors
- Glue stick

Africa is often portrayed by a media that thrives on depression and tragedy as a place of poverty, hunger, and war. Africa, like every continent, has its problems. It also has great beauty, kind people, lovely cities, and strong, functional societies. Africa is a big continent with 54 different countries, including six island nations. Each of them have unique characteristics and different governments, economies, cultural traditions, and strengths and struggles.

1. Read a book or watch a video about African cities.

2. Make a giant collage of African cities on your poster board. When you make a collage, you cover every inch of the background with pictures, colors, or words.

3. Give it a colorful, prominent title.

4. Start with cutting out and gluing on the "Cities in Africa" images from the Printable Pack. On a map of Africa from your student atlas, find each of the cities pictured.

5. You can include your own illustrations based on photos you find online. You can also print out pictures you find online.

6. Between the images, add in words that come to mind

Deep Thoughts

This is some of Karen's family with Ahmed, an African friend of ours on a visit to Alexandria. He was born and raised in Egypt and told us how he was very discriminated against throughout much of his life because his skin was not the right shade of brown for the region of Egypt he lived in. People thought he was a foreigner because the tone of brown did not match their perception of the ideal.

- Why do you think skin color has been such a defining feature of racism around the globe throughout much of the history of the world?
- Can you think of other physical features we use to judge people?
- Do you think there is a solution to stop this trend?

Fabulous Fact

Sub-Saharan Africa is the world's largest free trade area. Manufacturing, telecommunications, and agriculture are all on the rise. There are many thriving cities and industries. This is Port Louis, Mauritius.

Bookworms

Bravelands: Broken Pride by Erin Hunter is the first in a fantasy series set in the African savanna. The animals are personified characters who must set right an unthinkable act of betrayal. This book does contain some graphic fight scenes that may upset sensitive children.

Famous Folks

Elon Musk is a famous South African entrepreneur who is one of the wealthiest people in the world. He left South Africa when he was seventeen and went on to found many companies and become a household name in technology and business. Learn more about him.

about the pictures you've found. For example, you could write "glittering" next to a picture of high rises.

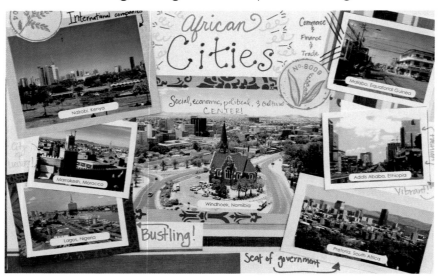

☺ ☺ ☺EXPLORATION: Flags of Africa

For this activity, you will need:

- Book or video about Africa from this unit's Library List or YouTube playlist
- "Flags of Africa" from the Printable Pack
- Scissors
- Glue stick
- World Explorer Journal
- Crayons or colored pencils
- Student atlas

Nations often include many different ethnic groups, cultures, tribes, and histories within their borders. Each of these groups may have profound differences that tend to separate them. Sometimes the groups even have a history of war, abuse, and conflict that creates deep tensions. Nations need ways to unite their people. A flag is a symbol for all of the people in a nation and can help unify them. Most flags contain symbols and colors that represent the nation meaningfully.

1. Read a book or watch a video about Africa.

2. In your World Explorer Journal, draw a curved line across the page, as though it is a string stretched across the page.

3. Cut out some of the flags from the "Flags of Africa" sheet. Choose your favorite. Find the country the flag represents on a map in your student atlas. Do a bit of research and find out the story or meaning behind the flag you chose.

4. Glue the hoist edge of the flag to the "string" you drew across your page in your World Explorer Journal. You can write the name of the country under the flag if you like. Later, you can quiz yourself on the flags and countries they represent.

5. Keep picking flags and finding them on a map of Africa until you have filled your "string." You can draw as many strings across your notebook as you have space for. You can also find out what the colors and symbols represent on each of the flags you chose.

6. Share the meaning or symbolism behind the flags you chose to research with your family or class. Discuss some of the things besides flags that can unite a nation together. Does your national flag mean anything significant to you?

Step 3: Show What You Know

During this unit, choose one of the assignments below to show what you have learned during the unit. Add this work to your Layers of Learning Notebook. You can also use this assignment to show your supervising teacher or your charter school as a sample of what you've been working on in your homeschool, if needed.

There are more ideas for writing assignments in the "Writer's Workshop" sidebars.

☺ ☺ **Coloring or Narration Page**
For this activity, you will need:

Additional Layer

The four color theorem says that any map can be completed with just four colors so that no two adjacent regions are the same color. It has been proved mathematically.

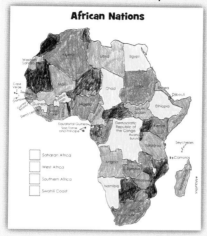

Try it with the map of Africa. Can you color all the countries with just four colors so that no touching borders are the same color?

Writer's Workshop

Write a story with this lion as your main character. Decide on his name and some personality traits he has. What problem does he need to overcome within the story? Does he have an enemy or any helpers along the way? When you're finished writing, share your story.

Unit Trivia

1. What is the highest mountain in Africa?

Mt. Kilimanjaro

2. True or false - Africa is a hot, dry desert continent.

False, although it has the largest desert in the world, the Sahara, Africa also has jungles, grasslands, mountains, and more.

3. Fill in the blank: An _____ is a group of islands.

Archipelago

4. What landform is found at the mouth of the Nile River?

A river delta

5. What is the biggest waterfall in Africa?

Victoria Falls

6. Name at least 6 African animals.

(answers will vary)

7. Fill in the blanks: A _____ is a grassy plain in a tropical or subtropical region. A _____ is even drier and gets less than ten inches of rain per year. A _____ is a dense forest in a tropical area that gets heavy rainfall. Also very wet, a _____ has marshes and swamps with ground that is saturated by water.

Savanna, desert, rainforest, wetland

8. True or false - At this point, all of the African nations are independent and don't have any leftover effects of imperialism.

False, although the nations are independent, there are many lingering effects.

- "Africa" printable from the Printable Pack
- Crayons, or colored pencils

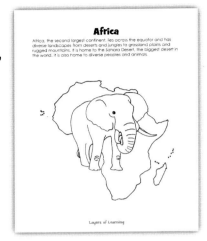

1. Depending on the age and ability of the child, choose either the "Africa" coloring sheet or the "Africa" narration page from the Printable Pack.

2. Younger kids can color the coloring sheet as you review some of the things you learned about during this unit. You might talk about the animals, food, people, or cities you learned about within Africa. On the bottom of the coloring page, kids can write a sentence about what they learned. Very young children can explain their ideas orally while a parent writes for them.

3. Older kids can write about some of the concepts you learned on the narration page and color the picture as well.

4. Add this to the Geography section of your Layers of Learning Notebook.

☺ ☺ ☺ Africa ABC Book

For this activity, you will need:

- A blank booklet with 26 pages (You can make your own by folding 8 sheets of paper, hamburger-style, and then sewing or stapling the folded seam.)
- Internet
- Markers, colored pencils, or crayons

1. Create your own ABC book filled with things you learned about Africa during this unit. The first page will say "A is for Africa" and you can illustrate it with a hand-drawn map of the continent.

2. Continue to create each page by thinking of something within Africa you learned about that begins with each letter of the alphabet in turn. Illustrate each page. If you have trouble thinking of something to go with each letter, you can use the internet to help you. You can use the names of cities, countries, landmarks, animals, famous people, industries, or anything else.

3. Add your book to your bookshelf as a keepsake and to read again and again as a family.

☺ ☺ ☺ Landforms Sticker Review

For this activity, you will need:

- "Landforms Sticker Review" printables from the Printable Pack, printed on full-size label paper and then cut apart into individual stickers
- Card stock

1. Give each child a set of the landform stickers and card stock and see if they can match up the pairs. You can use this as a simple review, a game, or a quiz. The printable can serve as your answer key as the two pages are aligned.

2. Add this page to your Big Book of Knowledge so you can continue to review the landforms regularly.

☺ ☺ ☺ Big Book of Knowledge

For this activity, you will need:

- "Big Book of Knowledge: Africa" printable from the Printable Pack, printed on card stock
- Markers
- Big Book of Knowledge

1. Color, draw on, or write on the Big Book of Knowledge page. Record concepts, definitions, and facts you learned during this unit. It's a record of the things you learned and hope to remember. Add the page to your Big Book of Knowledge.

2. Use your Big Book of Knowledge regularly to help you review, quiz, or create games that will help you commit the things you've learned to memory.

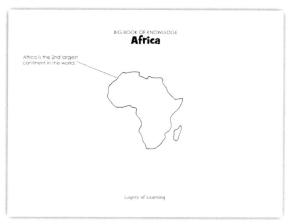

Big Book of Knowledge

The Big Book of Knowledge is a book for you, the mentor, to use as a constant review of all of the things you're learning about. You can use it to quiz your kids or prepare tests or review games. Whenever you learn something in Layers of Learning that you want your kids to remember, add it to your Big Book of Knowledge.

Assemble your Big Book of Knowledge in a binder or with binder rings. Divide it into sections for each subject.

In the Printable Pack for this unit you will find a "Big Book of Knowledge" sheet. You can add this sheet to others you collect or create yourself as you progress through the Layers of Learning curriculum. Customize the Big Book of Knowledge to your family by adding facts and topics that you enjoyed exploring as you were learning.

Visit Layers of Learning online to find more information on how to assemble and use your own Big Book of Knowledge.

You will also find cover and section pages to print along with creative games to play with your Big Book of Knowledge to keep school, even the tests, fun!

ASIA

Asia is the largest land mass on Earth. It stretches from tundra in the north through vast taiga forests and deserts, to grasslands, and then finally, to tropical rainforests in the south. Dramatic waterfalls, fascinating haystack-shaped mountains, jewel-like archipelagos, and rare species of plants and animals make Asia a wonderful part of the world to learn about. The continent is bordered by the Arctic Ocean in the north, the Pacific Ocean in the east, and the Indian Ocean in the south. The western border is a relic of ancient history when the Greeks defined Anatolia and everything to the east as "Asia." Today, we define the western border at the Ural Mountains and the Caucuses Mountains. The exact border is a matter of opinion, however, and is not completely agreed upon.

Altai Mountains, Russia

Central Mongolian Steppe

Tropical coast, Bali, Indonesia

Wadi Rum, Jordan

Cultures in Asia vary from the Chinese to Indonesians and Arabs to Mongols. Because of its vastness, Asia has a multitude of customs, languages, religions, and foods. People in Asia live in glittering high rise apartments, wooden huts on stilts, hovels made of corrugated metal and cardboard, western-style family homes, and movable tents made of animal skins and wood.

Asia also has the largest portion of the world's population at four and a half billion people. China and India are the two most populated countries on the planet. The people of Asia have long shaped world history. Powerful religious identities, including Christianity, Islam, Judaism, Hinduism, Buddhism, Confucianism, and Zoroastrianism, are all Asian. It was the lure of China that drove men like Christopher Columbus to seek a water route around the world and changed the face of the planet. Three of the world's five cradles of civilization - Yellow River, Mesopotamia, and Mohenjo-Daro - were in Asia. Asia is still a world economic and cultural driver to this day.

Step I: Library List

Choose books from your library that go with this topic. Here's a list of some favorites and also a list of search terms so you can utilize what your library offers. Read the books with your kids and/or assign them some to read independently. It is from these books your kids will learn most of the facts they need from this unit.

Search for: Asia, natural disasters, storms, earthquakes, hurricanes, tornadoes

☺ ☺ ☻ *Geography of the World* by DK. Read "Asia," "Peoples of Asia I," and "Peoples of Asia II" on pages 132-137 and "Natural Disasters" on page 272-273.

☺ ☺ ☻ *Draw Asia: Volume II* by Kristin J. Drager. This book shows you how to draw each of the Asian countries.

☺ ☺ ☻ *Coloring Book Animals of Asia: 20 Realistic Pictures + 60 Unique Facts About Animals* by Mark Shawe. This is a simple coloring book that teaches about Asian animals.

☺ ☺ ☻ *Asian Children's Favorite Stories: Folktales From China, Japan, Korea, India, The Philippines, and Other Asian Lands* by David Conger, et al. Short tales to read aloud to your children. Each tale is colorfully illustrated.

☺ ☺ ☻ *Tales Told in Tents: Stories from Central Asia* by Sally Pomme Clayton. This book shares twelve traditional folk stories from central Asia you can read aloud as a family.

☺ ☺ ☻ *Facts at Your Fingertips: Asia* by Derek Hall. An introduction to each of the Asian countries, one by one.

☺ *What Are Natural Disasters?* by Louise Spilsbury. Each page explains a specific natural disaster simply.

☺ *Fragile Planet* by Gerry Bailey. A perfect introduction to lots of the natural disasters we experience on planet Earth.

☺ *Introducing Asia* by Anita Ganeri. This is a book for little ones that answers all kinds of questions about Asia.

☺ *Explore Asia* by Bobbie Kalman and Rebecca Sjonger. This is an easy reader book with basic information about Asia.

Family School Levels

The colored smilies in this unit help you choose the correct levels of books and activities for your child.

☺ = Ages 6-9
☺ = Ages 10-13
☻ = Ages 14-18

On the Web

For videos, web pages, games, and more to add to this unit, visit the People & Planet Resources at Layers-of-Learning.com.

You will find a link to video playlists, web links, and more.

Bookworms

If you're looking for a family read-aloud, we'd like to suggest this one.

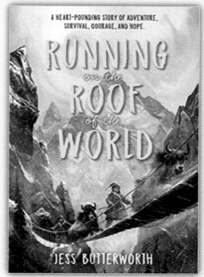

Running on the Roof of the World by Jess Butterworth is about a girl, Tash, and her friend, Sam, who flee through the dangerous Himalayas Mountains to safety in India after a crackdown on Tibet by the Chinese.

Teaching Tip

Here's a list of some natural disasters you may choose to focus on as you learn more about them in this unit:

- Tsunami
- Mudslide
- Earthquake
- Avalanche
- Drought
- Wildfire
- Blizzard
- Flood
- Volcano
- Tornado
- Hurricane
- Hailstorm
- Severe thunderstorm
- Heat wave
- Epidemic

Writer's Workshop

Choose one of the natural disasters listed above to write a report about. Include sections about causes, detection or prediction, and the aftermath and effects. Also, choose at least one famous instance of that natural disaster to highlight and tell the story of.

Memorization Station

Natural disaster: natural events that can cause great damage

Hurricane: a tropical storm with heavy rains and winds that are 74 miles per hour or greater

Tornado: a violently rotating column of whirling wind that is accompanied by a funnel-shaped cloud

The Seven Continents: Asia by John Son. A solid informational text for kids to read by themselves or with help. The pictures and large text will appeal to children.

A Is For Asia by Cynthia Chin Lee. This is a simple alphabet book that will introduce your youngest students to Asia and its people. Each page has colorful child-like illustrations.

Asia by Gary Drevitch. Teaches about the things that make Asia unique.

Asian Adventures A-Z: ABC through Asia by Yoke Qiu. This is an ABC book that highlights interesting cultural highlights about Asia.

Animals of Asia For Kids by Rachel Bubb. This is a sweet book that introduces you to twenty-four Asian animals through a simple narrative by a veterinarian and with hand-drawn illustrations.

Great Minds and Finds in Asia by Mike Downs. This picture book talks about inventions, technologies, foods, and other things that come from Asia.

Atlas of Natural Disasters by Jeff Groman. Explores each of the basic natural disasters, including hurricanes, tornadoes, volcanoes, earthquakes, landslides, avalanches, drought, and more.

Nature's Fury by Time Life Books. Tells the stories of many of the earth's natural disasters with actual photos.

Not For Parents Asia: Everything You Ever Wanted to Know by Lonely Planet Kids. Shares fascinating stories and facts about samurai, volcanoes, pirates, and other interesting bits about Asia.

The Geography of Thought: How Asians and Westerners Think Differently by Richard E. Nisbett. This is a readable, popular-level psychology book about fundamental differences that occur when people are raised in different cultures, right down to the thought patterns in your heads.

Step 2: Explore

Choose a few hands-on Explorations from this section to work on as a family. They should be appealing activities that will create mental hooks so your kids remember the information in the unit. Save the rest of the Explorations for the next time you do this unit in four years when your kids are older. You can also read the sidebars together and explore some little rabbit trails.

This unit includes printables. See the introduction for instructions on retrieving your Printable Pack.

Natural Disasters

Natural disasters are major events that are caused by natural processes of the earth. They include earthquakes, hurricanes, tornadoes, floods, volcanic eruptions, tsunamis, avalanches, and more.

Sometimes we can predict when these things will happen, but we are never sure exactly when one will strike. Even if we can see increased seismic activity, we aren't sure exactly when and where an earthquake will hit. We may see a storm coming but not anticipate the floodwaters rising as much as they do. We can often use technology to make some predictions, but even if we know a hurricane is coming, we can't predict its exact path. Natural disasters shape our world because they change the topography of the earth and affect the people, plants, and animals that lie in their path.

☺ ☺ ☺EXPLORATION: Natural Disasters Facts
For this activity, you will need:

- "Natural Disasters Facts" from the Printable Pack
- Books about natural disasters from the Library List
- Markers, crayons, or colored pencils
- Scissors
- Glue stick
- World Explorer Journal

1. Begin by cutting along the solid lines of the printable and folding along the dotted lines. On the front of each flap, write the name of a natural disaster and draw a picture to represent it. You'll be choosing six types of natural disasters, one for each flap.

2. Gather a few books about natural disasters and read through some together. As you are reading, listen for an interesting fact about each of the disasters you chose. Write the fact inside of the flap for that disaster.

3. Once all of your facts are written and you've read your

Fabulous Fact

We can't stop natural disasters from occurring, but we do our best to reduce their impact. For example, in areas where earthquakes are common, buildings are built with extra reinforcements and flexible foundations. In areas near volcanoes, roofs are built with steep slopes so heavy ash will slide off. In areas where hurricanes are common, most people have shutters or covers for their windows that they attach when a storm is on the way. In addition, scientists do their best to monitor and warn people ahead of time when they see a potential disaster on the way.

Teaching Tip

You can learn more about natural disasters, like earthquakes, in *Layers of Learning's Earth & Space: Plate Tectonics*.

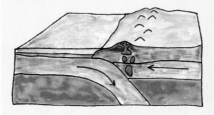

You can learn more about weather-related natural disasters in *Layers of Learning's Earth & Space: Weather*.

books, glue the back side of the booklet to a page in your World Explorer Journal.

☺ ☺ ☺EXPLORATION: Big Storms

For this activity, you will need:

- Chalkboard, white board, or large sheet of paper
- Books or videos about big storms (like hurricanes or tornadoes) from the Library List or YouTube playlist
- World Explorer Journal
- Markers, crayons, or colored pencils

1. Lots of natural disasters, like **hurricanes** and **tornadoes**, are caused by severe stormy weather. Can you think of any others? Brainstorm some together and write them down on a chalkboard, white board, or large sheet of paper.

2. Choose one of the examples you brainstormed and read a book or watch a video about the severe storm you chose. It could be tornadoes, hurricanes, blizzards, thunderstorms, or other severe weather storms. Find out how they form, how large they can become, and what kind of destruction they bring.

3. In your World Explorer Journal, draw a sketch of the storm you chose and then write some of the facts you learned near it.

4. Add a category chart to the page. Each kind of severe storm has its own category system. For example, blizzards can fall into five categories: extreme, crippling, major, significant, and notable. Find out the categories for the storm you chose and the criteria for each category. Make a table of them within your World Explorer Journal.

☺ ☺ ☺EXPLORATION: Natural Disasters Puzzle

For this activity, you will need:

- "Natural Disasters Puzzle" from the Printable Pack
- Book or video about natural disasters

1. Read each description on the printable and fill in the blanks with the natural disaster it is describing.

2. When you're finished,

Deep Thoughts

When a natural disaster strikes, it makes us become very aware of just how vulnerable we are. In one moment, life can change when you're in a fire, a flood, an earthquake, or another disaster.

How do you think a disaster like this would change your life?

What would you do to overcome something like this?

Are there things you can do to prepare now so you will be ready if something disastrous strikes where you live?

Memorization Station

Drought: a prolonged period of low rainfall that leads to a water shortage

Flood: a large amount of overflowing water that travels beyond its normal confines

Additional Layer

Your family may enjoy setting up a scene using toys and then causing a flood. Use Legos, Little People, or other similar toys and set up a scene with them outside. Use a hose or a bucket of water to flood the scene, then talk about the devastating damage a flood can bring.

unscramble the circled letters and write the word in the box at the bottom.

Answers: flood, tornado, earthquake, wildfire, hurricane, tsunami, landslide. Unscrambled word: DISASTER

3. Finish off your lesson by reading a book or watching a video about natural disasters.

4. Put the "Natural Disasters Puzzle" in your Layers of Learning Notebook in the geography section.

☺ ☺ ☺ **EXPLORATION: Too Much or Too Little Water**
For this activity, you will need:

- Two small, identical potted plants
- Two trays to hold the pots
- Water
- World Explorer Journal

We all need water to live, but sometimes we have too little or too much, and that can be disastrous. A **drought** is when there is too little water. Areas that don't get enough precipitation can have droughts, and they can change the face of the earth. When there's not enough rain, the land dries out, crops die, and dust storms can make areas nearly uninhabitable.

A **flood** is when there's too much water. Floodwaters saturate the ground, killing plants by making them drown and wilt. Some floods even fill streets, homes, and cities. Floods cause enormous damage and are expensive to clean up after.

Water plays a role in a lot of natural disasters, even beyond just floods and droughts. Landslides, tsunamis, extreme storms, heat waves, cold spells, avalanches, and many more disasters are all related to water in some way.

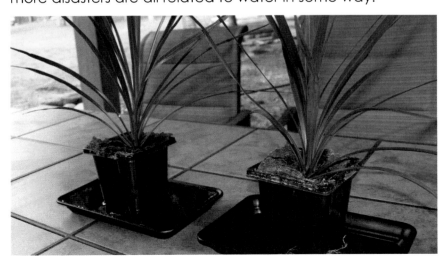

Writer's Workshop

Choose a natural disaster to sketch and then cut out. On the picture, write some tips for staying safe during that natural disaster.

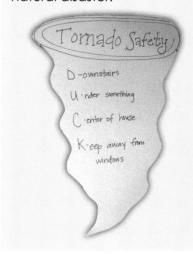

Tornado Safety

D -ownstairs

U -nder something

C -enter of house

K -eep away from windows

Writer's Workshop

Write a paragraph about a natural disaster.

- What do you think is the worst of all of the natural disasters?
- Is there one that you fear more than the others? Why?

Fabulous Fact

From 1876 -1879, there was a devastating drought in North China that caused around nine million people to die when they couldn't grow crops for food.

Memorization Station

Tsunami: a long high sea wave caused by an earthquake, underwater landslide, or another disturbance under the surface of the water

Additional Layer

The Wave by Hokusai is a famous woodblock print that depicts a large wave which some perceive to be a tsunami.

Bookworms

Five Epic Disasters by Lauren Tarshis is part of the I Survived True Stories series. It tells the personal stories of people who experienced huge disasters. Most, but not all of these, were natural disasters. You can read all of the stories or just select one or two.

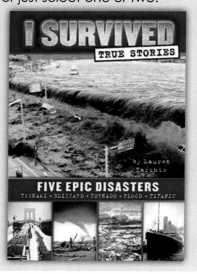

1. Begin with two identical potted plants. We are going to observe what happens when they receive too little water or too much water. Put both plants on their own small tray in a sunny, warm, place where you can observe them daily for at least a few weeks.

2. Give one plant water equal to the size of its pot every single day. For example, if the pot holds two cups of dirt, give the plant two cups of water. It doesn't have to be perfectly measured, but the plant needs to receive enough water that it is overflowing. You may have to empty the tray if it is overflowing. You are simulating flood conditions.

3. Don't give any water to the other plant at all. You are simulating drought conditions.

4. Observe the two plants and see how they do over time. Discuss your results and the effects of droughts and floods for life on earth - people, animals, and plants. Can water have effects on non-living things as well?

5. Write about your results in your World Explorer Journal and add a caption that describes some things you learned about floods and droughts.

☺ ☺ ☺EXPLORATION: Geology or Weather?

For this activity, you will need:

- Two flyswatters
- "Natural Disasters Flashcards" from the Printable Pack
- Scissors
- Tape (optional)

Some natural disasters are caused by weather. Big storms can create havoc in their paths. Too much or too little rain, high winds, lightning, and other harsh weather can be the cause of a variety of natural disasters.

Other natural disasters are caused by geological processes. Shifting plates under the earth's surface, moving rocks, land, or snow, and a variety of other geologic processes can cause disasters. For example, **tsunamis** are huge waves that can flood big areas, but the flood isn't caused by rain; it's caused by a sudden movement of the ocean's surface due to earthquakes, landslides below the ocean, or other underwater disruptions.

1. Cut out the "Natural Disasters Flashcards" from the printable and place them on a table or tape them up on a wall.

2. Have two kids face the cards, each holding a flyswatter.

Have another person call out either "Geology" or "Weather." When one is called, the kids holding the flyswatters must be the first to swat one that is caused by the called out word. The winner collects the card. You will keep calling out causes until all of the cards have been collected. The winner is the one who collects the most cards.

Answers:
Geology - Earthquake, Landslide, Tsunami, Volcano
Weather - Hurricane, Tornado, Flood, Wildfire, Drought

☺ ☺ ☺ **EXPLORATION: Natural Disasters in My Area**
For this activity, you will need:

- Internet
- Art paper
- Watercolor paints, paintbrushes, and a water cup

1. Some disasters, like fires caused by lightning strikes or severe windstorms, can happen anywhere. Specific regions of the world have a greater risk for certain types

The countries of Cyprus, Georgia, Armenia, and Azerbaijan lie on the border between Asia and Europe. Since Asia and Europe are really one land mass, technically, you could put these countries in either continent.

Layers of Learning has put all these countries in Europe because the people in these countries mostly identify with Europe more than Asia and say they are Europeans.

Can you find the Dead Sea on a map? It is the lowest point on earth, 423 meters (1,388 feet) below sea level. Besides being really low, it is also one of the saltiest bodies of water on the earth. It's nearly ten times saltier than the oceans. There are no fish, sea creatures, or even seaweed within it because of the high salt content.

Even though animals shy away from living there, people go visit it in droves. It's like a big spa that people visit to heal their skin and bodies from all sorts of ailments. Because of the high salt content, people float really well in it too. Find out more about buoyancy and why salt being in the water makes people float.

of natural disasters though. For example, if you live in Alaska, USA, you are more likely to be affected by a volcano, earthquake, or a tsunami than you are by a hurricane or tornado. The weather and geology of each region makes it more susceptible to certain disasters.

2. Search online for information about natural disasters that are more likely to occur in your region of the world. Find out the most likely disasters.

3. Paint a watercolor picture of the type of disaster that is most likely to occur in your area. On the back, write down the things you can do to prepare for it.

4. Do a bit more research about some things you can do to prepare for each of the disasters you are at risk for.

Asian Landscapes

☺ ☺ ☺ **EXPLORATION: Salt Dough Map of Asia**

For this activity, you will need:

- Student atlas
- Salt dough (1/2 cup warm tap water, 1/4 cup salt, 4 tablespoons cooking oil, 2 cups flour)
- Cardboard sheet
- Paints and paintbrushes
- Toothpicks
- "Toothpick Markers of Asia" from the Printable Pack
- Glue
- Markers
- Videos about Asia from the YouTube playlist for this unit

1. Cut a large sheet of cardboard, a bit larger than you want your map to be. Look at a map of Asia and draw

an outline of the continent on the cardboard using pencil.

2. Mix up a batch of salt dough for each child by combining 1/2 cup warm tap water, 1/4 cup salt, 4 tablespoons cooking oil, and 2 cups flour in a large bowl and kneading it with your hands until dough forms.

3. Using your pencil outline and a student atlas opened up to a relief map of Asia as guides, sculpt the continent in dough. Try to keep the dough thin so it won't take too long to dry. Add in mountains and make thin valleys for rivers. Make the plateaus higher land than the plains. Don't forget the islands of Asia.

4. While children work, play videos about Asia.

5. Paint the map to look like the landscape types. For example, paint deserts yellow, mountains brown, grasslands light green, and forests dark green.

6. Paint the cardboard surface around Asia blue, except for where Asia touches Europe. Paint that portion in a dark neutral color like gray or brown.

7. Cut apart the tags on the "Toothpick Markers of Asia" sheet. Glue the tags around the ends of toothpicks and put them in the correct places on your map of Asia.

8. Once the blue paint for the water is dry, label the seas and oceans with a marker.

9. Show your finished map to a friend or neighbor. Explain some of the important features of Asian geography.

☺ ☺ ☺**EXPLORATION: Asian Landscapes Map**
For this activity, you will need:

Bookworms

Giant: A Panda of the Enchanted Forest by Xuan Loc Xuan is a fairy tale about a panda bear that teachers respect for animals.

Additional Layer

The Arabian Desert occupies most of the Arabian Peninsula. It is the largest desert in Asia and the second largest on Earth. Do you know what the largest desert is?

The Sahara

Find the Arabian Peninsula on a map or globe and look at which seas surround it.

The Persian Gulf, the Gulf of Oman, the Arabian Sea, the Gulf of Aden, the Red Sea

There are camel trails going through the desert along with black lava flows, desert dunes, and bits of vegetation. There are even some mountains and plateaus too. Do you know what a plateau is?

An area of high, level ground

Memorization Station

Boreal forest: (taiga) a region of mostly coniferous trees in the high latitudes or in mountains with very cold winters and warm or hot summers

Tundra: a zone too cold for trees and where the ground remains frozen under the surface year round

Deciduous forest: a forest with trees that lose their foliage at the end of the growing season

Grassland: a zone that is too dry for many trees and the dominant vegetation is grasses

- Book or video about the physical geography of Asia from the Library List or the YouTube playlist for this unit
- "Asian Landscapes" from the Printable Pack
- Colored pencils or crayons
- Ruler

A map that shows the natural features of a place is called a physical map. The physical map of Asia helps us understand why people live where they do, the history of Asia, and the natural resources and diversity of the continent.

☺You can simplify this activity for younger children by having them color, but not label, the map as you talk through it. If they get tired, put it away to finish later in the day or week.

Asian Landscapes

1. Use a student atlas. Label these rivers of Asia and color them blue: Euphrates, Tigris, Indus, Ganges, Mekong, Yangtze, Yellow, Amur, Lena, Ob.

2. Label Lake Baikal, the Caspian Sea, and the Aral Sea. Color them blue.

3. Label the Arabian Peninsula and color it yellow, except for a strip of green on the southern and eastern coasts. The Arabian Peninsula is covered with a deep, dry desert.

4. Label the Indian Ocean, Pacific Ocean, Arctic Ocean, Persian Gulf, Arabian Sea, Bay of Bengal, South China Sea, and Sea of Japan. Color the oceans and seas blue.

5. Label the Zagros, Hindu Kush, Himalayas, Tien Shan, Altai, and Ural Mountains. Then, label the Tibetan, Iranian, Central Siberian, and Mongolian plateaus. Label Mount Everest. Color all of these brown.

6. Label the West Siberian Plain. Color it dark green. This is an area of dense **boreal forests**.

7. Color the northern edge of the continent purple. In this region, the ground is frozen year round. This is called **tundra**. Grasses and low bushes grow on it during the summer months, but it is too cold for trees.

8. The equator runs south of mainland Asia, right through the middle of the Indonesian Archipelago. Draw the equator on your map with a ruler. Label it.

9. Color the islands of the Indonesian Archipelago, Philippine Archipelago, and Thailand's peninsula dark green to show the rainforests in this area.

10. Label the Gobi, Takla Makan, and Thar deserts. Color them yellow.

11. Color the remaining land light green. These areas are **deciduous forests** or **grasslands**.

12. Read a book or watch a video about the physical geography of Asia.

13. Put your map of Asia in the Geography section of your Layers of Learning Notebook.

☺ ☺ EXPLORATION: Backpack Through Asia

For this activity, you will need:

- Globe or world map
- Video about Asian animals from the YouTube playlist for this unit
- Backpack for each child
- "Asian Animals" cards from the Printable Pack
- "Backpack Through Asia" from the Printable Pack
- Scissors
- Colored pencils or crayons
- Glue stick
- World Explorer Journal

1. Ahead of time, cut apart and hide the pictures of Asian animals around your yard or home. You will want one copy of the animals for each child. Hide all the panda bears together in one spot or hide them in many different places. Each child will get one copy of each animal.

Fabulous Fact

The rhinos in Africa have three horns, but the rhinos of India and Nepal have just a single horn. There aren't many of them left in the wild, so the governments of India and Nepal have created protected reserves to help increase their population again.

Additional Layer

Some people think of tigers as being African animals, but no tigers live in the wild within Africa. Tigers are actually native to Asia. They are apex predators, which means they are at the top of the food chain. They primarily eat animals like boars, bears, deer, antelopes, and young elephants. They live between 20-26 years in the wild and live out most of their lives alone. Tigers are great swimmers and really like the water, unlike most cats. Learn more about these fascinating creatures.

Writer's Workshop

Write a journal entry all about the Asian animal you would most like to see if you could see any of them.

Additional Layer

Learn to draw an Asian animal with an online tutorial. Here are some you could try:

- Komodo dragon
- Giant panda
- Orangutan
- Sun bear
- Snow leopard
- Japanese macaque monkey
- Malayan tapir
- Burmese python
- Red panda
- Gibbon
- Pangolin
- Bactrian camel

2. Find Asia on a globe or world map.

3. Watch a video about Asian animals.

4. Put on backpacks and go for a walk, looking for Asian animals and collecting them in your backpack as you go.

5. Color the "Backpack Though Asia" paper backpack.

6. Cut out the backpack, fold on the dashed lines, and glue the backpack together. Glue the backpack in your World Explorer Journal. Put your animals inside your backpack.

☺ ☺ ☺**EXPLORATION: Asian Animal and Art**
For this activity, you will need:

- Book or video about Asian animals from the Library List or YouTube playlist for this unit
- Internet for research and a how-to-draw
- Art paper or card stock
- Scissors
- Glue
- Crayons, colored pencils, markers, and/or paints

1. Choose a book or watch a video about

Asian animals.

2. Choose a specific animal from Asia and learn more about it and its habitat.

3. Use a "how to draw" from the internet to draw your animal on a sheet of card stock. Cut out your animal.

4. Use a book or the internet to find out what habitat your animals lives in within Asia. Use paints to create a habitat painting on another sheet of card stock or art paper.

5. Glue your animal to its habitat, then show your art to your family and teach them a bit about your Asian animal and its habitat. Does it live in a specific place within Asia?

☺ ☺ ☺ **EXPEDITION: Japanese Garden**
For this activity, you will need:

- Book or video about Japan from the Library List or YouTube playlist
- A public Japanese garden near you
- Camera (a phone camera is great)
- World Explorer Journal

This Japanese garden is in Spokane, Washington. It has pagodas, running water, meandering paths, trees, an arching bridge, koi fish, and plants that have structure and foliage that is beautiful year round. Above all, it has peace and calm.

Japan is a country in Asia. Like many other countries in east Asia, it has been heavily influenced by Chinese culture. In east Asia, serenity and beauty are highly valued and the

Fabulous Fact

Peacocks are the national bird of India and a symbol of immortality. Their plumage has tiny, microscopic crystal-like structures that reflect light and make them shimmer.

Bookworms

Feathers for Peacock by Jacqueline Jules is a story about how peacocks got their colorful feathers. This is a fun, folktale-style, humorous picture book.

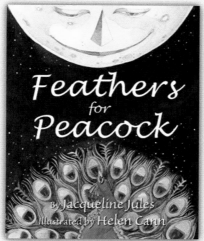

Writer's Workshop

Besides real animals, there are also mythological animals that are important to Asian cultures and stories. Draw your own dragon and write a vivid description of it with descriptive language.

Additional Layer

Mt. Everest is the highest mountain in the world at 29,032 feet (8848 meters), which is near the cruising height of a jumbo jet. It is on the border of Nepal and Tibet.

Learn more about this massive mountain.

- Who was it named after?
- What is its Napali name?
- Who was the first recorded person to climb to the top?
- During what months can people climb it?
- How much does it cost to climb it?
- Who is the youngest person ever to climb it?

Memorization Station

Rice paddy: a field planted with rice that grows in water

Most rice paddies are grown in flatlands. Farmers drain the fields, cut and thresh the rice, and store it. Rice is grown on all of the continents except Antarctica.

garden design of the region shows this. After World War II, many elements of Japanese culture came to the attention of the west and Japanese gardens were designed and grown in America and other places. Instead of lots of colorful flowers, Japanese gardens focus on serenity using rocks, trees, ponds, and running water. They often have bridges, fences, lanterns, and teahouses or pagodas as well.

1. Many larger cities have a public Japanese garden. Find out if your city has one. Visit it.

2. Before you go, read a book or watch a video about Japan.

3. Take pictures while you are there.

4. When you come home, print out your favorite picture and put it in your World Explorer Journal. Give it a caption that includes where you went and your favorite thing you saw there.

☺ ☺ ☺EXPLORATION: Rice Paddies

For this activity, you will need:

- Video about how rice is grown from the YouTube playlist
- World Explorer Journal
- Rice
- Rice cooker or pot with lid and a stove

People have been growing rice within Asia for thousands of years. It is the primary food staple for more than half of the world. Most of the world's rice is grown in **rice paddies** within Asia. China, Indonesia, and India are the top three rice-growing countries in the whole world. Rice grows in warm, wet climates and needs a long growing season. Many rice farmers flood their fields because rice grows really well in lots of water. Before it's time to harvest the rice, the fields are drained and given time to dry out. If rice is being grown on a hill, often the farmers will create stepped terraces so they can have flat areas to flood along the hill.

1. Watch a video on YouTube about how rice is grown.

2. Add an illustration with a caption in your World Explorer Journal about what you learned.

3. Cook some rice and taste it. Why do you think it is such an important food to so many people around the world?

☺ ☺ ☺ **EXPLORATION: Poster Map of Asia**

For this activity, you will need:

- Book or video about Asia from the Library List and YouTube playlist
- "Asia" from the Printable Pack (This is a simple outline of the continent. Print it using settings for "multi-page" or "poster" printing for an oversized map.)
- Tape
- Student atlas
- Colored crayons, pens, or pencils
- Glitter and school glue or glitter glue
- Colored paper
- Scissors
- Glue stick
- Oil pastels (optional)
- Paints and brushes (optional)

Bookworms

One Grain of Rice by Demi is a folktale that uses math to tell the story. It tells about a clever girl who saves her village with rice. It is a memorable story with charming illustrations.

Fabulous Fact

King cobras have their name because they kill and eat cobras.

Additional Layer

There are over 1,600 temples in Kyoto, Japan. Look some of them up online and notice their unique architecture. Find out which religious belief systems have temples and shrines in Japan.

Additional Layer

Use a map of Asia to find as many of these landforms as you can:

- Headland
- Cape
- Peninsula
- Strait
- Bay
- Sea
- Isthmus
- Gulf
- Archipelago
- Island
- Continent
- River
- River delta

Deep Thoughts

It has been said that religion causes conflict and war.

Does this mean religion is always a negative thing?

How can deeply held beliefs lead to clashes?

Can they also lead to peace?

Do you think the root cause of conflict is ideology or is it something deeper?

Fabulous Fact

The oldest known company in the world is Kongo Gumi. It has been building temples and shrines within Japan since 578 AD.

Here's a team of Kongo Gumi employees in the early 20th century.

1. Read a book or watch a video about Asia.

2. Tape the large Asia map together into one large map. Put the tape on the back of the sheets of paper so it won't get in the way of coloring and crafting.

3. Use a student atlas and your craft supplies to add the features to Asia that you want.

   Add rivers like the Yellow, Yangtze, Mekong, Ganges, Indus, Euphrates, Tigris, Ob, and Lena.

   Add mountains like Zagros, Himalayas, Tien Shan, and Qilian Shan. Add Mount Everest.

   Add the Equator.

   Add the Gobi Desert, Arabian Desert, and Siberia.

   Include cities like Jerusalem, Abu Dhabi, Baghdad, New Delhi, Beijing, Bangkok, Hong Kong, Singapore, Manila, and Tokyo.

4. Hang your completed map of Asia on the wall until the end of this unit.

People of Asia

☺ ☺ ☻EXPLORATION: Asian Religions

For this activity, you will need:

- "Religions in Asia" map from the Printable Pack
- Colored pencils or crayons
- Internet or a book about world religions

This is a thematic map. It shows just one aspect, or theme, of a place. Thematic maps are used to help explain something about the land or the people. This map of religions shows how people with different belief systems live in different places. Sometimes, but not always, the religions follow national borders. What this map doesn't show are all the people who believe in minority religions but live in a place with a majority religion. For example, there are Buddhists and Muslims who live in Russia, a majority Christian nation. Likewise, there are Jews and Christians living in Iran, a majority Muslim nation. This map also doesn't show the different sects of the major religions. For example, the Philippines is primarily Catholic Christian and Russia is primarily Orthodox Christian, but this map doesn't distinguish between the two. In addition, it can't show differentiations between specific locations and sects. Less than two percent of Indonesians are Hindu, but within Bali, a province of Indonesia, Balinese Hindu is practiced by over

85% of the population. There are also Muslim and Buddhist sects that are not differentiated in various parts of Asia.

1. Color the "Religions in Asia" map by number.

2. While you color, discuss:

   a. Why would the religion of people be important to know about?

   b. Does religion cause conflict between people in the real world? Why?

   c. Does religion affect government or the amount of freedom people have?

   d. How does religion affect the values or mores of a nation? (Mores are cultural norms like manners, clothing, and behaviors that everyone is expected to have).

3. Take each religion, one by one, and discuss the basic beliefs. Use the internet or a book about world religions to aid you. You don't have to do every religion on the map, a sampling is okay, depending on how much time you want to spend on this.

😊 😊 😊 **EXPLORATION: Asian Countries**

For this activity, you will need:

- Book or video about Asian Countries from the Library List, YouTube playlist, or a geography encyclopedia
- "Asian Countries" from the Printable Pack
- Colored pencils or crayons

Famous Folks

Buddha was a religious teacher from South Asia who founded Buddhism. He was born as Siddhartha Gautama, but was known by the title Buddha which means "enlightened." He taught morality, meditation, and wisdom and believed that these things led to truth. There are statues of Buddha in all shapes and sizes throughout much of Asia.

Fabulous Fact

Throughout Bali, an island province of Indonesia, you will see little offering plates. These are a ritual of the Balinese Hindu people who arrange fruits and flowers and leave them on a tray to offer thanks.

There are roughly 45 countries in Asia. Some countries are disputed, such as Palestine. Some people also include Georgia, Armenia, Azerbaijan, and Cyprus as Asian, but we include them with Europe. There isn't a clear line between the Eurasian nations. In addition, sometimes Egypt is listed as an Asian country, but we include it with Africa since most of the country and nearly all of the population is within Africa. Hong Kong, Taiwan, and Tibet are all sometimes claimed to be part of China and sometimes listed as independent nations. We listed Taiwan as an independent nation. Hong Kong and Tibet, however, are fully occupied by China, so we include them with China. Borders change and adapt over time, and many of these nations have been subject to border changes in recent years.

For the convenience of this curriculum, we have divided Asia into five regions which will be studied in more depth in future years. The five regions are Near East, Southeast Asia, Indian Subcontinent, Far East, and Asian Steppes.

Regions are useful for discussing areas of the world that encompass more than one country. Regions are arbitrary and defined by the person using them. There are no accepted geographical regions that everyone agrees on. Regardless of their continent, you can learn about each of these nations, its location, and its people.

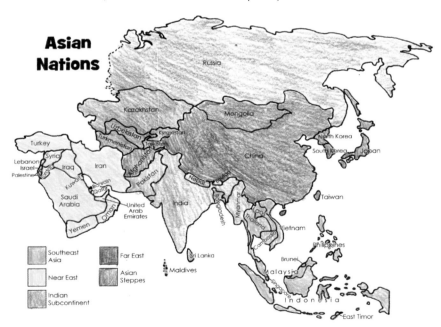

1. Read a book or watch a video about Asian countries.

2. Color the "Asian Countries" map by region. Use this chart and the image above to help you.

Southeast Asia	Near East

• Laos • Vietnam • Thailand • Cambodia • Singapore • Malaysia • Indonesia • Brunei • East Timor • Philippines	• Turkey • Syria • Lebanon • Israel • Palestine • Jordan • Saudi Arabia • Yemen	• Oman • United Arab Emirates • Qatar • Bahrain • Kuwait • Iraq • Iran
Asian Steppes	**Indian Subcontinent**	**Far East**
• Afghanistan • Turkmenistan • Uzbekistan • Tajikistan • Kyrgyzstan • Kazakhstan • Russia	• India • Pakistan • Nepal • Bhutan • Bangladesh • Myanmar • Sri Lanka • Maldives	• China • Japan • Mongolia • North Korea • South Korea • Taiwan

☺ ☺**EXPLORATION: Asian Cities**

For this activity, you will need:

- "Asian Cities" and "Plotting Asian Cities" from the Printable Pack
- Colored pencils or crayons
- Colored markers

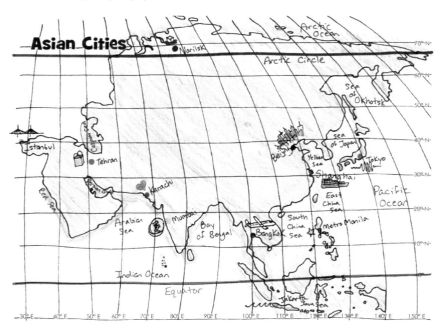

1. Follow the directions from the "Plotting Asian Cities" sheet using global coordinates to complete the "Asian Cities"

Fabulous Fact

Russia is a transcontinental nation. 77% of Russia is in Asia and the western 23% is in Europe.

There is a bridge over the Ural River in the town of Orenburg, Russia that is considered to be the border between the two continents.

In truth, the border between Asia and Europe has changed many times over the centuries, depending on who you ask. It has no real consequence other than for purposes of attracting tourists to the spots.

It is interesting, however, that Europe is considered to be in the western hemisphere and Asia is considered to be in the eastern hemisphere. That makes the line between the two also symbolic of East versus West.

Famous Folks

Marco Polo was a famous merchant from Venice, Italy who trekked across Asia and recorded his travels in the late 1200s. He described the lands and peoples of Asia along his way. He described amazing wealth and opulence as well as the advances, culture, and social structure he observed on his trip. Some experts question whether he exaggerated the stories, but his tales are a fascinating insight into Asia. Here is a page from *The Travels of Marco Polo*.

map.

2. Add the map to the Geography section of your Layers of Learning Notebook.

😊 😊 😊 EXPLORATION: Destination Asia

For this activity, you will need:

- Internet to look up an Asian country
- "Travel Brochure" from the Printable Pack
- Colored pencils or crayons

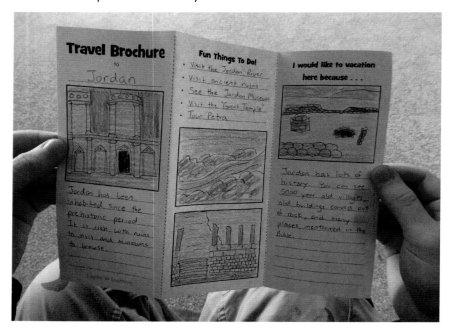

1. Choose an Asian country. Find out more about it online.

2. Write and illustrate a travel brochure showing the sights in that country that you would like to go see.

😊 😊 😊 EXPLORATION: Asian Greeting Game

For this activity, you will need:

- "Asian Greetings" from the Printable Pack
- Scissors
- Book or video about Asia from the Library List or YouTube playlist for this unit

Asia is not only big, it is also diverse, with many different cultures and customs. If you want to greet someone in South Korea, you bow if that person is older than you or in a respected position. In Yemen, you say "marhaba" (hello) and then shake their hand if they are the same gender as you. In India, you say "namaste" as you press your hands together, palm to palm, and give a slight bow.

1. Cut apart the "Asian Greetings" cards. Shuffle them and place them face down.

2. Each person picks up a card and performs the greeting on the card. The others try to guess which Asian country the greeting comes from. The person to guess the correct greeting gets to keep the card. Take turns until you've collected all of the cards.

3. Read a book or watch a video about Asia to finish off your lesson.

☺ ☺ EXPLORATION: Is It In Asia? Game

For this activity, you will need:

- Globe or world map
- "Is It In Asia?" map and the following page of image cards from the Printable Pack (one copy per child)
- Scissors
- Glue stick
- Colored pencils or crayons

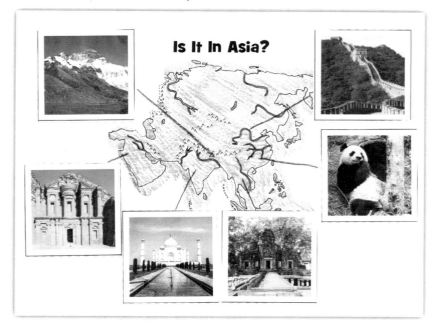

Is It In Asia?

1. On a globe or world map, find where you live and then find Asia.

2. Color the map of Asia.

3. Cut apart the picture cards, mix them up, then present them one at a time to the kids, asking, "Is this in Asia?"

   The first six are in Asia: panda bear, Taj Mahal, Great Wall of China, Petra in Jordan, Angkor Wat, Mount Everest.

   The Statue of Liberty, St. Basil's Cathedral, pyramids at

Famous Folks

Many famous athletes come from Asia. Ekaterina Gordeeva and Sergei Grinkov were two famous Russian ice skaters and Olympians with a tragic story. Learn more about them.

Fabulous Fact

Acupuncture, the practice of penetrating the skin with thin needles and gently moving them, began to be practiced anciently in China. It focuses on balancing the body's energy to promote healing.

Deep Thoughts

Discuss this quote by Confucius:

"What the superior man seeks is in himself. What the small man seeks is in others."

What you think it means? Do you think it's true? Do you have any real-life examples?

Writer's Workshop

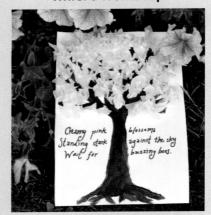

Write a haiku. This simple form of poetry comes from Japan. It has only three lines and seventeen syllables. The first line has five, the second has seven, and the final line has five syllables.

Haiku poems are usually about nature and try to capture a moment, much like taking a picture does.

Once you've written your poem, turn it into art by making a picture that surrounds it and captures the meaning of your haiku.

You can learn this form of poetry, as well as many others, in *Writer's Workshop Poetry*.

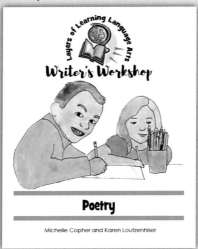

Giza, Uluru, Machu Picchu, and the Lalibela church are not in Asia.

4. Glue the cards that are in Asia to the spaces around the map of Asia.

5. Add it to the geography section of your Layers of Learning Notebook.

☺ ☺ ☺ EXPLORATION: Asian Countries Hangman

For this activity, you will need:

- Student atlas
- "Asia Countries Hangman" from the Printable Pack
- Clear page protector
- Wet erase or dry erase markers
- Paper towel or eraser
- Clipboard (optional)

1. Look at a map of Asia in your student atlas and point out each of the countries. How many of them have you heard of? Do you know where any of them are located?

2. Put the "Asian Countries Hangman" sheet inside a clear page protector so you will be able to write on it and then wipe it off to play over and over again.

3. Play Asia Country Hangman. Someone is "it" and chooses an Asian country. "It" keeps his or her country a secret and makes spaces for each letter in the name of the country on the bottom of the "Asian Countries Hangman" printable. Put the printable on a clipboard or surface where everyone can see it.

4. With the aid of a student atlas, students guess letters one by one, taking turns. "It" crosses the guessed letter off the Letter Bank. If the letter is in the name of the country, "It" writes the letter in the correct space. If the letter is not in the name of the country, "It" draws a body part on the stick figure.

5. If the Asian country is guessed before the stick figure is competed, then the students win; if it is not guessed, then "It" wins.

6. Make it harder by taking away the student atlas or by allowing cities or landmarks as well as country names.

☺ ☺ **EXPLORATION: Ten Asian Landmarks**

For this activity, you will need:

- Computer with the internet and a slideshow creator (PowerPoint, Prezi, Animoto, or OpenOffice Impress are some options)

1. Asia has many amazing landmarks. You will be choosing ten to create a slideshow presentation about. Go online to research each one, and then make one slide for each of your ten landmarks. On each of the slides, add a picture and a description or interesting facts about each of the landmarks you chose.

2. You can add fun elements to your slideshow like moving text, transitions, music or narration, and other design elements.

3. Present your slideshow to your family or another audience and teach them about each of the Asian landmarks you chose. Be prepared to answer any questions they have at the end.

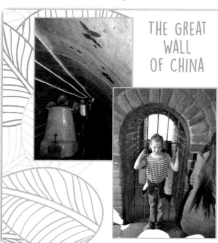

THE GREAT WALL OF CHINA

To see the Great Wall of China near Beijing, you ride on a little tram up the mountain. It goes through tunnels and has lights and drives slowly.

Along the wall there are lots of towers and guard stations you can explore. You can go inside some of them.

The entire wall is 13,171 miles long. We only explored about two miles of it. There are some parts of the wall that aren't continuous or have fallen into disrepair. That's not really surprising since it was built over 2,300 years ago.

☺ ☺ ☺ **EXPLORATION: Wan, To, Zum**

For this activity, you will need:

- Video about Asia from the YouTube playlist

Wan, To, Zum is a game that east Asian children play. It is similar to Rock, Paper, Scissors. In fact, Rock, Paper, Scissors

Memorization Station

Memorize some Asian landmarks and be able to point out their approximate locations on a map:

- Angkor Wat
- The Great Wall of China
- Borobudur
- The Grand Palace
- Marina Bay Sands
- Shibuya Crossing
- Petronas Twin Towers
- Mount Kinabalu
- Mount Krakatoa
- Mount Fuji
- Chocolate Hills
- Puerto Princesa Subterranean River
- Abhayagiri in Anuradhapura
- Taipei 101
- The Taj Mahal

Famous Folks

Rabindranath Tagore was Asia's first Nobel Prize winner. He was a brilliant polymath, poet, and writer.

Additional Layer

Karst mountains are mountains made of soluble rocks. Sinkholes, fissures, and underground streams and caves are common in karst mountains because parts of the bedrock dissolves away.

Fabulous Fact

Chopsticks were invented about 5,000 years ago in China and then their use spread to many other nations. They were initially used to stir and retrieve food from cooking pots, but are commonly used to eat with today. The round end symbolizes heaven and the square end symbolizes earth.

Additional Layer

Your kids can craft Asian paper fans by cutting a paper plate in half, decorating it with markers or paint, and then gluing two large craft sticks to the bottom to make a handle.

came from Asia and spread into the west.

1. Watch a video about Asia. Tell the kids they will be using facts from the video in a game to encourage them to pay attention and remember.

2. Play Wan, To, Zum. Each player hits his or her fist on his or her other open palm while chanting "wan, to, zum." On the fourth hit, throw a sign for one of the elements.

   - Bird - all five fingers bunched together at the tips
   - Rock - clenched fist
   - Water - face down palm

3. Have all the children throw at the same time. If one is dominant, he or she is the winner. Otherwise the weak player is out and you continue until there is a winner.

   - Bird beats water because birds drink the water
   - Rock beats bird because a rock can hit a bird
   - Water beats rock because the rock sinks in water

4. The one who wins Wan, To, Zum then gets to ask the others a question about Asia from the video you just watched. The one who answers correctly gets a point. If no one gets it right, then the asker gets a point.

5. Play to five points.

😊 😊 😊 EXPLORATION: Asian-Themed Party
For this activity, you will need:

- "Near East Naan Bread" and the other recipes from the Printable Pack
- Ingredients for the recipes from the Printable Pack
- Tablecloth
- Place settings
- Colored streamers, paper lanterns, or other decor (optional)
- "Asian Taboo" from the Printable Pack, printed onto card stock and cut apart

We recommend you have this party at the end of your Asia unit to culminate your fun projects and learning.

1. Ahead of time, plan the menu using the Asian recipes from the Printable Pack or use your own Asian recipes.

2. Get the ingredients together and have the whole family help in cooking.

3. Set the table with a tablecloth, place settings, and any other decorations you like. Hang paper streamers and paper lanterns from the ceiling. You may want to hang

maps, flags, artwork, or projects from this unit around your table as well.

4. Serve your Asian food. While you eat, play "Asian Taboo" with the cards from the Printable Pack. The first player draws a card and has to get the rest of the diners to guess the big bold word on the card without saying the word or any other word (or form of the word) listed on the card. For an added challenge, you can use a timer. Start at 2 minutes and then shorten the time so you have to get faster.

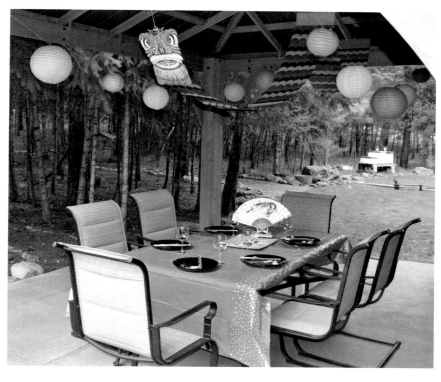

Step 3: Show What You Know

During this unit, choose one of the assignments below to show what you have learned during the unit. Add this work to your Layers of Learning Notebook. You can also use this assignment to show your supervising teacher or your charter school as a sample of what you've been working on in your homeschool, if needed.

There are more ideas for writing assignments in the "Writer's Workshop" sidebars.

☺ ☺ Coloring or Narration Page
For this activity, you will need:

*   "Asia" printable from the Printable Pack
*   Crayons, or colored pencils

Fabulous Fact

A yurt is a portable, round tent used by nomadic peoples within Asia. Traditionally, yurts have frames made of wood or bamboo and are covered in animal skins.

Bookworms

The Khan's Daughter by Laurence Yep is a Mongolian folk tale about a shepherd boy and the Khan's daughter.

Expedition

Go out to eat at an Asian restaurant to experience the food and ambiance. Try Thai, Indian, Japanese, Chinese, Korean, Vietnamese, or others.

People & Planet

Unit Trivia

1. What is the highest mountain in the world?

   Mt. Everest

2. True or false - China is Asia's largest country.

   False, although part of it is within Europe, Russia is Asia's largest country.

3. Fill in the blank: A _____ is a huge wave that stems from an underwater earthquake or disturbance.

   Tsunami

4. Name at least three world religions that originated in Asia.

   Christianity, Islam, Judaism, Buddhism, Hindu, Sikh, Confucianism/Taoism, Shinto

5. True or false - Plants die in droughts but thrive in floods.

   False - too little or too much water can kill many kinds of plants.

6. Which oceans touch Asia?

   Arctic, Pacific, and Indian

7. Fill in the blank: Mt. Fuji is the highest point in the country of _____.

   Japan

8. Which mountain range runs along the northern border of India?

   Himalayan Mountains

9. Which strait separates Asia from North America?

   The Bering Strait

10. Name at least five Asian animals.

    Answers will vary

1. Depending on the age and ability of the child, choose either the "Asia" coloring sheet or the "Asia" narration page from the Printable Pack.

2. Younger kids can color the coloring sheet as you review some of the things you learned about during this unit. You might talk about Asian landscapes, regions, religions, animals, or peoples. On the bottom of the coloring page, kids can write a sentence about what they learned. Very young children can explain their ideas orally while a parent writes for them.

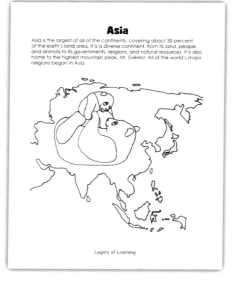

3. Older kids can write about some of the concepts you learned on the narration page and color the picture as well.

4. Add this to the Geography section of your Layers of Learning Notebook.

😊 😊 😊 **Writer's Workshop**

For this activity, you will need:

- A computer or a piece of paper and a writing utensil

Choose from one of the ideas below or write about something else you learned during this unit. Each of these prompts corresponds with one of the units from the Layers of Learning Writer's Workshop curriculum, so you may choose to coordinate the assignment with the monthly unit you are learning about in Writer's Workshop.

- **Sentences, Paragraphs, & Narrations:** Write a paragraph that compares Asia and another one of the continents. How are the two alike? How are they different?
- **Descriptions & Instructions:** Have you ever been in a natural disaster? Describe what your experience was like.
- **Fanciful Stories:** Dragons star in lots of Asian stories. Write your own story about a dragon.
- **Poetry:** Make a shape poem about Mt. Everest with your words climbing the side of the mountain slope and then descending down the other side.
- **True Stories:** Do some research about Confucius, Brahma, Abraham, Laozi, Jesus, Muhammad, or another

religious founder. Tell the true story of the person's life and the founding of the associated religion.

- **Reports and Essays:** Choose an Asian animal and create an animal mobile with picture cards and descriptions about habitat, diet, appearance, lifespan, and interesting facts.
- **Letters:** Write a pen pal letter to someone your age who lives in an Asian country of your choice. Describe what your life is like in your own country, then ask questions about theirs. There are pen pal services that can help connect you with real pen pals around the world; alternately, you can just do this as an exercise and not send your letter.
- **Persuasive Writing:** Write an opinion paragraph about whether or not you believe Asia is the most diverse continent in the world. Back up your opinion with reasons.

☺ ☺ ☺ Big Book of Knowledge

For this activity, you will need:

- "Big Book of Knowledge: Asia" printable from the Printable Pack, printed on card stock
- Markers
- Big Book of Knowledge

1. Color, draw on, or write on the Big Book of Knowledge page. Record concepts, definitions, and facts you learned during this unit. It's a record of the things you learned and hope to remember. Add the page to your Big Book of Knowledge.

2. Use your Big Book of Knowledge regularly to help you review, quiz, or create games that will help you commit the things you've learned to memory.

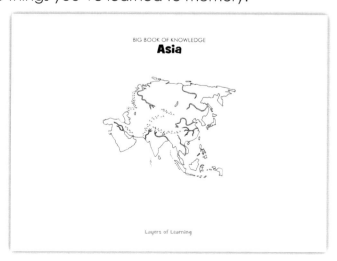

Big Book of Knowledge

The Big Book of Knowledge is a book for you, the mentor, to use as a constant review of all of the things you're learning about. You can use it to quiz your kids or prepare tests or review games. Whenever you learn something in Layers of Learning that you want your kids to remember, add it to your Big Book of Knowledge.

Assemble your Big Book of Knowledge in a binder or with binder rings. Divide it into sections for each subject.

In the Printable Pack for this unit you will find a "Big Book of Knowledge" sheet. You can add this sheet to others you collect or create yourself as you progress through the Layers of Learning curriculum. Customize the Big Book of Knowledge to your family by adding facts and topics that you enjoyed exploring as you were learning.

Visit Layers of Learning online to find more information on how to assemble and use your own Big Book of Knowledge.

You will also find cover and section pages to print along with creative games to play with your Big Book of Knowledge to keep school, even the tests, fun!

Unit Overview

Key Concepts:
- Soil is full of important minerals that give people, plants, and animals nutrients and provide people with the natural resources we use to make everything we need.
- South America is a continent that is biologically rich and diverse.
- It is the home of the Amazon Rainforest, the Amazon River, Lake Titicaca, Angel Falls, the Atacama Desert, and the Andes Mountains.

Vocabulary:
- Craton
- Shield
- Orogenesis
- Sedimentary basin
- Soil fertility
- Pampas
- Trade
- Harbor
- Port
- Desert
- Rain shadow
- Rainforest

Important Places:
- South America
- Amazon Rainforest
- Amazon River
- Lake Titicaca
- Angel Falls
- Atacama Desert
- Andes Mountains

SOUTH AMERICA

In this unit, we'll be learning a bit about continental rock and also explore the continent of South America.

Continents are very affected by the rock and soil they are built on. Diamonds, gold, oil, and rare earth elements are found only in certain types of rock. You will never find diamonds in anything but the oldest continental foundations. Productive farmland also depends on the type of soil that is present. The soil depends on the rock as well as on the plants and the climate in the area. In turn, these things affect wealth, jobs, food production, and how well the land can support populations of people.

South America straddles the equator, making most of the continent warm. The north is wet and home to the dense Amazon Rainforest. As you move further from the equator, the rainfall diminishes and, by the time you get to Argentina, grasslands dominate. The Andes Mountains, which run the entire length of the continent from north to south, form a rain shadow along the west coast of Peru and Chile, making the deserts there some of the driest on earth. In some places, rain falls only once every ten years or so. The Andes Mountains are high enough that they are snow covered all year round, and the highlands can be quite cool year round.

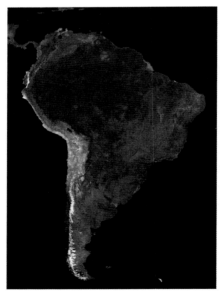 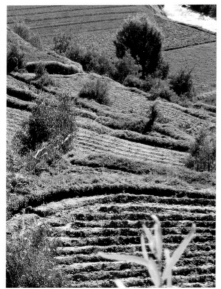

The terraced farms of Peru are necessary in the steep mountains of the young Andes on the western side of the continent.

The eastern half of South America consists of a series of cratons, or very old continental bedrock that once belonged to Pangaea and previous supercontinents. The northeast and east are ringed by the Brazilian and Guiana

Highlands, areas of old eroded mountains and plateaus. The west is lined with the young, still-forming Andes Mountains, some of the tallest mountains in the world.

Step I: Library List

Choose books from your library that go with this topic. Here's a list of some favorites and also a list of search terms so you can utilize what your library offers. Read the books with your kids and/or assign them some to read independently. It is from these books your kids will learn most of the facts they need for this unit.

Search for: soil, South America, Amazon River, Andes Mountains, Amazon Rainforest, rainforests, Patagonia

☺ ☻ ☻*Geography of the World* by DK. Read "Central and South America" and "Peoples of Central and South America" on pages 40-43.

☺ ☻ ☻*DK Student Atlas*. Use pages 58-65 to help you learn about and map South America.

☺ ☻ ☻*Smithsonian Children's Illustrated Atlas* by DK. Read "South America" on pages 22-33.

☺ ☻ ☻*Wild South America* from Amazon Prime. This is a fantastic documentary series about the nature of South America from the top to the southern tip. Suitable for everyone in the family. Also part of the *BBC Atlas of the Natural World: Western Hemisphere and Antarctica* DVD set.

☺ ☻ ☻*Eyewitness: The Amazon* by DK. This book teaches all about the Amazon River in a series of colorful pictures with interesting captions.

☺ ☻ ☻*Pebbles, Sand, and Silt* by Delta Education. A great read-aloud to introduce and discuss rocks and soil.

☺*Dirt: The Scoop on Soil* by Natalie Myra Rosinsky. A simple picture book that tells what soil is made of, how it is formed, and how to keep it healthy.

☺*Dirt* by Steve Tomecek. How soil is formed, the layers of soil, and its importance as a natural resource.

☺*3-D Explorer: Rainforest* by Joe Fullman. This is a gorgeous pop-up book about the Amazon River and plants and animals that live in and around it.

☺*This Place Is High: the Andes Mountains of South America* by Vicki Cobb. From what it's like to have so little oxygen to the animals that live there, this book explores what it would

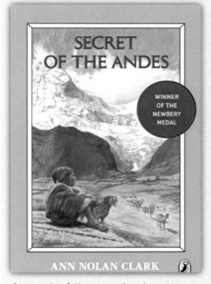

Secret of the Andes by Ann Nolan Clark is a fictional coming of age story of a boy who lives in the Andes Mountains and tends llamas. He finds out he has ties to the Incan past of Peru.

be like to actually live up in the Andes.

South America by Rebecca Hirsch. This is a simple beginner's guide to the continent. Includes full-color photos and just a little bit of text on each page.

South America by Libby Koponen. This is part of the "True Books" series. It has full-color photos and a medium amount of text.

South America by Madeline Donaldson. This is a part of simple continent series that gives basic, but interesting, information about the continent. It would make a great family read-aloud introduction to South America.

All The Way Down: Amazon Rainforest by Alex Wolf. This is a guide that takes you from the animals and plants that live high in the trees to those that live down under the ground and in the water. You explore the organisms that live in each level of the rainforest.

Atacama Desert Research Journal by Sonya Newland. The reader follows along as a scientist studies the Atacama Desert. You'll learn about the desert; its plants, animals, and people; plus how it may be in danger.

Where Is the Amazon? by Sarah Fabiny. Packed with information from the geology of the river to its history and environment. Contains lots of bright images and fairly dense text for good readers.

Bill Nye The Science Guy: Rocks & Soil. This is a video. You can often find these episodes on YouTube.

A Kid's Guide to South America by Jack L. Roberts. Learn about each country of South America with full-color photos of the people, scenery, and animals. A casual read.

Not For Parents South America: Everything You Ever Wanted to Know by Lonely Planet Kids. This is not a guidebook; it's more like a collection of true and fascinating stories about South America. Great for parents and kids to read together.

Atacama Desert by José da Silva de Magalhães. A book of photographs with captions of the best places to visit if you ever get a chance.

Soil: The Incredible Story of What Keeps the Earth, and Us, Healthy by Matthew Evans. This is a popular-level book written by a farmer all about how soil is essential and how we can care for it.

Dirt: The Ecstatic Skin of the Earth by William Bryant Logan. This book examines the importance of soil and also the human connection to it through the centuries, including architecture, medicine, farming, mining, and more.

Step 2: Explore

Choose a few hands-on Explorations from this section to work on as a family. They should be appealing activities that will create mental hooks so your kids remember the information in the unit. Save the rest of the Explorations for the next time you do this unit in four years when your kids are older. You can also read the sidebars together and explore some little rabbit trails.

This unit includes printables. See the introduction for instructions on retrieving your Printable Pack.

Rock & Soil

The rocks and soils of a continent affect the plants, animals, and people who live on it. The minerals available for mining are also dependent on the kind of rock the land is formed from, which greatly affects human economics and political power. The ease or ruggedness of terrain and coastlines also affects trade and transportation.

☺ ☺ ☺ **EXPLORATION: Building a Continent**
For this activity, you will need:

- "Cratons & Shields" from the Printable Pack
- Colored pencils
- Rock(s)
- Clay or salt dough (1/2 cup warm water, 1/4 cup salt, 4 Tbs cooking oil, 2 cups flour)
- Sand
- Plastic bin, shoe box size or bigger
- Water
- Blue food coloring

A **craton** is a very old, solid piece of ancient continental crust. Cratons are generally intrusive igneous rock, like granite. Every continent, including South America, has one or more cratons at its core. These cratons are from the Precambrian Period, some of them nearly as old as the earth itself. They have moved around the planet, being pushed into supercontinents and then pulled back apart repeatedly. They have extremely deep roots, plunging deep into the mantle and are the most stable parts of a continent, with the least tectonic activity. A craton that has rock exposed at the surface is known as a **shield**.

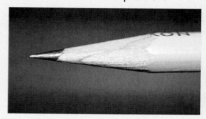

Fabulous Fact

Since soils take millions of years to form and humans cannot make soil, it is a precious resource. Without fertile soils we cannot grow enough food for our populations. If we pollute the soil, strip the soil away, or erode the soil through plowing and over watering, it cannot be replaced.

Memorization Station

Orogenesis: the formation of mountains by folding of the earth's crust and volcanoes

Sedimentary basin: place where sediment washes down and accumulates, becoming sedimentary rock

Soil fertility: how well the soil can support and grow plants

Pampas: a grassland region in South America with high soil fertility

New rock is also constantly being built through **orogenesis**, the formation of mountains by tectonic means. Mountains can be built with the uplift of continental rock or by volcanic activity. The old cratons and the newer orogenesis both crumble through the processes of erosion. The sediments created wash down into low lying areas, accumulate, and create large regions of sedimentary rock known as **sedimentary basins**.

1. Go outside and find at least one big, fist-sized or larger rock that has at least one flat side.

2. Color the "Cratons & Shields" printable. Make the craton gray, the sedimentary rock orange, and the volcanic rock purple. Color the oceans blue. Color the oceanic crust black. Then color the mantle area below the crust yellow.

3. The rock you found represents the craton of a continent. Inside a plastic box, place your rock or rocks with the flat side up. Then build at least one volcanic or fold mountain range out of clay or salt dough.

4. Between and around the volcanoes and the craton, fill in the land with sand, representing layers of sedimentary rock. The sand can cover or partially cover your craton.

5. Color a pitcher of water blue with food coloring. Then, carefully pour your "ocean" into your box. You have built a continent.

6. On the lower portion of the "Cratons & Shields" printable, draw a cross section diagram of the continent you built. Label your craton(s).

7. Put the "Cratons & Shields" printable into your Layers of Learning Notebook in the Geography section.

☺ ☺ ☺EXPERIMENT: Soil Fertility

For this activity, you will need:

- Book or video about soil from the Library List or YouTube playlist for this unit.
- "Soil Fertility" map from the Printable Pack.
- Colored pencils or crayons
- 3 jars or cups
- 3 different soils (potting soil, sand, soil from your yard, clay soil, etc.)
- Bean seeds (or another easy-to-grow plant)

Soil fertility is how well the soil can support and grow plants. Soils are full of microorganisms such as worms, bacteria, and fungi that break down organic matter like fallen leaves. As they break down the organic matter, they change it into inorganic nutrients. These nutrients are then taken up by the roots of living plants. If the soils are depleted of inorganic nutrients, then the soil will not grow plants very well. Soils in warm, tropical places or dry deserts are usually poor because they don't have enough organic matter. In warm places, the leaves and other debris break down too quickly and don't have a chance to accumulate. In deserts, there just isn't enough plant matter. Grasslands are usually the places with highest soil fertility. The **Pampas** region in southern South America is an example of a fertile soil region.

1. Read a book or watch a video about soil.

2. Color the "Soil Fertility" map according to the key. Where are the most fertile places on Earth? How do you think soil fertility might affect populations or economics and

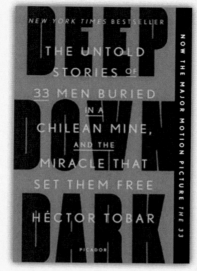
Expedition

Find out if there is a mine near you that lets people take tours. Often mines that aren't being used for mining anymore will have tours.

Go on a mine tour so you can see where the minerals you use every day come from. Go prepared with a really good question or two for the tour guide.

Deep Thoughts

Valuable minerals are found all over the earth, including in poor countries that don't have the resources or technological know-how to mine the minerals themselves.

Often rich companies or countries will come in and mine the minerals, abusing the people and leaving a mess behind. Often the reason poor countries are poor is because of corruption, so the leadership of the country welcomes the mining companies in because the few elites at the top get rich off the deal.

For an example of this, look up how the indigenous people of Ecuador are fighting back against Chinese mining companies and the local government officials. (China is not the only country that does this. The U.S., Britain, and many European countries also engage in this international abuse).

Discuss solutions.

trade among people? Put the map in your Layers of Learning Notebook behind the Geography divider.

3. Put three different types of soil into three different cups or jars. Label the cups with each type of soil.

4. Press a bean seed into the soil up to the depth of your first finger joint. Then water each cup.

5. Monitor the growth of the seeds for four weeks, while you study this unit. Which soils grew the strongest, biggest plants?

☺ ☺ ☺EXPLORATION: Mining Minerals

For this activity, you will need:

- Internet
- Video about how soap is made from this unit's YouTube playlist
- Bar of soap
- Sink
- World Explorer Journal

Minerals such as gold, tungsten, aluminum, copper, tin, iron, sodium chloride, manganese, and cobalt are essential to modern life. Everything from the machinery we use to the electronics in our pockets uses these minerals. Not a single thing you do, eat, or use could be accomplished without minerals. All of these minerals are obtained through mining.

1. Search around your home or classroom and determine which minerals the things around you were made of. You can use the internet to research.

   Pencils have graphite, knobs are made of aluminum or iron and tin, computers (including phones) contain tellurium, lithium, and cobalt, among others.

2. Watch a video about how soap is made. Which minerals are used in the process?

Answer: The steel the machines are made from is iron and carbon, plus often manganese, silicon, phosphorus, and oxygen, among others.

3. Place a bar of soap in a sink that you can leave alone over night. Turn the water on so it hits the soap at a slow drip. In your World Explorer Journal, draw a picture of your experiment and write down what you think will happen.

4. The next day, observe your soap bar. Relate the "erosion" of the soap to the erosion of the rocks on Earth, a process that frees the minerals so they are available to

plants and animals and for mining. These Earth minerals are used in all sorts of things we do every day, from manufacturing goods to providing the essential minerals we need in the food we eat.

☺ ☺ ☺EXPLORATION: Mining Makes a Mess

For this activity, you will need:

- Book or video about mining from the Library List or YouTube playlist for this unit
- Blueberry or chocolate chip muffins, one per child
- Toothpicks

Countries that have minerals can make a lot of money from the mining. However, that mining can also make a big mess. It can pollute the water, destroy the landscape, and harm the health of the people. It is important to mine, but we need to do it carefully and responsibly so we have a beautiful, healthy world for generations to come.

1. Watch a video about mining.

2. Using toothpicks, extract the blueberry or chocolate chip minerals from the muffin rock. Compare the chocolate chips or blueberries to the minerals we extract from mines within the earth.

3. Discuss:

   a. How messy was mining your muffin? Could you have been less messy? How?

   b. How is mining in your muffin like mining for minerals in the earth?

Writer's Workshop

Divide a sheet of paper into two columns. In one column, write a list of the benefits we get from mining. In the second column, write a list of the harmful environmental impacts of mining.

Below your list, write a paragraph about whether or not you believe the benefits outweigh the potential harm.

Additional Layer

In some South American countries, mining has become a family vocation. Even kids go deep into the mines to extract the minerals from the earth.

Look up some articles about child labor and mining online to learn more about this controversial practice.

You can search on your own or follow links from the Resources page for this unit.

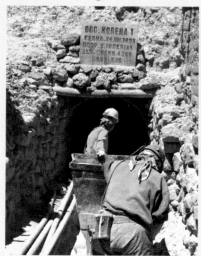

Potosi Mines, Bolivia. Shared under CC 2.0 license by Jenny Mealing

Additional Layer

The Andes Mountain Range is part of the Ring of Fire, a giant circle of volcanoes that surrounds the Pacific Ocean.

Learn what living on the Ring of Fire means for people in this region. Have there been any natural disasters on the west coast of South America recently?

You can learn more about the tectonic plates that cause the Ring of Fire in *Earth & Space: Plate Tectonics*.

Memorization Station

Memorize all of the countries and capitals of South America. You'll find videos on this unit's YouTube playlist that can help you. Spend a few minutes each day reviewing them. There's also a printable map to label in the Printable Pack.

4. Draw a picture of your muffin and the mess you made in your World Explorer Journal. Write a caption about what you did and about the need to clean up the messes we make on Earth.

☺ ☺ ☻ **EXPLORATION: Natural Harbors**

For this activity, you will need:

- Internet
- World Explorer Journal

One of the most important factors for economic success is **trade**. If a country can't or won't trade with other nations, then it will be poorer, have fewer goods, and have much less political power. One major factor for trade is the presence of **harbors**. Most global trade is conducted over the oceans, and protected harbors provide safe places for **ports** to be built where ships can load and unload cargo. Harbors are protected places along the coast that have deep water. Sometimes they are protected by islands or peninsulas, other times they are located up the mouth of a river. People also build artificial barriers to create or improve harbors.

1. Look up Santos, Brazil on an online map. Find the harbor.

   From the map, can you tell what makes this a good spot for shipping?

2. Next, look up Cartagena, Colombia on an online map. Examine the harbor. What makes it a good place for shipping?

3. Last, look at the coast of Suriname on the online map. Where would you build a shipping port? Why?

4. In your World Explorer Journal, draw a piece of imaginary coastline with a natural harbor. Draw landing places for your ships so they can load and unload cargo and people. Write a caption about what makes your harbor a good place for ships to stop.

South American Landscapes

☺ ☻ **EXPLORATION: Fabric Map of Geology and Biomes**

WARNING: This activity uses a hot iron. An adult or older teen should use the iron while children do other parts of the craft.

For this activity, you will need:

- "South America," "South America Geology," and "South

American Biomes" from the Printable Pack
- Fabric in various colors (You will need five colors, plus the blue for ocean. You might want yellow, greens, browns, and oranges for the biome map. The same colors can be used for the geology map.)
- Double-sided fusible webbing
- Sharp scissors (to cut fabric)
- Iron
- Tape measure or ruler

Make maps of South America out of fabric scraps. Start with the outline of South America from the Printable Pack.

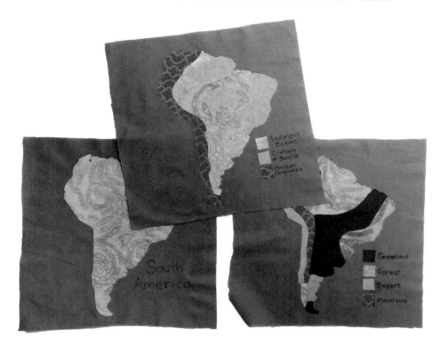

1. Cut three rectangles out of blue fabric, each 9 x 12 inches (23 x 30 cm).

2. Iron one side of the fusible webbing onto your remaining pieces of fabric so the fabric is stiff and easier to work with.

3. Use the "South America" outline to use as a stencil to make a simple fabric map of South America.

4. Cut apart the "South America Geology" printable on the solid lines like a puzzle.

   Place the pieces on the fabric, outline with a pencil or pen onto different colors of fabric according to the type of geology.

   Cratons and shields are both very old, Precambrian rocks that have been partially exposed by weathering. These should be one color of fabric.

Additional Layer

Potatoes are native to South America, where they grow over 200 varieties. Potato in Spanish is "patata" or "papa." Try these Chilean Papas.

Boil some diced potatoes until they are tender, then fry them in a pan with oil. Sauté them until they are brown and crispy all over. Combine 1 tablespoon white vinegar with 1 clove of garlic, 1 ½ Tbsp. paprika, ¾ tsp. oregano, and ¼ tsp. cumin. Toss over the potatoes, stir, and enjoy.

Additional Layer

There are over 200 varieties of fruits from the Amazon that are cultivated for humans. Have you heard of these?

- Camu camu
- Maracuya
- Acai berries
- Bacaba (kumbu)
- Capuazu
- Aguaje
- Cocona
- Pitahaya
- Pacay
- Cocona
- Mamey sapote

See if you can find any of these fruits to try while you learn about South America.

This is cocona fruit. It looks like a pepper on the outside but tastes like a cross between a tomato and a lemon.

The sedimentary basins are low lying areas where sediments have built up over the old rock. The sedimentary basins should be another color of fabric.

The Andean orogenesis is new rock that has more recently been added and is still growing on the South American continent. This should be a third color of fabric.

5. Cut apart the "South American Biomes" printable on the solid lines like a puzzle.

   Cut out each type of biome onto a different color of fabric.

   Peel the paper off the fusible webbing and iron onto your blue ocean piece.

6. Hang your maps to display them during this unit and tell about what each of the maps shows.

☺ ☺ EXPLORATION: Atacama Desert

For this activity, you will need:

- Student Atlas (or online map)
- Internet
- Plaster of Paris
- Sand
- Disposable cup or bowl and spoon
- Paper plate
- Chenille stems (pipe cleaners)
- Colored paper
- Glue
- Scissors

The Atacama **Desert** lies along the Pacific coast of northern Chile. The driest part is nestled between the Andes Mountains and the Chilean Coastal Range, making a double **rain shadow**. It is one of the driest places on Earth and normally receives less than .6 inches (15 mm) of rain each year. Some places in the Atacama have never received rain since people began recording.

1. Find the Atacama Desert on a map of South America. Then, look up pictures of the Atacama on the internet so you can see what it looks like.

2. Mix ½ cup Plaster of Paris with ¼ cup water in the disposable cup with a disposable spoon.

3. Pour the Plaster of Paris onto the paper plate and spread it evenly across the plate with the mixing spoon.

4. Sprinkle sand across the top of the Plaster of Paris, pressing it in gently with the back of a disposable spoon.

5. Research the Atacama Desert online and then craft a few plants and animals out of chenille stems. Make spiral bodies by wrapping a chenille stem around a pen or pencil. Then add paper faces, wings, or other features.

☻ ☻EXPLORATION: **Physical Map of South America**

For this activity, you will need:

- "South America Physical Map" and "South America Physical Map Labeling" from the Printable Pack
- Student atlas
- Black pen
- Colored Pencils

A physical map shows landscape features like mountains, forests, and rivers.

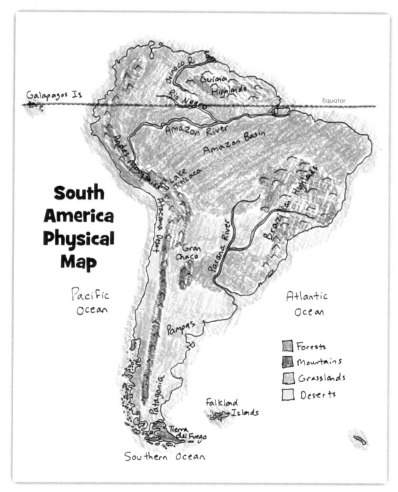

1. Trace over the equator with a red pencil on the "South America Physical Map" printable.

Deep Thoughts

In 2011, a tribe of about 200 individuals was discovered living on the border of Brazil and Peru, deep in the Amazon Rainforest. They have never had direct contact with the outside world. Brazil has a policy of maintaining their isolation because they fear the effects of disease and loss of freedom on these people, but the policy is under fire.

Does a tribe of a few dozen deserve the preservation of millions of acres of wilderness?

Does leaving these people isolated help or hurt them?

Can and should you protect people who are unaware they need protection?

Memorization Station

Desert: land with sparse vegetation that gets less than 10 inches (25 cm) of rain per year

Rain shadow: land that is blocked from receiving rain by mountain ranges

Additional Layer

Metals and mining have been an important part of human history. We even name our historical eras based on the metal tools people were making. Stone Age, Bronze Age, and Iron Age being the big three.

To make bronze, you have to mix copper and tin. Tin is only found in a few places on Earth. There is some tin in Mesoamerica and it can be found in South America in the Andes Mountains of Peru.

The Bronze Age in the Near East was from around 3300 BC until 1200 BC. Mesoamerica had a Bronze Age from about AD 1200 to 1500. South America also had a Bronze Age from about AD 100 to 1533. But in the Americas, bronze was never the primary material for making tools and is not a good indicator of their level of civilization or technological advancement.

This is a bronze figure from the Moche people of South America who flourished from AD 100-700.

Learn more about the Bronze Age in Layers of Learning *Ancient History: Bronze Age Near East.*

2. Use the "South America Physical Map Labeling" checklist and an atlas to label each of the features in South America carefully with a black pen.

3. Color the water blue.

4. Make a key on the map for each of the types of landscape: forests, mountains, grasslands, deserts.

5. Color the map according to your key. Add it to the Geography section of your Layers of Learning Notebook.

☺ ☺ ☺ **EXPLORATION: Landforms Map of South America**
For this activity, you will need:

- "South American Landforms" from the Printable Pack
- Scissors
- Glue stick
- Book or video about South America
- Watercolor paints

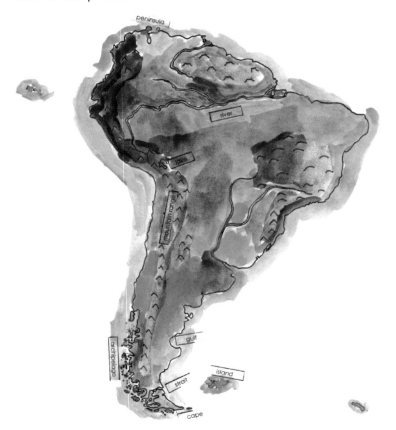

1. Cut out the tags at the bottom of the "South American Landforms" map. Glue them on next to an example of that landform on the map.

2. While you let the glue dry, read a book or watch a

video about South America.

3. Paint the map with watercolor paints. Once the map is dry, put it in your Layers of Learning Notebook in the Geography section.

😊 😊 😊 EXPLORATION: South American Rainforest Scene

For this activity, you will need:

- Books or internet sites about rainforests
- Cardboard box (shoe box or similar in size)
- Paint in various colors, green, brown, blue, etc - spray paint can be nice for painting a base coat on the box
- Colored paper
- Crayons, markers, or colored pencils
- Glue
- Scissors
- World Explorer Journal

Much of South America is covered in **rainforest**. The Amazon Rainforest is the largest in the world. The Mata Atlantica is another rainforest that extends along the coast of Brazil from the hump on the South American western coast almost to Argentina in the south. The Valdivian Rainforest is in Southern Chile and is a temperate rainforest. Rainforests are dense with plants and animals, many of which haven't even been described and cataloged by scientists yet.

1. Research one of these rainforests. Find out details about several plants and animals that live in the forest you chose.

The Shaman's Apprentice: A Tale of the Amazon Rain Forest by Lynne Cherry has lovely drawings of real plants from the Amazon. This is a fictional story about real traditions and healing plants and the need to protect them for future generations.

Memorization Station

Rainforest: a dense forest in a tropical area with heavy rainfall and high biodiversity

Deep Thoughts

A lot of people are worried about the health of the rainforests in South America. Why? How are the rainforests important to the world? What is the land that used to be rainforest being used for now? Research solutions people have come up with and discuss what you think could solve the problems.

In this photograph, the dark green is healthy rainforest. The brown or light green areas are cleared farmland.

Famous Folks

Edson Arantes do Nascimento of Brazil, better known as Pelé, is perhaps the world's top fútbol (soccer) player of all time.

He used his fame to work on behalf of Brazil's poor.

Fabulous Fact

The Amazon River carries so much water that it accounts for one fifth of the river water in the entire world. It puts out more water than the next seven biggest rivers combined.

Writer's Workshop

Pretend you are traveling on the Amazon River by canoe and write a letter home telling about the animals you see. You may need to research to find out which animals live in or near the Amazon River.

Writer's Workshop: Letters can help you hone your letter writing skills.

2. Make a diorama in a box tipped on its side. Start by painting the whole box inside and out with paint in colors of your choice.

3. Once the paint has dried, add a background inside the shoe box with paper and more paint so it looks like a rainforest.

4. Add trees, plants, animals, water, and other elements you design with paper.

5. Give each plant or animal a tiny paper label so you can describe your diorama and the things in it to an audience.

6. Add an entry in your World Explorer Journal with a rainforest picture and a narration that includes what you learned about the South American rainforest you researched.

☺ ☺ ☺ EXPLORATION: Amazon River Roller Box

For this activity, you will need:

- Books, websites, or videos about the Amazon River
- "Amazon River Roller Box Canoe" from the Printable Pack
- Cardboard box
- Long roll of paper or printer paper taped, end to end
- Wooden dowels
- Scissors
- Spray paint
- Crayons, markers, or paints and paintbrushes
- Tape

The Amazon River is the largest river, by volume, in the world. It has hundreds of tributaries and its drainage area covers over 2.7 million square miles (7 million square kilometers). The river is so big and so deep that large ocean vessels can travel as far upriver as the city of Manaus, 930 miles (1500 kilometers) upriver.

1. Cut off one wide side of a cardboard box. Paint the whole box, inside and out, with any color spray paint you like.

2. Read books, explore websites, or watch videos about the Amazon River. Pay attention to the animals, plants, and people you might meet along the river.

3. If necessary, trim your long paper roll down so it will fit in the box.

4. Draw a long river along the length of the paper. Along the paper, draw animals, plants, and people you might meet as you travel down the river.

5. Color the river blue and the banks green. Color the animals and people.

6. Cut a pair of holes on each side of the box, sized so the dowel rods can go through these holes. Insert your dowels through the holes, top and bottom. Tape one end of your paper roll to one dowel and the other end of your paper roll to the other dowel. Roll the paper up.

7. Color the "Amazon Roller Box Canoe" and cut it out on the big dashed lines, then glue it at the bottom of your box so the canoe appears to be traveling up the river.

8. Roll dowels to make the background move behind your canoe. Tell the story of what you see as your audience watches.

☺ ☺ ☺EXPLORATION: Angel Falls
For this activity, you will need:

• Videos about Angel Falls from this unit's YouTube playlist
• Watercolor paints, brushes, and a water cup
• World Explorer Journal

Angel Falls is the highest waterfall in the world. You would have to hike through the Venezuelan rainforest to see it, but today, we'll explore it through videos.

1. Watch some videos from this unit's YouTube playlist about Angel Falls. Watch at least one that shows people either climbing up or base jumping from the falls.

2. Add an entry in your World Explorer Journal with a drawing of the falls and a caption or narration that tells what you learned about it from the videos.

Fabulous Fact

All of South America used to be claimed by European governments. Suriname, the most recently independent, won its independence from the Netherlands in 1975. Today, only French Guiana, a department of France, is still under European leadership.

These boys are getting ready to celebrate Suriname's first independence day in 1975.

South American countries all have big celebrations on their independence days. People close all the businesses, have parades, and throw parties.

Additional Layer

The Galapagos Islands are actually nineteen volcanic peaks that have emerged from the surface of the water, forming the island archipelago. Learn more about them and the studies of Charles Darwin's travels there. There were no native humans there when he went, so he spent a long time just observing the animals that lived there on the islands.

Bookworms

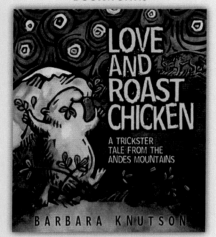

Love and Roast Chicken: A Trickster Tale from the Andes Mountains by Barbara Knutson is the story of a guinea pig who has to outfox the fox who wants to eat him. The story is a retelling of an ancient myth from the region.

3. Write a journal entry on a separate sheet of paper that answers this question: If you had a chance to climb up or base jump off of Angel Falls, would you do it? Why or why not?

4. Add your journal entry to the Geography section of your Layers of Learning Notebook.

Additional Layer

Machu Picchu is one of the amazing landmarks of the Andes Mountains. It was an Incan city that was abandoned around the time the Spanish conquistadors invaded South America.

☺ ☺ ☺**EXPLORATION: Andes Mountains**

For this activity, you will need:

- Internet
- World Explorer Journal
- "Andes Mountain Trivia" from the Printable Pack

The Andes Mountains run all of the way from the southern tip of the continent to the northernmost coast along the Caribbean Sea. The range is comprised of a series of smaller mountain chains that were formed when two tectonic plates collided. Among the mountain peaks are also a series of high-elevation plateaus.

1. Read books, explore websites, or watch videos about the Andes Mountains. Take some notes about what you learn.

2. Quiz yourself on some Andes Mountains facts using the "Andes Mountain Trivia" page from the Printable Pack. If there are any answers you don't know, look them up to learn even more.

3. Add the trivia sheet to the Geography section of your Layers of Learning Notebook.

☺ ☺ ☺**EXPLORATION: Lake Titicaca**

For this activity, you will need:

• Videos about Lake Titicaca from this unit's YouTube playlist
• World Explorer Journal

Lake Titicaca is a lake high in the Andes Mountains that sits at about 12,507 feet (3,812 meters) above sea level. That means it is the highest navigable lake in the world. It is also South America's largest lake. It is most famous for its man-made islands, made using totora reeds by the Uros tribe.

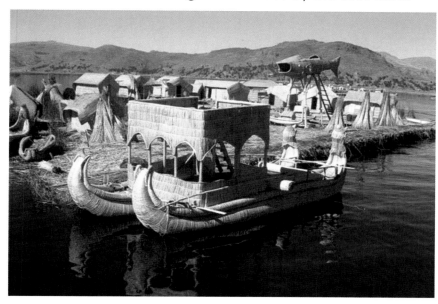

1. Go watch a video from this unit's YouTube playlist about Lake Titicaca. While you watch, take notes in your World Explorer Journal about what you learn.

Famous Folks

Paulo Coelho is a Brazilian author, famous for his book *The Alchemist,* which we can happily recommend to your high schoolers.

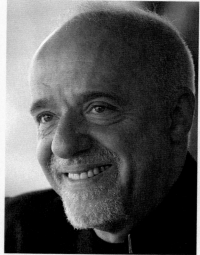

Photo by Paul Macleod, CC by SA 3.0, Wikimedia

Fabulous Fact

The Kapok tree can get as high as 200 feet (61 meters) with a diameter of nearly 11 feet (3.5 meters). They can grow up to 13 feet (4 meters) a year! It is the biggest tree in the Amazon Rainforest.

The majestic trees provide a home to many species of birds, insects, amphibians, monkeys, sloths, jaguars, and bats.

Famous Folks

The indigenous people of South America rarely have political power, but in 2006, Evo Morales, an Aymara, was elected president of Bolivia.

He focused his policies on reducing dependence on world organizations and the United States and increasing indigenous rights.

Fabulous Fact

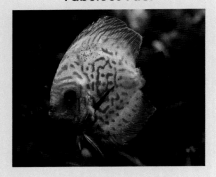

The Amazon Rainforest has the highest density of plant and animal species anywhere on the planet. The Amazon River that runs through it is the home of the largest number of freshwater fish species in the world. This region is the planet's most varied biological zone.

2. The elevation of Lake Titicaca, the highest lake on Earth, is 12,507 feet (3,812 meters). The elevation of the Dead Sea, the lowest lake on Earth, is about 1,412 feet (430 meters) below sea level. Do the math and figure out the difference in elevation between the highest and lowest lakes on the planet.

☺ ☺ ☺ **EXPLORATION: South American Animals Memory**
For this activity, you will need:

- "South American Animals Memory" from the Printable Pack, 2 copies on card stock
- Scissors
- Glue stick
- World Explorer Journal

There are thousands of animal species that live within South America in the wide range of habitats on the continent.

This tamarin monkey lives in the Amazon Rainforest. It uses its long fingers to swing through the trees and forage for insects, fruit, birds, and little lizards to eat. It is quick and hides in tree hollows to sleep. It is just one of many species of monkeys that are known to live within the Amazon Rainforest.

1. Cut apart the animal cards from the "South American Animals Memory" and take a few minutes to look at each one. Can you name the animals? What do you know about each one? You might enjoy taking a few minutes to read about each of them online and learn something new.

   Answers in order from left to right and top to bottom: toucan, llama, jaguar, sloth, anteater, capybaras, anaconda, spectacled bear, Amazon River dolphins, piranhas, macaw, and red-eyed tree frog

2. Next, play a memory game by taking the two sets of cards you created and turning them upside down in rows on a playing surface. Each player will take turns flipping two cards and trying to find a matching pair. If you make a match, you can try a second time on your turn. Take turns until all of the matches have been made, then see who got the most matches.

3. For an extra challenge, see if each player can name each animal she or he collected a match for and share one fact about it.

4. Once you're done playing, choose some of the South American animal cards to glue on to a page of your World Explorer Journal. Add each name and write a sentence or two about each South American animal.

People of South America

☺ ☺ ☺**EXPLORATION: Flag Garland**
For this activity, you will need:

- "Flags of South America" from the Printable Pack (seven pages)
- White card stock
- Hole punch
- String
- Scissors

There are 12 independent countries in South America: Columbia, Venezuela, Guyana, Suriname, Ecuador, Peru, Brazil, Bolivia, Chile, Argentina, Paraguay, and Uruguay. There are also 2 territories. French Guiana is a department of France and the Falkland Islands are a territory of the United Kingdom.

1. Print the flags from the Printable Pack onto card stock paper. Cut out the flags.

2. Punch two holes on the hoist side (left side) of each flag. Thread string through the holes, in one side and out the other, of all of the flags to make a long garland to hang

Additional Layer

The Christ the Redeemer statue is the most famous South American landmark. It is a statue of Jesus Christ that looks down over the city of Rio de Janeiro, Brazil. It is an art deco statue that was completed in 1931. It stands 98 feet (28 meters) tall.

Do a bit of research and find out why it was built.

Bookworms

The Great Kapok Tree: A Tale of the Amazon Rain Forest by Lynne Cherry is the story of a man who tries his best to cut down a giant kapok tree.

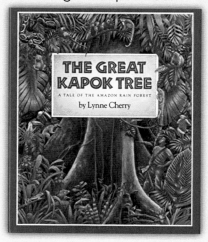

The forest animals around him whisper in his ear about how living things are connected and need each other, and the man learns about the importance of trees.

Famous Folks

Shakira Isabel Mebarak Ripoll, know as Shakira to her fans, is a singer from Colombia.

She sings in both Spanish and English and is one of the best-selling music artists of all time.

Additional Layer

Arepas are a little thicker than tortillas but made in a similar way. Look up a recipe and make some to try.

Fabulous Fact

Brazil is the largest country in South America, covering more than half of the continent. It is just a bit smaller than the United States of America.

on your wall.

3. Match each flag to its country on a map of South America.

☺ ☺ ☺ **EXPLORATION: Tortillas**

For this activity, you will need:

- 5 cups all purpose flour
- 1 Tablespoon salt
- ½ cup shortening, coconut oil, butter, or lard
- 2 cups water
- Bowl for mixing
- Spoon and fork for stirring
- Rolling pin or tortilla press
- Griddle and stove

Nearly everyone in South America eats flat bread. The thinnest flat bread is a tortilla. Tortilla means "small cake" in Spanish. Tortillas were made in South America before European contact and are still a daily staple for most people who live there. Beans, rice, beef, chicken, peppers, and onions are cooked and seasoned, then wrapped in the tortilla. You can make homemade tortillas.

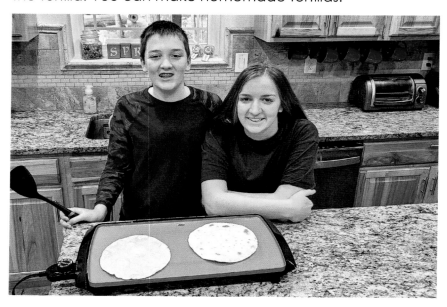

1. Mix the flour and salt together, then add in the shortening. Cut the shortening into the flour using a pastry cutter or the tines of a fork.

2. Stir in the water until the flour holds together in a ball.

3. Divide the dough into 24 equal pieces.

4. Roll each piece out on a floured countertop with a rolling pin or press them in a tortilla press. The rolled

dough should be very thin and roughly round.

5. Place the rolled tortilla on a hot, ungreased griddle. Cook until the dough just begins to bubble up, then flip and cook for another minute.

6. Taste your tortillas. If you'd like, you can even add a filling or just spread a bit of butter and then sprinkle it with a mixture of cinnamon and sugar for a sweet treat.

☺ ☺ ☺EXPLORATION: Andes Poncho

For this activity, you will need:

- Bright fabric with stripes or a fun pattern (enough to drape to the wearer's thighs in front and back - 1.5 to 3 yards or 1.4 to 2.7 meters)
- Trim color fabric (optional)
- Sharp scissors for cutting fabric
- Needle and thread, sewing machine and thread, or hemming adhesive (glue made for fabric hemming)

Since ancient times, the people who live high in the Andes Mountains have worn ponchos. Traditional ponchos are woven of alpaca wool in bright, colorful patterns. Ponchos are a large rectangular piece of cloth with a hole in the center for the head to go through. They are warm and can shed rain and snow, making them perfect for the cold, wet climate of the mountains.

1. Wash and dry your fabric. Press it with an iron, if needed.

2. Fold the fabric in half the short way, hamburger-style.

3. In the center of the fold and perpendicular to it, cut

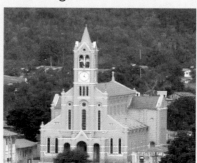

Expedition

Fútbol (soccer) is the most popular sport in South America. It was introduced to the area of Buenos Aires in Argentina in the late 1800s and then spread throughout the continent. It has become an integral part of the culture there. Go to a park and have a game with your friends or family.

Bookworms

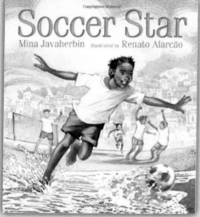

Soccer Star by Mina Javaherbin is the story of a boy who works hard and helps his family, but loves playing soccer above everything else. During the game, Maria, a girl, wants to play too. Will she get to play with the boys?

a slit 6 inches (15 cm) long. A small child will need a smaller hole and a large adult may need a bigger hole. Start with a small slit, test it, then make it longer bit by bit until it fits over the head but doesn't slip off the shoulders.

4. Hem the cut edges of the fabric with a needle and thread, a sewing machine, or hemming adhesive.

5. If you'd like, add a contrasting fabric as trim around the edges.

☺ ☺ ☺ **EXPLORATION: Curupira, the Forest Guardian Doll**

For this activity, you will need:

- "Curupira Doll Pattern" from the Printable Pack
- Red yarn
- Brown fabric
- Green fabric
- Cotton stuffing (cotton balls, batting, pillow stuffing, etc)
- Needle and thread or sewing machine
- Scissors
- Permanent marker or paint pens.
- Hot glue (optional)

Curupira is a folk creature from the Amazon basin. He has bright red hair and his feet are backward. He likes to trick travelers by making them think he is going one way when really he is walking the other. He lives in the forest and cares for the living things in it. He might play a prank on you if you are traveling through because he likes to have his fun, but he won't hurt anyone except those who abuse the forest by killing when they shouldn't.

If he thinks a forester has cut too many trees or a hunter has killed more animals than he needs to survive, he will cast an illusion or an enchantment to confuse and frighten him or her. He can turn a hunter into a helpless rabbit or squirrel so the hunter becomes the hunted.

1. Use the "Curupira Doll Pattern" from the Printable Pack. Cut out the pieces of the pattern. Fold your fabric in half so it is double-layered. Pin the pattern pieces to the fabric. The legs need to be pinned along a folded edge

of the fabric on the side that says "fold." Cut the fabric out around the pattern pieces. Re-pin the arms and legs and make another set of arm and leg pieces.

2. Stitch the pairs of fabric pieces together all around the edge, leaving a 2 inch (5 cm) gap on one side of each piece.

This shows the doll in stages. On the furthest left, an arm is sewn together and a gap is left at the end to put stuffing in. The next piece over is the legs, sewn together with a gap near the center and turned right side out so the seams are inside the doll. Next, there is an arm as well as the body, both stuffed and ready to be assembled into the doll.

3. Turn the doll pieces inside out so the seams are on the inside.

4. Stuff with cotton. Use a pencil or end of scissors to get stuffing down into the ends.

5. Sew up the gaps. Then, sew the legs and arms onto the body. The legs are attached in the center at the bottom of the body piece. Make sure the legs are backwards before you sew it together.

6. Wrap red yard around a small box, we used a crayon box, about 20 times. Remove the wrapped yarn from the box and tightly tie off the yarn in the center. Snip through the yarn on both sides so there are no more loops in the yarn. Glue or sew the yarn to the top of the head in the center where the yarn is tied.

7. Add facial features with a permanent marker or paint pens.

8. Use the green fabric to make a skirt for the doll. Glue or sew the skirt on.

9. Use the doll to make up stories about how the Curupira might have adventures saving forest creatures and trees from people, storms, fires, or savage predators.

Writer's Workshop

Look up a recipe from South America and try making it. Write your own version of it, including the ingredient list and numbered instructions. If there's anything you would change from the original, make sure to include your changes.

Here are a few you might like trying:

- Ham & cheese arepas
- Arroz con leche (sweet rice)
- Tortas fritas (fry bread)
- Feijoada (Black bean stew)
- Grilled Brazilian Pineapple

Fabulous Fact

South America's main natural resources include iron ore, gold, silver, copper, tin, and petroleum. In addition, the major crops grown are corn, coffee, wheat, soybeans, and cocoa. Fruits like pineapple and papaya, as well as nuts like cashews and Brazil nuts, are also commonly grown.

Writer's Workshop

Paraguay and Bolivia are the two landlocked countries within South America.

Write a paragraph about the challenges landlocked countries face. You may want to do research online to help you.

Teaching Tip

If you don't have the time, supplies, or means to make a full-sized hammock, consider making a miniature version for a little toy or stuffed animal.

You can learn the same lesson using a smaller-scaled project.

This one was made with a pillowcase and paracord.

☺ ☺ ☺EXPLORATION: Hammocks

For this activity, you will need:

- A twin-size, flat bed sheet
- Rope (paracord works well), 2 pieces cut 15 feet (7.6 meters) long each (depending on the distance of your trees, you may need more or less)
- Trees or posts spaced about 14 feet (4 meters) or so apart
- Book about South America

A hammock is a length of cloth or woven net slung between two trees or poles with rope. A person can climb into the hammock and sleep. Hammocks are comfortable and cool in hot climates. They also keep you off the ground, safe from snakes, scorpions, and crawling insects. They were invented by the people of the Caribbean and South America and are still popular for sleeping all over the continent.

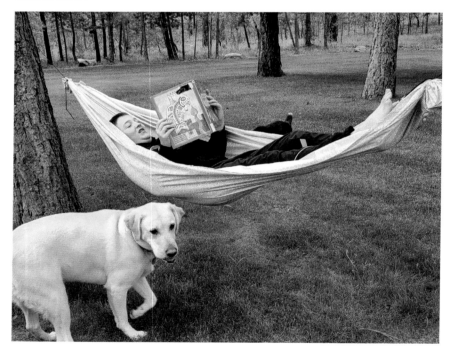

1. Make an accordion-fold along each short end of the sheet, then firmly tie a piece of paracord tightly around each bunched end. You'll have a knotted cord at each short end of the sheet.

2. Wrap each end of the paracord around a tree and tie another firm knot to secure each end of the hammock.

3. Tie your sheet up to trees or poles.

4. Read a book about South America while lounging in your hammock.

😊 😊 😊**EXPLORATION: Maracas**

WARNING: This activiy uses a hot glue gun. Be careful!

For this activity, you will need:

- Small gourd (It needs to have a fat end and slim "handle.")
- Dried beans or pebbles
- Knife or power saw
- Small, long handled spoon
- Hot glue and hot glue gun
- Acrylic paints and paintbrushes
- World Explorer Journal

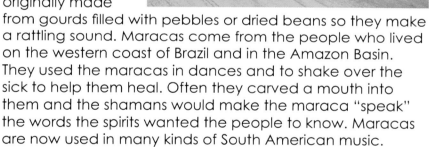

Maracas are a percussion instrument originally made from gourds filled with pebbles or dried beans so they make a rattling sound. Maracas come from the people who lived on the western coast of Brazil and in the Amazon Basin. They used the maracas in dances and to shake over the sick to help them heal. Often they carved a mouth into them and the shamans would make the maraca "speak" the words the spirits wanted the people to know. Maracas are now used in many kinds of South American music.

1. Cut the handle off the gourd.

2. Remove the seeds and pulp using a narrow, long-handled spoon.

3. Let your gourd dry out for several days. In a humid environment you may need to place your gourds in your oven on a low temperature for a hour or two.

4. Add a handful of pebbles or dried beans to the gourd.

5. Glue the "handle" of the gourd back on with hot glue.

6. Once the glue has dried, paint your maraca with South American inspired designs.

7. Add an entry in your World Explorer Journal about maracas and draw the gourd maracas you made.

Fabulous Fact

Even though Bolivia is a landlocked country, they have a navy. They do drills and naval exercises on Lake Titicaca.

Additional Layer

Because it doesn't have any harbors or safe places to dock a ship, Easter Island is one of the most remote islands in the world. It lies off the coast of Chile about 2361 miles (3800 km), a five-hour flight from Santiago, Chile. It was settled by Polynesians long ago, who traveled there by canoe. Learn more about this fascinating island and its moai statues.

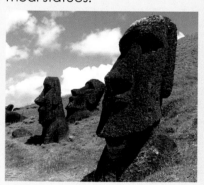

Writer's Workshop

Choose any one of the South American countries to learn about. Write a country report with eight sections: geography, politics, religion, climate, daily life, holidays, popular foods, and interesting facts.

Writer's Workshop

Carnival is a week-long festival in which followers of Catholicism indulge in drinking, eating, dancing, and fun before beginning Lent, a month of abstinence from indulgences leading up to Easter. Carnival is a huge celebration where masses of people gather to celebrate. Carnival festivities happen all over the world, but the biggest one is in Rio de Janeiro, Brazil.

Watch a video of a Carnival celebration in Brazil. Imagine you are really there in person and write a journal entry about all you saw and did.

Fabulous Fact

Tierra del Fuego is the archipelago that is at the southern tip of South America, across the Strait of Magellan. The islands are divided between Chile and Argentina.

☺ ☺ ☻ EXPLORATION: Languages of South America Map

For this activity, you will need:

- "Major Languages of South America" from the Printable Pack
- Colored pencils

Portuguese and Spanish are the most commonly spoken languages in South America, but there are also dozens of other European languages and hundreds of native languages spoken throughout the continent.

Quechua is spoken by 25 million people in South America and was the language of the Inca. Many people who speak Quechua, do not know Spanish beyond a few scattered words. Aymara is spoken mostly in Bolivia and has nearly 2 million speakers. Mapuche is spoken in central Chile and parts of Argentina by about 260,000 speakers.

1. Color the "Major Languages of South America" map from the Printable Pack. This map only shows a few of the most common languages and where they are mostly spoken. The numbers in the key correspond to the numbers on the map.

2. Get a taste for each language with the chart below. You can make a larger chart and add more words if you like.

English	Hello	Welcome
Portuguese	Oi!	Bem-vindos
Spanish	Hola	Bienvenidos
Quechua	Rimaykullayki	Haykuykuy
Aymara	Laphi	Jallallt'atapxtawa
Guarani	Maitei	Eguahe pora
Mapuche	Mari mari	Kümey mi akun
Dutch	Hallo	Welkom
French	Bonjour	Bienvenue

Step 3: Show What You Know

During this unit, choose one of the assignments below to show what you have learned during the unit. Add this work to your Layers of Learning Notebook. You can also use this assignment to show your supervising teacher or your charter school as a sample of what you've been working on in your homeschool, if needed.

There are more ideas for writing assignments in the "Writer's Workshop" sidebars.

☺ ☺ Coloring or Narration Page

For this activity, you will need:

- "South America" printable from the Printable Pack
- Writing or drawing utensils

1. Depending on the age and ability of the child, choose either the "South America" coloring sheet or the "South America" narration page from the Printable Pack.

2. Younger kids can color the coloring sheet as you review some of the things you learned about during this unit. On the bottom of the coloring page, kids can write a sentence about what they learned. Very young children can explain their ideas orally while a parent writes for them.

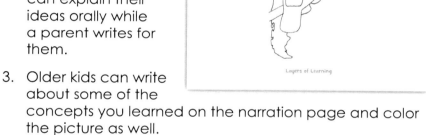

South America

South America contains twelve independent countries and two territories. People of South America speak hundreds of different languages, including Spanish, Portuguese, Dutch, French, English, Quechua, and many native languages. The continent ranges from towering mountains to vast flat plains and from tropical rainforests to the driest desert outside Antarctica.

Layers of Learning

3. Older kids can write about some of the concepts you learned on the narration page and color the picture as well.

4. Add this to the History section of your Layers of Learning Notebook.

☺ ☺ ☺ Writer's Workshop

For this activity, you will need:

- A computer or a piece of paper and a writing utensil

Choose from one of the ideas below or write about something else you learned during this unit. Each of these prompts corresponds with one of the units from the Layers of Learning Writer's Workshop curriculum, so you may choose to coordinate the assignment with the monthly unit you are learning about in Writer's Workshop.

- **Sentences, Paragraphs, & Narrations:** Write a narration that describes several of the main landmarks within South America.
- **Descriptions & Instructions:** Create a set of written instructions, travel guide-style, about taking a trip to Machu Picchu.

Additional Layer

Capoeira is a Brazilian martial art that combines music, dance, acrobatics, and exercise. Learn more about this unique martial art.

Additional Layer

Learn all about Magellan, the Portuguese explorer whom the Strait of Magellan is named for.

Additional Layer

To celebrate all you've learned about South America, take an afternoon off of your normal school routine and enjoy one of these fun movies:

- *The Emperor's New Groove*
- *Encanto*
- *Rio*
- *Jungle Cruise*

Unit Trivia Questions

1. The ancient core rock of a continent is called the:

    a) shield

    b) continental crust

    c) sedimentary basin

    d) craton

2. Which large, high-elevation lake in South America has man-made floating islands on it?

    Lake Titicaca

3. Name at least five animals that live within South America.

    Toucan, jaguar, monkey, sloth, piranha, etc. (answers will vary)

4. This region of South America is comprised of grasslands that have very fertile soil.

    a) Amazon Basin

    b) Pampas

    c) Andes

    d) Coastal plains

5. What is the most popular sport within South America?

    Fútbol (Soccer)

6. True or False - All trading between nations happens at ports within harbors, where goods are stored and exchanged.

    False - Some nations, like landlocked Bolivia and Paraguay still trade even without any ports or harbors. Ports are the most important trading locations though.

7. What is the name of the highest waterfall in the world?

    Angel Falls

- **Fanciful Stories**: Write a fable whose main character is a monkey from the Amazon Rainforest.
- **Poetry:** Write an acrostic poem about South America by writing the continent's name vertically and then finding landmarks within it or special things about it that begin with each of those letters.
- **True Stories:** Write a true story about one of the encounters between Spanish conquistadors and native peoples within South America.
- **Reports & Essays:** Make a mobile that includes interesting facts about some of South America's world-record geographic features - Angel Falls (the world's highest waterfall), the Amazon River (the world's largest river by volume), the Amazon Rainforest (the world's largest rainforest), Lake Titicaca (the world's highest navigable lake), and Atacama Desert (the world's driest desert).
- **Letters:** Make a post card that highlights the spot in South America you would most like to go.
- **Persuasive Writing:** Write a persuasive essay about mining and how to protect the earth that provides us with valuable natural resources.

☺ ☻ **South America Crowns**

For this activity, you will need:

- "South America Crowns" from the Printable Pack
- Green construction paper
- Colored pencils or crayons
- Scissors
- Clear tape or stapler

1. Cut out each of the pieces on the "South America Crowns" printable. Color them any way you like.

2. Cut out a length of green construction paper sized to fit the head of each child. Make the green bands into a ring using a stapler or tape, as needed.

3. Attach each piece on to the band to create South America crowns. As you do, review the concepts you learned from the unit. For example, as you add the toucan, ask what other animals live in South America. Make sure each person gets a turn to share some of what they learned about South America.

☺ ☺ ☺ **Big Book of Knowledge**

For this activity, you will need:

- "Big Book of Knowledge: South America" printable from the Printable Pack, printed on card stock
- Writing or drawing utensils
- Big Book of Knowledge

1. Color, draw on, or write on the Big Book of Knowledge page. Record concepts, definitions, and facts you learned during this unit. It's a record of the things you learned and hope to remember. Add the page to your Big Book of Knowledge.

2. Use your Big Book of Knowledge regularly to help you review, quiz, or create games that will help you commit the things you've learned to memory.

Big Book of Knowledge

The Big Book of Knowledge is a book for you, the mentor, to use as a constant review of all of the things you're learning about. You can use it to quiz your kids or prepare tests or review games. Whenever you learn something in Layers of Learning that you want your kids to remember, add it to your Big Book of Knowledge.

Assemble your Big Book of Knowledge in a binder or with binder rings. Divide it into sections for each subject.

In the Printable Pack for this unit you will find a "Big Book of Knowledge" sheet. You can add this sheet to others you collect or create yourself as you progress through the Layers of Learning curriculum. Customize the Big Book of Knowledge to your family by adding facts and topics that you enjoyed exploring as you were learning.

Visit Layers of Learning online to find more information on how to assemble and use your own Big Book of Knowledge.

You will also find cover and section pages to print along with creative games to play with your Big Book of Knowledge to keep school, even the tests, fun!

Key Concepts:
- It is our responsibility to take care of the earth.
- Coral reefs are fragile environments that need protection and restoration.
- Oceania is a continent region made up of Australia and thousands of islands in the Pacific.
- There are fourteen countries and ten territories in Oceania.
- Each of the countries of Oceania has a unique history and culture, including dances and foods.

Vocabulary:
- Biodiversity hotspot
- Endemic
- Habitat
- Habitat loss
- Atoll
- Oceanic island
- Continental island
- Coral island
- Archipelago

Important Places:
- Great Pacific Garbage Patch
- Great Barrier Reef
- Australia
- New Zealand
- Papua New Guinea
- Palau
- Micronesia
- Nauru
- Solomon Islands
- Vanuatu
- Fiji
- Tuvalu
- Marshall Islands
- Tonga
- Samoa
- Kiribati

OCEANIA

Oceania is a region that includes the continent of Australia and the islands of the South Pacific. It stretches across almost half of the globe, more than 7,300 miles (11,800 km) from west to east. The defining characteristic of this region is the ocean. Historically, these islands have been isolated from the major world landmasses, leading to unique animal and plant life as well as unique human cultures.

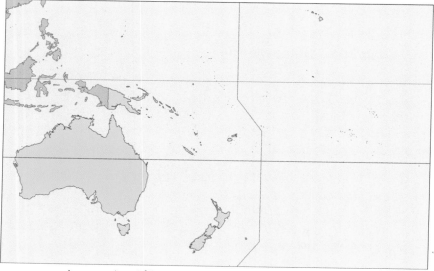

Image by Júlio Reis, CC by SA 3.0, Wikimedia.

There are thousands of islands in the region, many of them tiny and uninhabited. Landscapes range from deserts and rugged snowcapped mountains to tropical beaches and rainforests. Oceania includes fourteen countries plus many territories and protectorates with more than 41 million inhabitants. The nations range from highly developed and economically powerful to less developed and poor.

On the left is Mount Cook in New Zealand and on the right you see a beach in Fiji.

Most of the islands in this region were subjugated and colonized by Europeans, which had a profound effect on their history and ecology. Likewise, the Europeans who settled in this region were enormously influenced by their landscape and the people they came to live among. The result is unique cultures and environments unlike anywhere else on Earth.

Many of these environments, such as coral reefs and rainforests, are fragile and easily damaged by human activity. Unique species such as the Guam Micronesian kingfisher and the Mariana eight-spot butterfly are only found in small habitats. Learning to care for our planet while also using its resources is one of the struggles of humanity, especially as we increase our technology to the point where it is easier to harvest natural resources.

Step 1: Library List

Choose books from your library that go with this topic. Here's a list of some favorites and also a list of search terms so you can utilize what your library offers. Read the books with your kids and/or assign them some to read independently. It is from these books your kids will learn most of the facts they need from this unit.

Search for: Oceania, Australia, Pacific Islands, environment, pollution, marine conservation, coral reefs, Great Barrier Reef

☺ ☺ ☺*Geography of the World* by DK. Read "Australasia and Oceania" and "Peoples of Australasia and Oceania" on pages 254-257.

☺ ☺ ☺*Draw Oceania* by Kristin J. Draeger. Using a step-by-step progression, your kids will learn to draw Oceania from memory with this book.

☺*Australia and Oceania* by Barbara A. Somervill. This is part of a series about the seven continents. Includes lots of full-color pictures and about a paragraph of text per page.

☺*Explore Australia and Oceania* by Bobbie Kalman. Learn about the countries, climate, and ecosystems of Oceania.

☺*The Mess That We Made* by Michelle Lord. This is a beautiful picture book about an the ugly problem of pollution, including the Great Pacific Garbage Patch.

☺*Zobi and the Zoox: A Story of Coral Bleaching* by Alisa Wild, et. al. Set on the Great Barrier Reef, this book explains the science and problem of coral bleaching through the story of a rhizobia bacterium named Zobi.

☺ ☺*Maui, Kakamora and Other Legends of Oceania* by

Family School Levels

The colored smilies in this unit help you choose the correct levels of books and activities for your child.
☺ = Ages 6-9
☺ = Ages 10-13
☺ = Ages 14-18

On the Web

For videos, web pages, games, and more to add to this unit, visit the People & Planet Resources at Layers-of-Learning.com.

You will find a link to video playlists, web links, and more.

Bookworms

If you're looking for a family read-aloud, we'd like to suggest this one.

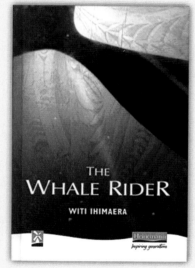

THE WHALE RIDER
WITI IHIMAERA

The Whale Rider by Witi Ihimaera is a fictional story about a young Maori girl who is next in line to be the Whale Rider, except that she's a girl. She has to prove herself to her grandfather and the rest of the tribe. Infused with Maori legend and culture, this is a book with universal themes.

Additional Layer

Additional Layer

The Great Barrier Reef off of Australia's eastern shore is the largest coral reef system in the world.

Learn more about the reef.

Fabulous Fact

The biggest city in Oceania is Sydney, Australia with more than five million people.

It is one of the most popular tourist cities in the world.

On the Web

Watch Enric Sala's TED talk entitled "Glimpses of a Pristine Ocean."

Sala talks about the difference between a pristine coral reef and one visited by even a few humans.

Richard Sweetman. These are the legends of Polynesia, retold in simple language for children. There are a few simple illustrations, but we think this is best shared as a read-aloud.

☺ ☺*The Great Barrier Reef* by Dr. Helen Scales and Lisk Feng. This is a non-fiction picture book about the Great Barrier Reef, its ecological importance, and how we can protect it. The illustrations are charming.

☺ ☺*The Night Marchers and Other Oceania Stories* by Kate Ashwin, et. al. This is a graphic novel-style book of seventeen real, spooky legends from the Pacific. Pictures are in black and white and one is told only in the native language instead of English.

☺ ☺*Can You Protect the Coral Reefs?* by Michael Burgan. This is part of the "You Choose: Eco Expeditions" series where the reader is the main character and makes choices throughout the book.

☺ ☺*The Great Pacific Garbage Patch* by Laura Perdew. This book is filled with charts, maps, photos, and the truth about the mess we've made of our oceans.

☺*Among the Islands: Adventures in the Pacific* by Tim Flannery. The author is a world-renowned biologist from Australia who searched out rare species on Pacific Islands so they could be cataloged and perhaps saved before their habitats were destroyed. This is a record of anecdotes about his quest and the animals, plants, and people he met along the way.

☺*Plastic Ocean: How a Sea Captain's Chance Discovery Launched a Determined Quest to Save the Oceans* by Charles Moore. This is written by the sea captain and researcher who discovered the Great Pacific Garbage Patch in 1997. The book describes the pollution problem, the persistence and health problems with plastics, and calls for change.

☺*Living Planet* by David Attenborough. This book explains in detail the myriad of communities of life on Earth and how they are interconnected, unique, beautiful, and worth caring for.

Step 2: Explore

Choose a few hands-on Explorations from this section to work on as a family. They should be appealing activities that will create mental hooks so your kids remember the information in the unit. Save the rest of the Explorations for the next time you do this unit in four years when your kids are older. You can also read the sidebars together and explore some little rabbit trails.

This unit includes printables. See the introduction for instructions on retrieving your Printable Pack.

Fragile Planet

Humans often destroy fragile ecosystems and species through our lack of care. Even though life on this planet, as a whole, is resilient, adaptable, and hardy, it is our responsibility to not leave a mess or wreak wanton destruction as we go through our lives. If humans were to completely pollute the earth to the point of a mass extinction event, life would recover, but we wouldn't. When we speak of saving the planet, we're really talking about saving ourselves.

☺ ☺ ☻ EXPLORATION: Biodiversity Hotspots

For this activity, you will need:

- Video about biodiversity hotspots from the YouTube playlist for this unit
- "Biodiversity Hotspots" map from the Printable Pack
- Colored pencils or crayons
- World Explorer Journal
- Glue Stick
- Scissors

When humans threaten many species in one place we call it a **biodiversity hotspot**. There are 36 identified biodiversity hotspots around the world. Conservationists work to protect these places from further destruction, but it's hard. The reason these habitats are threatened is usually economic.

Additional Layer

The National Park of American Samoa protects 8,257 acres of tropical rainforest and coral reef on three islands.

Preserves, parks, and nature reserves serve as untouched or lightly touched places for wild things to have rest and thrive without humans. These spots provide oases where nature can recover and from which it can recolonize other, degraded locations.

Learn more about the difference between an untouched coral reef and a highly used one.

Memorization Station

Biodiversity hotspot: a place where many species are threatened by human activity

Biodiversity refers to the variety of living things. These hotspots are places with high numbers of species, all being threatened as a whole.

A biodiversity hotspot is a clearly defined place with at least 1500 endemic vascular plants and 30% or more of its original vegetation.

People & Planet

Fabulous Fact

Palau has some of the highest biodiversity in the Pacific with more than 500 species of coral and 1,200 species of fish. It has an ancient history of caring for the earth that has continued into the present day. Ngardok Nature Reserve was the first park established in modern times. It contains a tropical forest, a freshwater lake, and marshes.

Memorization Station

Endemic: a species that is native and only lives in one place on earth

Habitat: the natural home of a living thing

Habitat loss: the damage of a habitat

There are three types of habitat loss. Habitat destruction is when a habitat is completely gone because of construction, a volcano, a landslide, logging, dredging.

Habitat fragmentation is when tiny isolated bits of habitat are left after roads, farmers' fields, dams, and cities, have been built.

Habitat degradation is when a habitat is damaged through introduced species, pollution, or fire suppression and native species can no longer live and reproduce effectively.

Forests are cleared, mines are opened, and reefs are fished to feed people's families. These people are often from poorer places and they are harvesting resources they require to survive. Most of the region of Oceania is considered a biodiversity hotspot.

1. Watch a video about biodiversity hotspots.

2. Cut apart the "Biodiversity Hotspots" maps. Color the map on the outlined hashed areas. Glue it into your World Explorer Journal. Write the definition of "Biodiversity Hotspot" next to the map.

3. As a group, go online and research **endemic** species of New Zealand, southwest Australia, eastern Australia temperate forests, east Melanesian islands, or Polynesia. Identify why you think these areas of abundant life are important for people to protect.

4. In your World Explorer Journal, draw a picture with a caption of at least one endemic species from the biodiversity hotspot you researched. Endemic species are only found in one place, so if their home is destroyed, they are gone forever.

☺ ☺ ☺ EXPEDITION: Habitat Loss

For this activity, you will need:

- A trail to hike near you (a wilderness area is best, but a park will do)
- Water, appropriate clothing for your area, and a cell phone
- Snacks, a first aid kit, and a flashlight (optional, but recommended if you are hiking in the wilderness)
- Camera (a phone camera is great)
- World Explorer Journal
- Glue stick

A **habitat** is the place where an animal or plant lives. It includes the water, soil, rocks, air, and other living things that nurture the organism so it can thrive and reproduce. Most living things have very specific needs. If their habitat is destroyed or disturbed, they often struggle to survive. **Habitat loss** is a major cause of extinction. Human beings are one cause of habitat destruction and, in the modern world, we are the main cause. Our challenge is to learn to use the resources of the earth that we need without destroying the whole environment as we do so.

1. Go to a nearby trail to hike. Remember to bring water, appropriate clothing, and a cell phone. At the trailhead, before you begin, discuss the habitat you are in.

a. What kinds of plants and animals live in the area? How much rainfall does it get? What are the seasonal temperatures like?

b. Is the habitat you are in extensive and widespread or is it a small, unique habitat?

c. How much do you think the habitat has been affected by humans? Are buildings and roads nearby? Have people harvested natural materials from the area? Have people suppressed wildfires or introduced species?

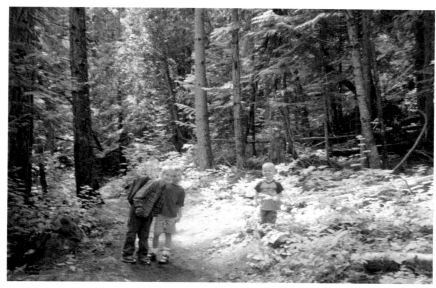

2. Hike the trail, watching for animals and plants that you find interesting. Keep an eye out for signs of human touches such as trash, roads, power lines, water mitigation, noise, and so on.

3. Take a rest partway through your hike to discuss the human touches you have noticed during your hike.

a. How much do you think humans have affected the wild things in your habitat even though you are in an area that is lightly touched?

b. What do you know about coral reefs? Are they alive?

Coral reefs, such as the Great Barrier Reef in Australia, are in danger from pollution, rising sea temperatures, illegal fishing practices, and careless tourists.

Coral is a symbiosis of a living polyp and certain kinds of algae. They excrete a hard exoskeleton which forms the body of the coral. Thousands upon thousands of fish, plants, and other sea creatures live among the coral and depend on it for habitat. If the

Additional Layer

Coral reefs and the things living on them are fascinating. Spend some time learning more about these vital habitats. What will we lose if we lose the reefs?

Writer's Workshop

Write up a scientific report about the human touches you found in your natural place. Your last paragraph should be an idea for an experiment you could perform to determine how much humans have impacted your spot.

Bookworms

Stuff by Maddie Moate is about all the things we use in daily life, where it goes when we are done with it, and where it could go to be gentler on the planet. Ages 6-10.

Famous Folks

Boyan Slat was 18 years old when he started a company called The Ocean Cleanup.

Photo by DWDD, CC by SA 3.0, Wikimedia

The idea started to form when Slat was 16 years old on a dive and found more plastic than fish. Everyone told him it was impossible to clean up the oceans. He decided to prove them wrong.

coral is destroyed, so are the other living things.

   c. Do you think you can affect the coral reefs even if you never go near one? How?

4. Take a photo of your hike. Print it and paste it into your World Explorer Journal with your thoughts about the importance of habitats and protecting them.

☺ ☺ ☻ **EXPLORATION: Great Pacific Garbage Patch**
For this activity, you will need:

- Book or video about the Great Pacific Garbage Patch from the Library List or YouTube playlist for this unit
- Internet for research
- Card stock paper
- Markers, colored pencils, or crayons

The currents of the oceans carry floating things along until they wash up on a beach or collect in the swirling gyres in the midst of these great bodies of water. Since the 20th century, the vast majority of things floating in the oceans have been man-made plastics. These plastics have collected into large patches up to ten meters deep and covering thousands of square miles. The largest and most famous is the Great Pacific Garbage Patch in the northern Pacific Ocean.

1. Read a book or watch a video about the Great Pacific Garbage Patch.

2. Choose one type of plastic marine debris to research. It could be plastic straws, grocery bags, polyester fabric, water bottles, or any other common plastic item.

3. Make an illustrated fact sheet showing how it travels from its intended purpose to the ocean.

4. Then, on the reverse side of the paper, show what happens to it once it is in the ocean.

5. Present your research and your illustrated fact sheet to an audience. Then, put the illustrated fact sheet in your Layers of Learning Notebook in the Geography section.

☺ ☻EXPLORATION: Nuclear Testing In the Pacific

For this activity, you will need:

- Internet
- "Nuclear Testing At Bikini Atoll" from the Printable Pack
- Colored pencils

From the 1940s through the 1960s, the United States, France, China, the USSR, and other nations tested nuclear weapons by detonating bombs in remote locations. One of these remote locations was Bikini **Atoll** in the Marshall Islands, where the United States detonated 23 nuclear devices over a period of twelve years.

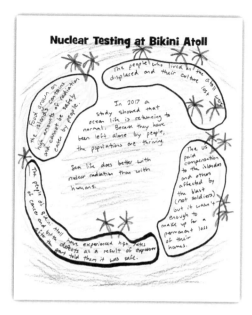

Nuclear Testing at Bikini Atoll

Fortunately, the marine environment appears to be healing from the damage, but Bikini Atoll may not ever be able to safely support human communities again.

1. Search online for "Bikini Atoll nuclear testing" and read an article about the tests that went on there. Discuss:

   a. What were the reasons for the nuclear testing? Do you think they were compelling?

   b. What were the costs to the people who lived on the islands?

   c. What were the costs to the soldiers who did the testing or helped with clean up later?

   d. What were the costs to the natural environment?

   e. What is being done to clean up the nuclear waste now?

2. Use the "Nuclear Testing at Bikini Atoll" sheet to write down four effects the nuclear testing has had on people, one fact for each piece of the island. Then, in the central lagoon on the sheet, write the effects the nuclear testing has had on animals and plants.

3. When you are finished writing, color your sheet to look like a tropical island. Put the finished paper in the Geography section of your Layers of Learning Notebook.

Deep Thoughts

The people who lived on Bikini Atoll were forcibly relocated to Rongerik Atoll, where there was not enough food or water. After abandoning them for a year, the Navy discovered the people were starving and hurriedly moved them to another island. Some returned home to Bikini Atoll in 1970, but the government later found that the high levels of strontium-90 and cesium-137 in the soil and water were giving the islanders cancer and causing other health problems.

Bikini Atoll and other sites in the Pacific are still contaminated with the after effects of nuclear testing. The U.S. government is still paying reparations to the Pacific Islanders who are affected.

Find out more about the reparations being paid. Do you think it is enough? Explain your position.

Memorization Station

Atoll: a ring-shaped island formed of coral on the top of a sunken undersea mountain

They are often formed on the rim of an undersea volcano.

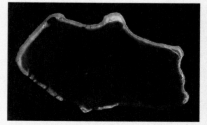

Above is a NASA image of Bikini Atoll. The land is built of eroded coral with a central lagoon.

First published in 1857, *The Coral Island* by R.M. Ballantyne is about three teen boys who become stranded on a Pacific Island after a shipwreck. They have harrowing adventures including a battle, pirates, and cannibals.

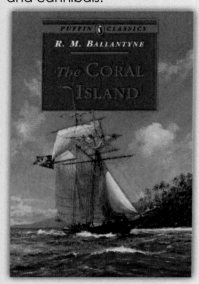

This book influenced Robert Louis Stevenson, author of *Treasure Island*, and William Golding, author of *Lord of the Flies*.

Additional Layer

El Niño and La Niña cycle of the Pacific Ocean has had affects on the sea levels in Kiribati. In El Niño years, the prevailing ocean currents cause downward pressure on the sea levels and Kiribati's sea levels lower. The reverse happens in La Niña years. If a rare tropical cyclone also occurs in a La Niña year, you can have massive degradation of the coastline, as happened in 2015.

Learn more about the El Niño cycle.

☺ ☺ ☺**EXPLORATION: Sinking Islands of Kiribati**

For this activity, you will need:

- Book or video about sea level rise from the Library List or YouTube playlist for this unit
- Internet
- Salt dough (½ c. warm water, ¼ c. salt, 4 tablespoons cooking oil, 2 cups flour) or play dough
- Deep pan or dish
- Water with blue food coloring added
- World Explorer Journal
- Colored pencils or crayons
- Ruler

The islands of Kiribati (pronounced Kir-ee-boss)are low-lying coral atolls, none more than about 6 feet (2 meters) above sea level. The islands are eroding and, at the same time, sea levels are slowly rising at about an eighth inch (.3 cm) per year. It doesn't sound like much, but when your entire island is only 3 feet above sea level, even a few inches can be a big deal. It is predicted that the entire nation will be underwater within a hundred years. We have no way to know for sure if current trends will continue, if a catastrophic event will wipe out the islands more quickly, or if the islands will actually gain ground. But we do know that the people of Kiribati are vulnerable.

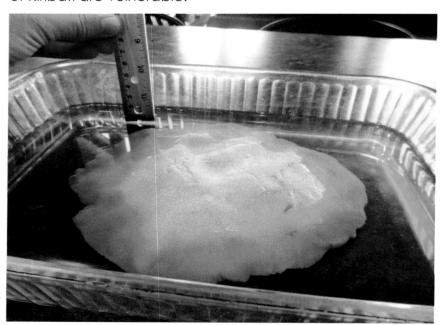

1. Watch a video about the causes of sea level rise.

2. Use an online map to find Kiribati in the middle of the Pacific. Zoom in on some of the islands. Notice how low-lying and isolated they are.

3. Make a scale model of a coral island using salt dough in a pan. Every 1 cm will equal 1 meter in the real world. Your island should be flattened at the edges and very low-lying, with the highest point no more than 2 cm tall.

4. Pour in just enough water to barely cover the bottom. This is the "normal" sea level, or the base level. What happens if your sea level rises 1 cm (the equivalent of 1 meter in the real world)? How much of the island do you lose? Pour in water to see what happens.

5. In your World Explorer Journal, draw a picture of a Kiribati Island with rising sea levels. Add a caption about the potential problem for the people living there.

☺ ☺ ☺ **EXPLORATION: Bleaching of the Great Barrier Reef**

For this activity, you will need:

- Globe or world map
- Video about the Great Barrier Reef and one about coral bleaching from the YouTube Playlist
- Synthetic sponges
- Scissors
- Paints
- Card stock paper or art paper
- "Fish Against Coral Bleaching" from the Printable Pack
- Glue stick
- World Explorer Journal (optional)

Coral polyps are living animals. They host algae inside their bodies and the algae provide part of the food the corals use to survive. If ocean temperatures are too hot or too cold for a particular species of coral, the coral expels the

Bookworms

Life in a Coral Reef by Wendy Pfeffer is a sweet, little non-fiction picture book about animals that live on tropical reefs.

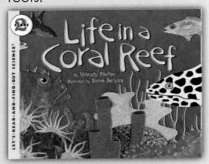

For kids 4 to 8 years old.

Additional Layer

The Great Barrier Reef is a UNESCO World Heritage site. Find out who UNESCO is and their mission.

Famous Folks

Australian Steve Irwin was a nature documentary maker, conservationist, and zookeeper.

Photo by Sheba_Also 43,000 photos, CC by SA 2.0, Wikimedia

Irwin and others like him have done a great deal to make people understand and care about the natural world and all the things that live in it.

algae. Algae may also be kicked out if nutrients or light levels are wrong or if pollutants are present. The corals are delicate and human activities can easily damage them. The algae give the corals their color, so coral without algae is said to be "bleached" because it is white. The coral doesn't die right away, but it is much more likely to die from not having enough food. Every few years, the Great Barrier Reef experiences a massive bleaching event and huge swaths die off. The frequency of these events seems to be increasing.

1. Paint a sheet of card stock or art paper with a thin layer of blue paint. Set it aside to dry.

1. On a globe or map of the world, find Australia and then the Great Barrier Reef on its eastern coast.

2. Watch a video about the Great Barrier Reef.

3. Cut pieces of sponge into coral reef shapes. Dip them in paint and then press onto the blue painted piece of paper. Use many different colors and shapes.

4. Sponge a light brown or yellow along the bottom to represent the sand or rock.

5. Watch a video about coral bleaching.

6. On several of the fish from the "Fish Against Coral Bleaching" printable, write one way coral can become bleached and die. Color the fish, cut them out, and glue them into your coral reef. You don't need to use all of the fish, three or four is enough.

7. Once it is completely dry, display your art on your wall throughout this unit or put it into the Geography section of your Layers of Learning Notebook.

8. Optionally, you may also press one painted coral into your World Explorer Journal and give it a caption about coral bleaching once the paint has dried.

Oceania Landscapes

😊 😊 😊 **EXPLORATION: Oceania Pebble Map**

WARNING: This activiy uses a hot glue gun. Be careful!

For this activity, you will need:

- Pebbles and small rocks, washed and dried
- Large sheet of cardboard
- Blue spray paint
- Paints & brushes
- Hot glue and glue gun
- Student atlas
- Permanent marker

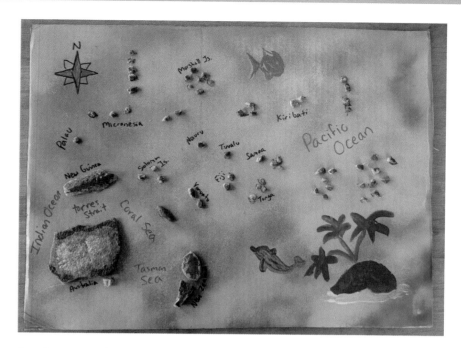

1. Spray paint a large sheet of cardboard blue. Let it dry.

2. Use a student atlas opened to a map of the South Pacific to design a map of the Pacific with pebbles on your blue cardboard. Each pebble or rock represents an island.

3. Glue the pebbles and rocks to the correct places with a hot glue gun.

4. Paint each island nation and rock to match its landscape. Most islands will be green, but also show the deserts of Australia, the mountains of New Zealand, and so on.

5. Use dark blue paint in the oceans to mark where the deepest undersea trenches are.

6. Add decorative elements like fish or palm trees to the cardboard ocean background.

7. Display your map until the end of this unit.

☺ ☺ ☺EXPLORATION: Oceania Physical Map

For this activity, you will need:

- Book or video about Oceania from the Library List or the YouTube playlist
- "Oceania" from the Printable Pack
- Student atlas
- Colored pencils or crayons

1. Use a student atlas. Label the Great Dividing Range and the Southern Alps and color them brown.

Bookworms

The Happy Isles of Oceania by Paul Theroux is a travelogue about the author's journey by kayak through Oceania.

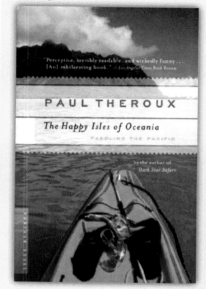

The story begins with the author's divorce and his need to get away from it all. This is for older teens and adults.

Fabulous Fact

Oceania is the smallest continent (except for Antarctica) in both land area and in population.

If you count the surface area of the ocean though, then it is the largest.

Additional Layer

On our map, the island of New Guinea is cut in half.

This is a satellite image of New Guinea, an island that includes the countries of Papua New Guinea and Indonesia. Image by SaltedSturgeon, CC by SA 4.0, Wikimedia.

The other half is part of Indonesia, which is part of Asia, so we just don't show it on this map.

The geology of New Guinea is interesting because it is continental rock, part of the same landmass as Australia. Learn more about New Guinea.

Writer's Workshop

In New Guinea, you can travel from glaciers to tundra to tropical rainforest to savanna to coral reef all in one day.

Write about someone having a single day adventure in all of these places.

2. Label Uluru rock. Label the Great Sandy Desert, Great Victoria Desert, and Simpson Desert, and color them yellow.

3. Label the Great Barrier Reef and color it pink.

4. Use a ruler to mark the Equator; label it and color it red.

5. Label these seas and color them blue: Pacific Ocean, Indian Ocean, Torres Strait, Tasman Sea, Coral Sea.

6. Color the rest of the land green.

7. Put this map in your Layers of Learning Notebook in the Geography section.

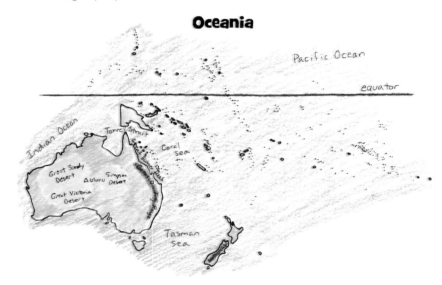

☺ ☺ ☺ **EXPLORATION: Poster Map of Oceania**
For this activity, you will need:

- Book or video about Oceania from the Library List or YouTube playlist
- "Oceania" map from the Printable Pack, printed on multiple sheets of paper (Your printer should have settings for "multi-page" or "poster" printing.)
- Tape
- Student atlas
- Colored crayons, pens, or pencils
- Glitter and school glue or glitter glue
- Colored paper
- Scissors
- Glue stick
- Oil pastels (optional)
- Paints and brushes (optional)

1. Read a book or watch a video about Oceania.

2. Tape the large map of Oceania together with the tape on the back of the sheets.

3. Use a student atlas and your craft supplies to label and color the map of Oceania any way that you want.

4. Display your completed map of Oceania on your wall throughout this unit.

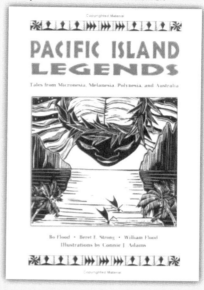
☺ ☺ ☺EXPLORATION: Types of Islands

For this activity, you will need:

- "Islands Vocabulary" from the Printable Pack
- Internet
- Globe or world map
- Colored pencils or crayons
- Scissors
- Dinner plates
- Blue gelatin dessert
- Various cookies, crackers, or candies
- World Explorer Journal
- Envelope
- Glue stick

Islands can be formed in three main ways. **Oceanic islands** are made with tectonic processes, usually volcanoes from the ocean floor, but sometimes uplifted sea floor. **Continental islands** are made of continental crust and are located on the edges of continental shelves, or in the case of New Zealand, the middle of a submerged continent. **Coral islands** are built entirely of coral reefs that have formed on submerged volcanoes or continental land. They are low-lying and usually very small. In some places, they are called cays or keys. An **archipelago** is a group of islands all clustered together. Archipelagos can be in lakes, rivers, or oceans.

Memorization Station

Oceanic island: formed from tectonic activity, usually volcanoes, in the middle of the ocean

Continental island: lies on the continental shelf and is completely surrounded by water

Coral island: built of coral reef that has emerged from the sea

They are low lying and usually small. Sometimes they are called cays (pronounced keys)

Archipelago: a group or chain of islands that occur in a cluster

Writer's Workshop

During World War II, Japan conquered most of Melanesia and Micronesia. Pick an island in this area, research what happened to it during WWII, and write a one-page report about the war years.

This is a picture of U.S. troops getting ready to invade Kwajalein Island in the Marshall Islands in 1944.

You might be interested in Guam, Palau, Papua New Guinea (Port Moresby), Solomon Islands (Tulagi), or the Marshall Islands.

Expedition

Gather some gloves and garbage bags and select a place nearby that you could go to clean up trash or litter. Walk around the area together cleaning up the garbage others have left. It could be a park, picnic area, trail, or along a street nearby.

Make sure to stay together, avoid picking up anything dangerous, and watch out for cars or strangers.

When you're finished, dispose of or recycle the trash properly. If everyone did small things to help our planet, it would make a big difference.

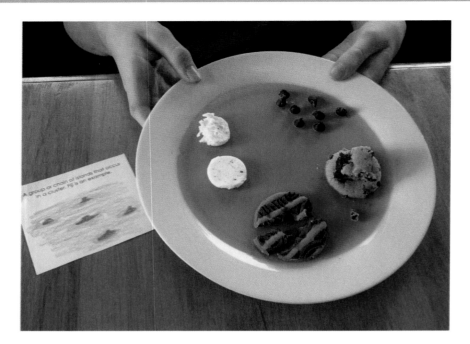

1. Ahead of time, prepare the blue gelatin dessert and pour it onto dinner plates to set up in the refrigerator, one for each child.

2. Read the definitions on the "Island Vocabulary" cards. Go online to look up images of the example islands given on the cards. Find the example islands on a globe or world map.

3. Then draw a picture of the definition on the card. Cut the cards apart.

4. On the reverse side of each vocabulary card write the word that is being defined. Make sure to match your definitions correctly. If you need help, look at the Memorization Station sidebars within this unit.

5. On the blue gelatin, design examples of each island vocabulary definition using cookies, crackers, and candies. Explain your islands to your group and then eat your treat!

6. Put the Island vocabulary cards in an envelope glued inside your World Explorer Journal.

☻ ☻ EXPLORATION: Island Latitude & Longitude

For this activity, you will need:

- Student atlas
- "Island Latitude and Longitude" from the Printable Pack
- Internet

1. Use a student atlas to find the coordinates from the

"Island Latitude and Longitude" sheet. Identify each island and write its name beneath the coordinates.

Answers:
1. **American Samoa**
2. **Coral Islands**
3. **Fiji**
4. **Kingman Reef**
5. **New Zealand**
6. **Tonga**

7. Use the internet to find one interesting fact about each island. Write the facts in the spaces.

8. Put the completed sheet in your Layers of Learning Notebook in the Geography section.

🙂 🙂 🙂 **EXPLORATION: Pacific Island Beach Comber**

For this activity, you will need:

- Brown or yellow butcher paper, 6-10 feet long
- Washable paint in bright colors
- Bucket of water
- Internet or library to research animals
- Colorful paper
- Crayons, colored pencils, or markers
- Scissors
- Glue

1. Lay a long piece of butcher paper out on a flat, outdoor surface.

2. Paint a child's feet at one end of the paper and then have the child walk along the paper to other end where you can use a bucket of water to wash their feet. Repeat once for each child. The painting represents footprints on a sandy beach.

3. Let the paint dry and then hang the beach on your wall.

4. Each child can then research one animal or plant that

Fabulous Fact

Butterfly fish are common on coral reefs. There are 129 different species.

There are 30 species of clownfish, all of which have a special symbiosis with anemones.

Other common reef fish include Batlett's anthias, lionfish, yellow tang, mandarin fish, harlequin tuskfish, Moorish idols, and the blue tang.

Additional Layer

The crown-of-thorns starfish feeds on coral reef polyps. Learn more about these fascinating animals.

Fabulous Fact

The flags of New Zealand, Papua New Guinea, Australia, and Samoa all feature the Southern Cross constellation.

Famous Folks

Abbé Nicolas Louis de Lacaille was the French astronomer who named most of the constellations of the southern hemisphere.

lives on or in the ocean near a Pacific island. Draw a picture of the animal or plant and color it. Post it on the beach that is on your wall.

5. Draw some large circles on sheets of colorful paper, cut them out, and write facts about the animal or plant you drew in the circles. Glue the circles around the picture of the animal or plant.

☺ ☺ ☺ EXPLORATION: Southern Constellations

For this activity, you will need:

- "Southern Constellations" from the Printable Pack, printed on card stock paper
- "The Tale of the Tohunga" from the Printable Pack
- Scissors
- Flashlight
- Book of Pacific Islander or Aboriginal tales (optional)

Oceania is mainly in the Southern Hemisphere, so when the people of Oceania look up at night, they see different stars from those in the northern hemisphere. The people of Oceania used the stars as a map, much more than even the ancient people of the continents. They had only the ocean's trackless surface and the stars to guide themselves by. Experts in the stars spent their lives memorizing the sky, its patterns, and how to interpret them for the good of their people.

1. Cut the "Southern Constellations" circles out. Punch holes where the star dots are.

2. In a darkened room, hold the constellation cards over the lit end of a flashlight and shine them on a ceiling or wall to see each constellation.

3. As you view the constellations, read "The Tale of the Tohunga."

4. If you have a book of Pacific Islander or Aboriginal tales, read one aloud while the children continue to look at their constellations.

5. Glue one of the constellations to your World Explorer Journal and write a caption next to it about constellations in the Southern Hemisphere.

☺ ☺ ☺ EXPLORATION: Ring of Fire Hydrothermal Vents

For this activity, you will need:

- Video about undersea hydrothermal vents from the YouTube playlist
- Globe or world map
- Egg carton
- Paint & brushes
- Paper
- Tissue paper
- Scissors
- Glue
- Other craft supplies, as desired

The Ring of Fire is a zone of volcanoes and earthquakes that circles the Pacific Ocean. Many of the islands in Oceania, such as the Marianas, Papua New Guinea, Solomon Islands, Tuvalu, Samoa, Fiji, and New Zealand, were formed because of this seismic activity. There are thousands of islands around the Pacific that were formed from the Ring of Fire, but even more volcanoes are still lying under the surface. This area is full of hydrothermal activity on the ocean floor.

1. Watch a video about the undersea hydrothermal vents near the Mariana Islands.

2. Find the Mariana Islands on a globe or world map. This area is rich in hydrothermal vents.

3. Using an egg carton as a base, create an undersea scene with hydrothermal vents. The upright portions between the egg cups can be the vents. Make the ejecta from the vents from tissue paper.

4. Use paper to make the kinds of creatures that live near hydrothermal vents.

5. Show your project off to an audience and describe where the hydrothermal vents are located along with some of their unique features.

People of Oceania

☺ ☺ ☺ **EXPLORATION: Oceania's Countries**

For this activity, you will need:

- Book or video about Oceania from the Library List or YouTube playlist for this unit
- "Oceania's Countries" from the Printable Pack
- Colored pencils or crayons

Oceania consists of fourteen countries and ten territories. These countries and territories can be divided into three cultural areas: Micronesia, Melanesia, and Polynesia.

Oceania's Nations

1. Read a book or watch a video about Oceania.

2. Color each of the countries of Oceania green. They are Australia, New Zealand, Papua New Guinea, Palau, Micronesia, Marshall Islands, Solomon Islands, Nauru,

Vanuatu, Tuvalu, Samoa, Tonga, Fiji, and Kiribati.

3. Color each of the territories in Oceania yellow. They are Northern Mariana Islands, Guam, New Caledonia, Wallis & Futuna, Tokelau, American Samoa, Niue, Cook Islands, French Polynesia, and Pitcairn Islands.

4. Color the sea around the Polynesian islands light blue. Polynesia includes: New Zealand, Tonga, Niue, Samoa, American Samoa, Wallis & Futuna, Tuvalu, Tokelau, Cook Islands, French Polynesia, and Pitcairn Islands.

5. Color the sea around the Micronesian islands dark blue. Micronesia includes: Kiribati, Nauru, Marshall Islands, Micronesia, Guam, Northern Mariana Islands, and Palau.

6. Color the seas around the Melanesian islands purple. We are including Australia for convenience and because its islands are part of Melanesia. Melanesia includes: Australia, Papua New Guinea, Solomon Islands, Vanuatu, New Caledonia, and Fiji.

7. Put this map in your Layers of Learning Notebook in the Geography section.

😊 😊 😊 EXPLORATION: Rugby

For this activity, you will need:

- Video about rugby game clips and one of the All Blacks doing the haka from the YouTube playlist for this unit
- Rugby ball or American football or any playground ball
- Globe or world map

The most popular sport in Oceania is rugby. It's a rough game that is similar to American football but faster paced and with fewer rules or protective gear.

1. Watch a video of rugby game clips to get an idea of what the game is about.

2. To start a game, the ball is bounced off the field at the mid-line and then a player kicks it while it is in the air. Go outside and practice until you can kick the ball off a bounce.

3. Take a break inside and find New Zealand on a globe or world map. New Zealand's national rugby team is called the All Blacks. They are the most successful rugby team in the world. Before each match, the All Blacks perform a haka dance, a Maori challenge given to opponents before war.

4. Watch a video of the All Blacks performing the haka.

Deep Thoughts

New Zealanders have melded an ancient tradition of the haka dance with the modern sport of rugby.

Photo by Alasdair Massie from Cambridge, UK, CC by SA 2.0, Wikimedia

How does this preserve a culture and how does it change it?

Is cultural change usually good, bad, or does it depend?

What do you think of New Zealand's approach to blending two old cultures to make a new one?

Famous Folks

Jonah Lomu of New Zealand is one of the biggest superstars to play rugby ever.

He played professionally from 1994 until 2007. He died of heart failure associated with a serious kidney disorder he battled most of his adult life.

Tupaia was a priest and navigator from the Society Islands in modern-day French Polynesia.

He joined Captain James Cook's expedition in 1769, guiding the ship from island to island and negotiating on behalf of both parties.

Before he met Cook, he had already traveled extensively and knew many different languages. He was also a priest of the god 'Oro and traveled to bring his worship to other islands.

Additional Layer

Ia ota is a favorite dish in Tahiti, made of raw tuna marinated in lime juice and coconut milk then mixed with diced vegetables such as tomatoes and carrots.

Photo by HinanuiOB, CC by SA 4.0, Wikimedia

Try making this or other Pacific Islands seafood recipes during this unit.

5. Go outside and play a modified game of rugby.

- Players can kick, throw, bounce, or run with the ball.
- You can move the ball toward your team's goal by running or kicking it forward, but never throwing it forward.
- If you kick it forward, all your teammates must be behind you.
- If the ball touches the ground, any player can pick it up and play continues.
- The ball must touch the ground in the end zone to score a point.
- Normally you can tackle, but for your game, just two-hand tag players to stop them from moving further.
- Make up your own rules as needed.

☺ ☺ ☺ EXPLORATION: Living Off The Ocean

For this activity, you will need:

- Colored paper
- Circular object like a dish
- Colored pencils, crayons, or oil pastels
- Hole punch
- Metal brad
- Scissors
- Internet

As you would expect of people living in the middle of an ocean, seafood is popular in Oceania. More than 300 varieties of fish are eaten, along with crabs, shellfish, and sea weed. Many islanders live subsistence lifestyles where they farm garden plots and fish off the shore or off small boats for their living.

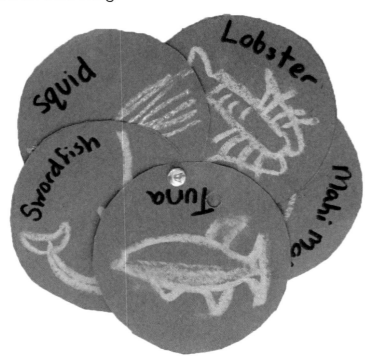

1. Use a circular object to trace five circles onto colored paper. Cut out the circles.

2. Together, as a group, brainstorm as many different kinds of fish and seafood as you can. Make a list that everyone can see.

3. On each circle, draw one type of food the people of Oceania get from the ocean. Write the name of the sea creature on the front of each circle.

4. Hole punch each circle in one spot. Then, fasten all the circles together with a metal brad to make a fan book.

5. On the back of each card, write a few facts about the seafood. It could be about the animal or about how it is caught or eaten. Use the internet to research.

6. Glue the back of the bottom circle to your World Explorer Journal.

☺ ☺ ☺ EXPLORATION: Tourism

For this activity, you will need:

- Travel or tourism videos about several Pacific islands from the YouTube playlist
- "Tourist Shirt" from the Printable Pack, printed on white or colored card stock
- Colored pencils or crayons
- Scissors
- Glue stick
- World Explorer Journal

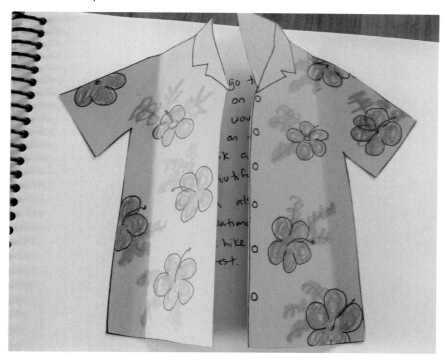

Writer's Workshop

Palau announced in 2015 that 80% of its waters would be off limits for commercial fishing. In Palau, they call this practice "bul" and it is an old concept of limiting harvests so that there will be harvests in the future for your children and grandchildren.

Draft a public policy for the place where you live that would limit harvests (of fish, trees, wild berries, deer, or whatever is common where you live) so that future generations could also have those resources.

How will you balance current needs with future needs?

Deep Thoughts

Tourism can have good impacts on a place, such as preserving a local culture as tourists go to see it. Tourism can also be bad, such as higher prices in local shops.

Brainstorm more good and bad things about tourism. Would you want your neighborhood to be a tourist hot spot? Why or why not?

Tourists are watching men in Yap perform dances. The dances are performed and preserved, in part, because tourists go watch them, but the dances also may lose some of their meaning as their purpose changes.

Tourism is the main industry for much of Oceania. People come for the gorgeous beaches, relaxed island vibe, and snorkeling or scuba adventures. In some countries, like Vanuatu and Fiji, tourism makes up more than half of the income for the people of the islands. Other islands struggle to get any tourists because of inadequate airports, electric grids, food supply lines, and hotels and restaurants.

1. Watch travel or tourism videos from several Pacific islands. Choose one that you would like to visit.

2. Draw and color designs on the "Tourist Shirt." Make it something tropical like surfboards, pineapples, palm trees, or hibiscus flowers.

3. Cut the shirt out around the outside, and then cut up the middle of the shirt to make two halves.

4. Glue the outside edges of the shirt and the sleeves to your World Explorer Journal so that it makes two flaps that close to show your tourist shirt.

5. Inside the flaps of the shirt, write where you would visit and what you would do there.

☺ ☺ ☺EXPLORATION: Music & Dance of Oceania

For this activity, you will need:

- Videos of four different types of dance from Oceania from the YouTube playlist
- "Dance of Oceania" from the Printable Pack
- Colored pencils or crayons
- Scissors
- Glue stick
- World Explorer Journal

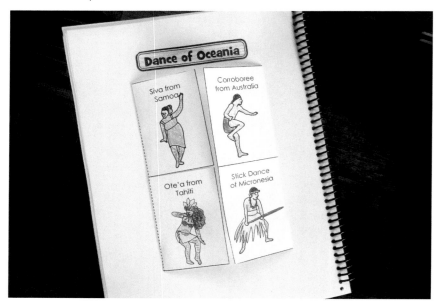

The islands of Oceania each have a distinct culture, including dance styles ranging from the smooth soft motions of Samoa to the militant stick dances of Micronesia. Dance in the islands is used to tell stories, celebrate events, memorialize, or even ask for favors.

1. Cut out the "Dance of Oceania" title and foldable on the solid lines. Fold on the dashed lines.

2. Glue the back of the booklet to your World Explorer Journal. You will have four flaps, one for each type of dance. Glue the title above the booklet.

3. Color the dancers.

4. Watch the four types of dances in the videos. After each one write down the characteristics of the dance and music under the flaps.

☺ ☺ ☺ **EXPLORATION: Oceania Feast**

For this activity, you will need:

- Book or video about Oceania or specific countries in Oceania from the Library List or the YouTube playlist for this unit
- "Oceania Recipes" from the Printable Pack
- Tropical fruits like bananas, plantains, coconut, breadfruit, papaya, or mango
- Ingredients and cooking implements from the recipes you chose
- Brightly colored tablecloth
- Plastic leis
- "Surfboard Trivia" cards from the Printable Pack, printed on card stock

The people of Oceania love food, parties, and big groups of people enjoying time together. If you're in Australia, you might be invited to a "barbie," an outdoor barbecue. In Samoa on Sunday afternoon, you might eat at an extended family's umu. And in Papua New Guinea, you might get to go to a mumu feast and watch a sing-sing of music and dance performers.

1. Prepare some foods from Oceania. You can use the "Oceania Recipes" or find your own.

2. Set your table with a brightly colored tablecloth, plates, cups, utensils, and a colorful lei on each plate, along with three or more surfboard trivia cards for each person.

3. Have each person write down a trivia question with the answer on each surfboard card. The trivia questions

Bookworms

Haka: A Living Tradition by Wira Gardiner is about the history of the haka, its meanings, and the many ways it is a living, changing tradition that is used in ritual today, not just shown off as a museum piece.

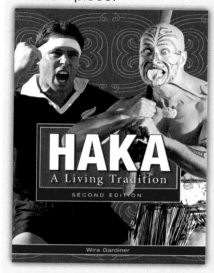

This book has photographs and illustrations accompanying dense text.

Additional Layer

The main crops grown in Oceania are potatoes, sweet potatoes, taro, coconuts, and tropical fruits.

Many people of Oceania still grow their garden plots that, along with the sea, provide most of their food.

This is a taro plot. Learn more about taro and other staples of Oceania.

should come from things you have learned during this unit.

Fabulous Fact

People in many nations of Oceania greet one another with kisses on the cheeks, forehead touches, or hugs rather than the more distant handshakes and bows of the rest of the world.

This is a normal greeting among the Maori of New Zealand.

Photo by Raimond Spekking, CC by SA 4.0, Wikimedia.

Writer's Workshop

The wealthiest nations in Oceania are Australia, New Zealand, French Polynesia, and New Caledonia. The poorest are Kiribati, Papua New Guinea, Tuvalu, and Vanuatu.

Make a comparison chart of education between Papua New Guinea and French Polynesia or any other wealthy vs poor places in Oceania.

Children from Papua New Guinea rarely have access to books. Buk bilong Pikinini has established a library for these children to help them gain literacy. Photo by Ness Kerson/ madNESS Photography for AusAID, CC by SA 4.0.

should come from things you have learned during this unit.

4. While you eat, play your surfboard trivia game.

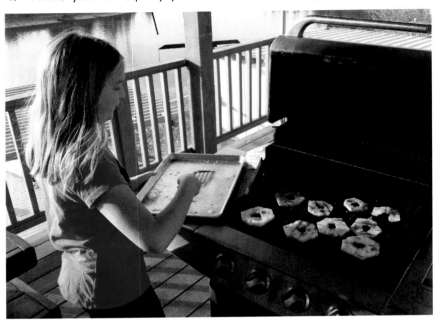

Step 3: Show What You Know

During this unit, choose one of the assignments below to show what you have learned during the unit. Add this work to your Layers of Learning Notebook. You can also use this assignment to show your supervising teacher or your charter school as a sample of what you've been working on in your homeschool, if needed.

There are more ideas for writing assignments in the "Writer's Workshop" sidebars.

☺ ☺ **Coloring or Narration Page**
For this activity, you will need:

- "Oceania" printable from the Printable Pack
- Writing or drawing utensils

1. Depending on the age and ability of the child, choose either the "Oceania" coloring sheet or the "Oceania" narration page from the Printable Pack.

2. Younger kids can color the coloring sheet as you review

some of the things you learned about during this unit. On the bottom of the coloring page, kids can write a sentence about what they learned. Very young children can explain their ideas orally while a parent writes for them.

3. Older kids can write about some of the concepts you learned on the narration page and color the picture as well.

4. Add this to the Geography section of your Layers of Learning Notebook.

☺ ☺ ☺ Writer's Workshop

For this activity, you will need:

- A computer or a piece of paper and a writing utensil

Choose from one of the ideas below or write about something else you learned during this unit. Each of these prompts corresponds with one of the units from the Layers of Learning Writer's Workshop curriculum, so you may choose to coordinate the assignment with the monthly unit you are learning about in Writer's Workshop.

- **Sentences, Paragraphs, & Narrations:** Stretch a Sentence. Begin with the phrase: *Beautiful Oceania.* Then add "what," "where," "when," and "why" to expand your sentence.
- **Descriptions & Instructions:** Write down directions on how to get from your home to a hotel in Fiji. Include driving to the airport, changing planes midway, landing in Fiji, and then driving to your hotel. You can research details or just make it up.
- **Fanciful Stories**: Pick a creature that lives on a coral reef. Give it a personality and a goal. Then pick a different creature to be its nemesis. Write character sketches for both.
- **Poetry:** Recycle "Mary Had a Little Lamb" into a poem about an island child who has a little fish, dolphin, or crab as a pet.
- **True Stories:** Find a recent news story about something from Oceania. Rewrite the news story as a narrative, as though it is a story with plot, characters, and setting.
- **Reports and Essays:** Create note cards with facts about a Pacific Island dance style that you have researched.
- **Letters:** Create a resume for a job as a marine conservationist working for Ocean Conservancy, Pacific Marine Mammal Center, or another organization. Pretend you have completed the

Famous Folks

Most countries in Oceania are republics with elected parliaments or senates that help a president rule.

However, Tonga has a king. Here is his royal majesty King Tupou VI and his wife, Queen Nanasipau'u.

Photo by Governor-General of New Zealand, CC by SA 4.0.

Additional Layer

Most people in Oceania are Christians. British and American missionaries brought the religion to the region in the early 1800s.

Learn more about religion in Oceania. You may also enjoy researching the Prince Philip Movement in Vanuatu and the emergence of "cargo cults" in the 20th century.

These men worship Prince Phillip. Photo by Christopher Hogue Thompson.

Unit Trivia Questions

1. What is the Great Pacific Garbage Patch?

   A region where plastic trash collects and floats in the Pacific Ocean. There are garbage patches in all of the oceans.

2. True or false: Even heavily damaged coral reefs can be restored.

   True. Coral reefs quickly restore themselves when the pollutants and harmful practices are removed.

3. How many countries are in Oceania?

   Fourteen

4. The most important source of income for most nations in Oceania is _____.

   Tourism

5. Which of these is not a popular food in Oceania:

   a) Rice

   b) Fish

   c) Taro

   d) Cornmeal grits

6. Which country in Oceania has a king?

   a) Tonga

   b) Fiji

   c) Solomon Islands

7. Name the three regions of Oceania.

   Micronesia, Melanesia, Polynesia

8. Explain the difference between an oceanic and a continental island.

   Oceanic islands are volcanic or uplifted sea floor. Continental islands are made of granite-based continental crust.

training and are looking for an entry-level position.

- **Persuasive Writing:** Would you rather go scuba diving on the Great Barrier Reef or attend a dance festival in Samoa? Think about your reasons for your opinion and then write a journal entry explaining your choice.

😊 😊 😊 **Oceania Countries Quiz**

For this activity, you will need:

- "Fill In Oceania's Countries" from the Printable Pack

1. Fill in the names of the countries of Oceania. For younger kids, you can give a word bank to make it easier and to help with spelling.

2. Give each answer up to two points, one for being the correct name and one for spelling & neatness.

3. These are the answers:

   1. Australia
   2. New Zealand
   3. Papua New Guinea
   4. Palau
   5. Micronesia
   6. Nauru
   7. Solomon Islands
   8. Vanuatu
   9. Fiji
   10. Tuvalu
   11. Marshall Islands
   12. Tonga
   13. Samoa
   14. Kiribati

😊 😊 😊 **Oceania On One Hand**

For this activity, you will need:

- Paper and pencil
- Colored pencils, crayons, or markers

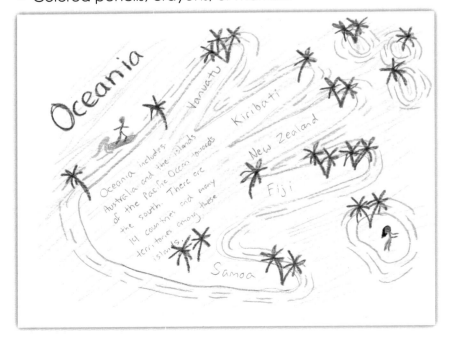

1. Trace your hand on a piece of paper.

2. In the palm write, from memory, a sentence that summarizes what you learned about Oceania.

3. On each finger write down a country from Oceania.

4. Decorate your page to look like scenes from Oceania.

5. Take turns reading the summaries and naming the countries and one fact about each country.

6. Put the page in the Geography section of your Layers of Learning Notebook.

☺ ☺ ☺ Big Book of Knowledge

For this activity, you will need:

- "Big Book of Knowledge: Oceania" printable from the Printable Pack, printed on card stock
- Writing or drawing utensils
- Big Book of Knowledge

1. Color, draw on, or write on the Big Book of Knowledge page. Record concepts, definitions, and facts you learned during this unit. It's a record of the things you learned and hope to remember. Add the page to your Big Book of Knowledge.

2. Use your Big Book of Knowledge regularly to help you review, quiz, or create games that will help you commit the things you've learned to memory.

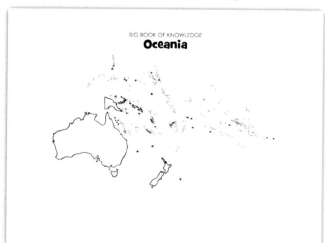

BIG BOOK OF KNOWLEDGE
Oceania

Big Book of Knowledge

The Big Book of Knowledge is a book for you, the mentor, to use as a constant review of all of the things you're learning about. You can use it to quiz your kids or prepare tests or review games. Whenever you learn something in Layers of Learning that you want your kids to remember, add it to your Big Book of Knowledge.

Assemble your Big Book of Knowledge in a binder or with binder rings. Divide it into sections for each subject.

In the Printable Pack for this unit you will find a "Big Book of Knowledge" sheet. You can add this sheet to others you collect or create yourself as you progress through the Layers of Learning curriculum. Customize the Big Book of Knowledge to your family by adding facts and topics that you enjoyed exploring as you were learning.

Visit Layers of Learning online to find more information on how to assemble and use your own Big Book of Knowledge.

You will also find cover and section pages to print along with creative games to play with your Big Book of Knowledge to keep school, even the tests, fun!

NORTH AMERICA

North America includes the Canadian Arctic to the Isthmus of Panama and the nations of the Caribbean Sea. The Rocky Mountain range runs from the far north down through Mexico and Central America, forming a spine that separates the continent into two halves. The land in the east is generally wetter and flatter than the land in the west. The largest river is the Mississippi and its tributaries, which drains the central part of the continent and empties into the Gulf of Mexico.

This is a view from the top of Pike's Peak in the Rocky Mountains, USA. This part of North America has a continental climate.

North America includes arctic, continental, temperate, dry, and tropical climates as it stretches from the North Pole to regions close to the equator. Climate is the average temperature and precipitation in a region. The types of plants and animals that live in a place depend on the climate. Certain species thrive in cool temperatures and others in hot places. North America's animals and plants vary widely and many are unique to the continent because of its climates and its isolation from Asia and Europe.

On the left is a beach in Costa Rica, which has a tropical climate.

On the right is a polar climate on Baffin Island, Canada.

Though people of nearly every heritage and culture live in North America, the predominant cultures are of European descent, mostly England, France, Germany, and Spain. The three most commonly spoken languages are English, French, and Spanish. In spite of their European heritages, the people of North America have made their own unique cultures, adopting parts of many cultures from around the world, including the cultures of indigenous peoples and the many immigrants.

Step I: Library List

Choose books from your library that go with this topic. Here's a list of some favorites and also a list of search terms so you can utilize what your library offers. Read the books with your kids and/or assign them some to read independently. It is from these books your kids will learn most of the facts they need from this unit.

Search for: North America, Central America, Caribbean, climate

☺ ☺ ☻*Geography of the World* by DK. Read "Climate and Vegetation" on page 14, "North America" on page 20, "Peoples of North America" on page 22, and "Central America and the Caribbean" on page 44.

☺ ☺ ☻*Small Animals of North America Coloring Book* by Elizabeth Anne McClelland. This is a detailed coloring book of real animals, not cartoony. Each page includes brief information about the animal. Use this for kids who love coloring or animals.

☺ ☺ ☻*Amazing Places to See in North America* by Publications International Ltd. This is a small square 320-page book with full-color photos and descriptions of natural beauties, man-made architecture, and artistic wonders. Perfect from browsing at any age.

☺*Introducing North America* by Chris Oxlade. Exactly what you would expect, this is a quick overview of the stats and various landmarks and people of the continent.

☺*Discover the Continents: North America* by Emily Rose Oaschs. Large, bright pictures of places, plants, and animals around North America are paired with just a few large print sentences and captions on each page. This book highlights the various climates of North America.

☺*Native American Stories for Kids* by Tom Pecore Weso. This book includes twelve tales from tribes within the United

Family School Levels

The colored smilies in this unit help you choose the correct levels of books and activities for your child.

☺ = Ages 6-9
☺ = Ages 10-13
☻ = Ages 14-18

On the Web

For videos, web pages, games, and more to add to this unit, visit the People & Planet Resources at Layers-of-Learning.com.

You will find a link to video playlists, web links, and more.

Bookworms

If you're looking for a family read-aloud, we'd like to suggest this one.

Esperanza Rising by Pam Munoz Ryan is about a girl who grows up wealthy in Mexico until circumstances and the Great Depression drive her family to a farm labor camp in California. But she won't stay down, no matter what happens.

Fabulous Fact

If you have ever traveled from a forest to a grassland or from the desert to the mountains, you have seen the transition between climate zones. On a map, it looks like there is an abrupt boundary but, in the real world, there is usually a gradual transition from one climate to the other.

This is a photo of the outskirts of Spokane, Washington, USA.

Photo by Joe Mabel, CC SA 3.0

Spokane is on the boundary between the forested mountains of Idaho and the grasslands and deserts of central Washington. In the photo above you can see how the trees (dark patches) are interspersed with grasses.

As you travel west to east, you go from no trees to thick forests.

Writer's Workshop

If you could design a perfect climate, what would it be like? Would it have snow? Would it rain a lot? When would summer start and end? Would it be dry?

Write about your perfect climate.

States. It was written by a Native American author. It also has playful full-page illustrations, one for each tale.

☺*Nature's Treasures of North America* by Alison Limentani. Adorably illustrated, this book highlights animals from various habitats across North America from tundra to coral reefs.

☺*Climate & Weather* by Barbara Taylor. Discusses the difference between climate and weather, maps and explains the world climates, and discusses violent weather and weather pollution.

☺ ☻*The Seven Continents: North America* by Karen Kellaher. This is a solid introduction to the continent with pictures and paragraphs on every page.

☺ ☻*Wild Animals of North America* by Karl Meyer. Each page has a full color photo and a description of the animal on the back side. The pages can be removed from the book to become posters.

☺ ☻*The Climate Zones* by Kristen Rajczak. This book is specifically about the mapping and geography of climate zones, teaching how, where, and why certain climates exist. Uses examples mostly from North America.

☺ ☻*Why We Live Where We Live* by Kira Vermond. This book is a deep thinker for kids. It discuses climate, economics, natural resources, politics, city planning, and more all about why people live where they live. Highly recommended.

☺ ☻*Using Climate Maps* by Rebecca E. Hirsch. Explains how to read climate maps, what they show and what they don't show, and how climate maps are used.

☺ ☻*The Science of Weather: The Changing Truth About Earth's Climate* by Ian Graham. The weather affects farms, rivers, coastlines, transportation, and makes climates over time.

☺ ☻*Paddle to the Sea* by Hollling C. Holling. A young native boy carves a canoe with a paddler and sets it in the melting snow above a mountain stream. Over four years, Paddle-to-the-Sea travels through the Great Lakes and St. Lawrence River to the Atlantic. We also recommend *Minn of the Mississippi* by the same author.

☺ ☻*North American Maps for Curious Minds* by Matthew Bucklan and Victor Cizek. This is a series of maps and keys that show random things like which country you would land in first if you swam from every point on the North American shore or a map of every show the Beatles played in North

America. Fun for browsing.

☺*Lonely Planet's Best of Central America* by Ashley Harrell, et. al. This is a travel guide for Central America with photos and descriptions of places to go and cultures to see.

☺*Caribbean Islands* by Paul Clammer et. al. This is a Lonely Planet travel guide about the region. It includes photos and descriptions of some of the best sights in the Caribbean.

☺*Explore the Americas* by Lonely Planet. This is a guide to sixty different trips and experiences across the Americas, from Canada to Argentina. Browse it for information on places and people of the region.

☺*The Whole Story of Climate* by E. Kirsten Peters. The author is a PhD geologist and university professor. She explains the earth's climate history over hundreds of millions of years. Why the earth's climate changes, what we do know, and what don't we know are discussed. She also explains that we don't have any idea what is coming next except that climate change is normal. We should still be concerned about human pollution that may have repercussions on the earth's systems. This is a popular-level science book.

☺*A Cultural History of Climate* by Wolfgang Behringer. This is about the history of climate change and how human societies reacted to events like the desertification of the Sahara and the Little Ice Age in Europe. From witch hunts to migration and war, the author argues that changing climates have deep effects on human societies.

Step 2: Explore

Choose a few hands-on Explorations from this section to work on as a family. They should be appealing activities that will create mental hooks so your kids remember the information in the unit. Save the rest of the Explorations for the next time you do this unit in four years when your kids are older. You can also read the sidebars together and explore some little rabbit trails.

This unit includes printables. See the introduction for instructions on retrieving your Printable Pack.

Climates

A **climate** is defined by the amount of rainfall and the temperatures an area receives on average over the years. It is the cumulative average of the **weather**. North America has all five of the major climates: **tropical**, **desert**, **temperate**, **continental**, and **polar**.

Famous Folks

The most widely used climate classification system was developed by Wladimir Köppen, a Russian botanist and geographer.

He was born and educated in Russia and then spent his career in Germany and Austria.

Additional Layer

Ancient art can be evidence of climate change. This painting of cattle is from the Sahara desert.

Memorization Station

Climate: the average temperature and precipitation a place receives over a 30-year period

Weather: the temperature, precipitation, humidity, pressure, and wind at a particular time

Bookworms

Why Geography Matters More Than Ever by Harm de Blij is about the importance of geographical knowledge for navigating the everyday world whether you are a big wig politician, a voter, a captain of industry, or just navigating daily life and geopolitics.

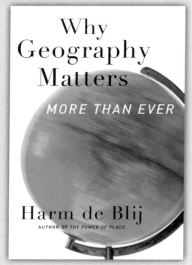

We highly recommend this book for teens and adults.

Memorization Station

Memorize the five major climate types:

Polar climate: very long, cold winters and short cool summers

Continental climate: cold, snowy winters, warm to hot summers

Temperate climate: cool winters, warm to hot summers

Desert climate: cold to warm winters and hot summers, very little rain

Tropical climate: warm to hot winters and hot summers, moderate to heavy amounts of rain

☺ ☻ EXPLORATION: Climate Match of North America

For this activity, you will need:

- "Climate Match Map" and "Climate Match" from the Printable Pack
- Book or video about each type of climate: polar, continental, temperate, desert, and tropical (You can find recommendations in the Library List or YouTube playlist.)
- World Explorer Journal
- Colored pencils
- Glue stick
- Scissors

Some places are cold and snowy, others are hot and dry, and others are warm and wet. Each of the differences in climate, or weather over time, means that there will be differences in plants and animals that live in these places. Some plants need lots of water and constant warmth to thrive, while others do well with hot temperatures and very little rain. Still others need a deep cold season to successfully complete their life patterns.

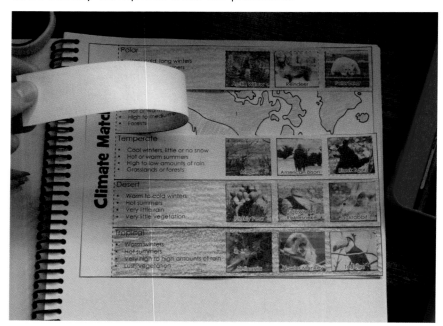

1. Color the "Climate Match Map" map according to the key. Use any colors you like.

2. Cut out the "Climate Match" rectangle on the solid lines. Glue the title edge next to the "Climate Match Map" so that the long flaps cover the map in your World Explorer Journal.

3. Read a book or watch a video about each type of climate.

4. Cut out the animal and plant squares and see if you can match the animals and the plants to the climates they live in. Glue them in the correct spots.

Answers: Polar- arctic willow, polar bear, reindeer
Continental- ponderosa pine, red squirrel*, mallard duck
Temperate- maple*, black bear*, American bison*
Desert- prickly pear, jackrabbit, sidewinder rattlesnake
Tropical- helicona, toucan, howler monkey
*some species live in more than one climate

5. Discuss why animals and plants live in different climates.

☺ ☺ ☺EXPLORATION: Defining Climate

For this activity, you will need:

- Books or videos about climate from the Library List or YouTube playlist
- "Climate & Weather" from the Printable Pack
- Scissors
- Glue stick
- Colored pencils or crayons
- World Explorer Journal

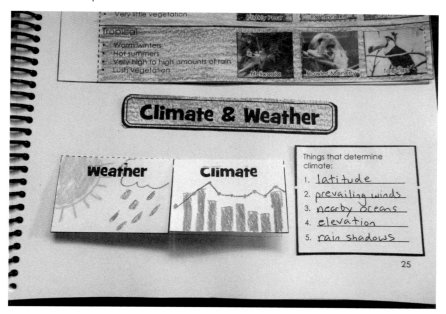

1. Read a book or watch a video about climate. Come up with a definition of climate and a definition of weather, individually on paper or together on a white board. As you do, compare the two words and talk about how they are similar and how they are different.

2. Color and cut out the title of the "Climate & Weather" page and glue it into your World Explorer Journal.

3. Cut out the "Weather Climate" flaps on the solid lines

Additional Layer

Climates change and we only partially understand why. For example, North Africa has cycled from wet to dry for as long as we can tell. Sometimes, like now, the Sahara is a desert, and sometimes it is a grassland.

This is part of the Great Green Wall. Photo by Agenzia Dire, CC by SA 4.0.

Right now, the Sahara is expanding and countries in the region are trying to stop the expansion. They have begun a project called the Great Green Wall, a planted forest to border and contain the Sahara. Do you think they will be successful?

Learn more about the Orbital Monsoon Hypothesis and the Great Green Wall project.

Bookworms

Here are five books, each taking place in a different North American climate.

Julie of the Wolves by Jean Craighead George takes place in a polar climate.

Hatchet by Gary Paulson takes place in a continental climate.

Summer of the Monkeys by Wilson Rawls takes place in a temperate climate.

Sing Down the Moon by Scott O'Dell takes place in a desert climate.

The Jumbies by Tracey Baptiste is set in a tropical climate.

In each of the books, the reader is immersed in the natural world of the setting.

and fold on the dashed lines. Glue the back of the flaps down to your World Explorer Journal. On the cover of each flap, draw a graphic or picture that helps you remember the definition of weather and the definition of climate. Inside the flaps, write the definitions.

4. Come up with a list of five things that determine what the climate of a place will be based on your reading or viewing. Your list should include things like latitude, nearby oceans, mountain rain shadows, mountain elevation, and prevailing winds. But you should make the list your own; it doesn't have to exactly match ours. Write it on the provided rectangle and then cut and paste into your World Explorer Journal. Make sure kids understand each of the terms in the list.

☺ ☺ EXPLORATION: Köppen Climate Classification

For this activity, you will need:

- Video on the Köppen Climate Classification system from the YouTube playlist for this unit
- "Köppen Climate Classification," "Climate Data Set 1," "Climate Data Set 2," and "Köppen Climate Map of North America" from the Printable Pack
- Colored pencils
- Student atlas
- Internet (optional)

Climate Data Set I

Classification **Cfb**

Vancouver, Canada

MONTH	AVERAGE TEMPERATURE	AVERAGE PRECIPITATION
January	37.2 °F (2.9 °C)	12 in (312 mm)
February	37.7 °F (3.2 °C)	7 in (200 mm)
March	40.9 °F (4.9 °C)	10 in (257 mm)
April	46.1 °F (7.8 °C)	7 in (181 mm)
May	53.2 °F (11.8 °C)	4 in (120 mm)
June	58.4 °F (14.7 °C)	4 in (103 mm)
July	64.2 °F (17.9 °C)	2 in (56 mm)
August	64.7 °F (18.2 °C)	2 in (75 mm)
September	58.7 °F (14.8 °C)	4 in (123 mm)
October	50.1 °F (10 °C)	9 in (253 mm)
November	42 °F (5.5 °C)	14 in (362 mm)
December	36.9 °F (2.7 °C)	12 in (309 mm)

49.2°F   87 in

Russian climatologist Wladimir Köppen invented a way to classify climates based on temperature and precipitation levels. There are five main climates: tropical, desert, temperate, continental, and polar. Each of these climates is given a letter designation: A-tropical, B-desert, C-temperate, D-continental, and E-polar. Within each main climate type, there are sub-climates. For example, within the tropical climate, there are tropical rainforest, tropical monsoon, and tropical savanna sub-climates. The sub-climates are indicated with more letters. Rainforest is indicated with an f. So a tropical rainforest climate would be Af.

1. Watch a video about the Köppen climate classification system and how it works.

2. Find the average temperature for the year for Vancouver, Canada using the "Climate Data Set 1" sheet. To find the average yearly temperature, add up all the average monthly temperatures and divide by 12, the number of months.

   Note that the average temperature is the daily high plus the daily low averaged.

3. Circle the coldest month in blue and the hottest month in red.

4. On the "Köppen Climate Classification" sheet, read the definitions for each 1st Level set. Determine which classification Vancouver belongs in. Write the letter in the "Classification" box at the top of the data set.

5. Next, circle the month with the highest precipitation in green and the month with the lowest in brown.

6. Add up the total amount of rain for the year. Using the Köppen Climate Classification chart, determine which category Vancouver falls into, first based on total rainfall and then based on seasonal variations.

7. Finally, use the third level column to determine which sub-temperature group the climate fits into. Tropical and Polar climates don't have a third level.

8. Summer in the Northern Hemisphere is June, July, August, and September. Look at the average temperatures in those months. If the average temperature is above 70 °F, color it pink. If the average temperature is between 50 and 70 °F, color it yellow. If the average temperature is below 50 °F, color it light blue. These are the hot, warm, cold designations for Level 3. Determine which Vancouver fits in.

9. Repeat the process for the other three city's data sets.

   Answers: Vancouver Cfb, Phoenix BWh, Kingston Aw/As (It is on the border between these climates and you may have gotten either answer), Nuuk ET

Deep Thoughts

The Köppen Climate Classification System is not the only way to categorize climates. Charles Thornthwaite developed a climate classification system based on precipitation effectiveness. If you divide the amount of precipitation each month by the amount of evaporation, you get how much water remains in the ground for plants to use.

The major classifications are microthermal, mesothermal, and megathermal, having to do with heat and evaporation levels.

Think about the Köppen system. What weaknesses does it have? Does it fail to explain climates? Is it hard to understand? What would you do to make it better?

Additional Layer

Gardeners use special climate zone maps called plant hardiness zones to determine which plants will survive and thrive in their gardens.

This is a plant hardiness zone map of the United States.

Find out what plant hardiness zone you live in. Design a small vegetable or flower garden on paper with plants that would thrive in your zone.

Additional Layer

Climate influences human culture, from clothing choices to home construction to social norms. Agriculture, a major step in human civilization, flourished first in mild climates such as Mesopotamia, Egypt, and the Indus Valley.

Think about early civilizations and the biggest empires on earth. What climates did they appear in. Why?

Fabulous Fact

This is a diagram of how rain shadows work. Copy it into your World Explorer Journal.

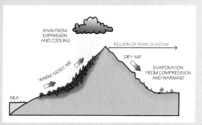

Image by Wade Greenberg-Brand/Paleontological Research Institution

Memorization Station

Memorize the five climate factors.

Latitude: distance north or south of the equator

Prevailing winds: surface winds that mostly blow in one direction

Ocean effect: ocean water absorbs and releases heat from the sun, moderating the temperature and providing rain

Elevation: distance above sea level

Rain shadow: land that is blocked from receiving rain by mountain ranges

10. Look at the "Köppen Climate Map of North America" to see the climate map for the whole continent. Plot the cities of Vancouver, Phoenix, Kingston, and Nuuk on the map. You will need a student atlas and its gazetteer to find their locations.

11. If you want to see the Köppen Climate map of North America larger, you can look it up online and put it on a big screen. You may also want to examine the Köppen Climate map of the world or of your part of the world online.

12. Put your papers from this Exploration in your Layers of Learning Notebook in the Geography section.

☺ ☺ ☻EXPLORATION: 5 Climate Factors
For this activity, you will need:

- "Climate Factors" map from the Printable Pack
- Colored pencils or crayons
- Internet

Places near the equator are hotter than places near the poles because they receive much more direct sunlight, and therefore, more heat from the sun. But, **latitude** is only one factor that determines climate. Other things such as **prevailing winds**, **ocean effect**, **elevation**, and mountain **rain shadows** also determine temperature and rainfall.

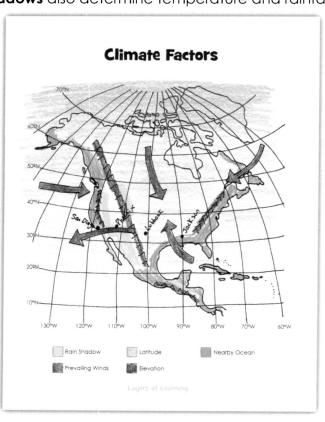

1. Plot the locations of these four cities on the "Climate Factors" map.

    - Jackson, Mississippi 32°N 90°W
    - Lubbock, Texas 33°N 101°W
    - Phoenix, Arizona 33°N 112°W
    - San Diego, California 32°N 117°W

    These four cities are at about the same latitude, but they all have different climates. Jackson is humid subtropical. Lubbock is cool semi-arid. Phoenix is a hot desert climate. San Diego has a mild Mediterranean climate.

2. Color the prevailing winds arrows dark blue. Winds change the temperature as they bring cold air from the poles or warm air from near the equator. Clouds and rain are also carried on the winds, so they determine the amount of rainfall.

3. Color the mountains purple. Higher elevations are cooler than lower elevations because the atmosphere is thinner higher up. Fewer air molecules means it can hold less heat.

4. Mountain ranges block wind, making air rise higher, which cools the clouds and makes them drop their water just before or on the mountains. On the far side of the mountains there is a rain shadow, a place where much less rain falls because the mountains have blocked it. On the side of each mountain range farthest from the prevailing winds, color the land yellow to show that it is drier. The Appalachians, in the eastern part of North America, don't have a rain shadow because the prevailing winds run parallel to the mountain range.

5. Color all the coastal areas up to 60°N green. The oceans absorb heat energy from the sun, which cools the air and adds moisture to it. In the winter, the heat is released back into the atmosphere, warming the coastal areas. Coastal areas are usually mild and wet, unless the prevailing wind does not blow against the region; then, they are mild and dry.

6. Use light blue to color the rest of the map, making the color progressively darker and heavier as you reach higher latitudes. This shows that latitude does strongly affect climate. As the sun's rays become less direct near the poles, the temperatures cool dramatically.

7. Look at the four cities you plotted on the map. Discuss why each city has the climate it does based on the five factors you learned about.

Fabulous Fact

Within any climate, there are little zones with climate variations, like a lake shore that is milder than land just a few hundred feet further from the lake or a city that is hotter than the surrounding countryside because of all the asphalt and concrete. These are called microclimates.

Writer's Workshop

Make a list of places around the world you would like to visit. Organize the list by climate.

Polar

- Greenland
- Antarctica

Tropical

- US Virgin Islands
- Bora Bora

Additional Layer

Very little is known about North American history during the ancient period. There were thriving civilizations, especially in Central America, but we have no written records that we can read and archaeology in the Americas is still in its infancy.

The Olmecs are the earliest known civilization in North America. Learn more about them. Find their ruins on a map and look up images.

Bookworms

The Day the World Came to Town by Jim DeFede is about real events in the town of Gender, Newfoundland, Canada on September 11, 2001.

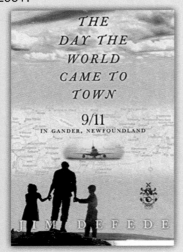

THE DAY THE WORLD CAME TO TOWN

9/11
IN GANDER, NEWFOUNDLAND

JIM DEFEDE

Thirty-eight jetliners on their way to the United States were grounded in this town of 10,000, causing an overnight population boom. This book is a heartwarming recounting of the kindness and humanity of the Canadians who welcomed the world into their homes for the four days travelers were trapped there.

For ages 14 and up.

8. Look up and compare the climates of Vancouver and Winnipeg in Canada.

9. Put the "Climate Factors" map in the Geography section of your Layers of Learning Notebook.

😊 😊 😊 EXPLORATION: Six Awesome Climates

For this activity, you will need:

- "Six Awesome Climates" from the Printable Pack
- Book or video about climates from the Library List or YouTube playlist
- Atlas or online map
- Card stock
- Scissors
- Glue stick
- Internet
- String
- Hole punch

The Hoh Rainforest, Saguaro National Park, Everglades National Park, Tikal National Park, Grasslands National Park, and Ivvavik National Park each showcase a different kind of climate in North America. These are all places that people decided were important for preserving because of their beauty and because they are unique.

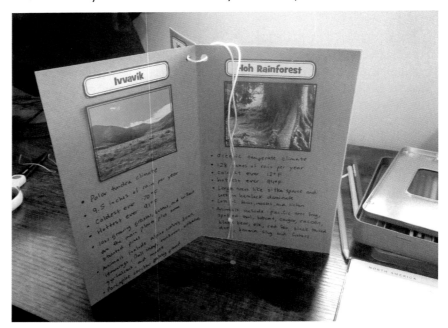

1. Read a book or watch a video about climates.

2. Find each of the national parks in a student atlas or online map.

3. Fold three pieces of card stock in half the short way, hamburger-style.

4. On the front side of each half, glue the titles of the six different climates and their pictures.

5. Research each climate and make a bulleted list of facts about each to write below the pictures and titles. You can include things like average summer and winter temperatures, average yearly rainfall, and plants and animals.

6. Glue the three panels together, back to back, to make a six-part display. Hole punch the middle and tie a string to the project. Hang it from your ceiling until the end of this unit.

☺ ☺ ☻ EXPLORATION: Climate Zone Documentary

For this activity, you will need:

- Clip of a nature documentary from the YouTube playlist for this unit
- Websites and books about climate zones
- Clothing items that match a chosen climate zone

1. Watch a clip of a nature documentary. Notice how the presenter talks and the kinds of information they give. You will be mimicking this style.

2. Research information about a climate zone. Young kids can learn about one of the five main Köppen climate zones (polar, continental, temperate, desert, and tropical) and older kids can learn about a more precise climate zone.

3. Write a script for yourself in the style of a documentary presenter.

4. Prepare either a slide show or several printed images to show your audience.

5. Dress up for the climate you are presenting. Shorts, tee, and sandals for a tropical climate, parka and snow boots for a polar climate, etc.

6. Read your script like a documentary presenter while showing your audience the images about your climate zone. Put your script in the Geography section of your Layers of Learning Notebook.

☺ ☺ ☻ EXPLORATION: Fantasy Planet Climates

For this activity, you will need:

- "Fantasy Planet" grid from the Printable Pack (no title because you will add one, but look for the blank grid)
- Colored pencils or crayons

1. On the "Fantasy Planet" grid, draw a fantasy world map. Add at least two continents.

Teaching Tip

Keeping student work to display during a unit, taking a picture, and then tossing the project when the unit is over keeps the clutter under control.

It also teaches kids to let go of things and keep their possessions to a level where they can be cared for.

Additional Layer

Climate change is not covered in this unit because here, the purpose is to learn about geographic climate zones.

You can find out more about climate science in *Earth & Space: Seasons & Climate*.

Writer's Workshop

Southern California, a dry climate, has a big problem with water shortages.

Research the problems and write a report explaining why they never have enough water.

Propose a solution.

Famous Folks

Louis Agassiz was a Swiss biologist and geologist who, in 1837, proposed that Earth had once been in an ice age.

This was an astonishing idea because people had always thought climate was pretty static and the earth was unchanging. Now we know that change is normal.

Expedition

Take a trip to a climate or micro-climate that is different from the one you live in. Take photos of your home climate and photos of the climate you visit. Put one photo of each climate in your World Explorer Journal and explain the differences you observed.

Writer's Workshop

Adapting to new climates can be difficult for people. Imagine moving from Cuba to Winnipeg, Canada.

Write a paragraph about all the new equipment and habits you would need to survive in your new climate.

2. Trace over the equator with a red pencil, 30°N and S with a yellow pencil, and 60°N and S with a blue pencil.

3. Draw large arrows to show the prevailing winds. Because of planet rotation, winds tend to blow southeasterly between the equator and 30°S, northeasterly between the equator and 30°N, westerly between 30° and 60° in the northern and southern hemispheres and towards the equator from the poles.

4. Draw mountain ranges on your continents.

5. Create a key on your map, one color for each major climate zone: tropical, desert, temperate, continental, and polar.

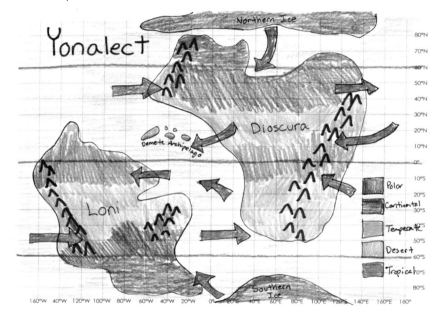

6. Where you have rain shadows from the mountains, color desert climates. Desert climates are also most likely to be at around 30° north and south because these are zones where winds diverge toward the poles or toward the equator, preventing rain from being carried into these latitudes.

7. Near the equator, color tropical climates.

8. Near ocean coasts or where warm ocean winds are carried, color temperate climates.

9. In the middle of large landmasses or where land is sheltered from ocean winds, color continental climates.

10. Above and below 60°, color polar climates. Remember, even these high latitudes can be tempered by winds from the lower altitudes.

11. Give your planet a name and write it on your map.

North American Landscapes

☺ ☺ ☺**EXPLORATION: Watercolor Collage of North America**

For this activity, you will need:

- Poster board
- Watercolor paper
- Watercolor paints & brushes
- Scissors
- Glue
- Student atlas

1. Paint sheets of watercolor paper with colors you will use to make a physical map of North America. You could use light green for grasslands, purple for mountains, dark green for forests, and so on.

2. Freehand draw an outline of North America on a piece of poster board, using a student atlas as a guide.

3. Paint the water on the poster with blue paint. It's okay if the lines aren't neat because they will be covered with paper anyway.

4. Cut or tear the painted watercolor sheets and glue them to the map of North America to show where the mountains, tundra, forests, grasslands, deserts, and rainforests are located. Tear thin strips of blue and add the major rivers and the Great Lakes.

5. Use a black marker to label the major features, such as the Great Lakes, Rocky Mountains, Hudson's Bay, Atlantic Ocean, and so on. Use a student atlas to identify important features.

☺ ☺ ☺**EXPLORATION: North American Landscapes**

For this activity, you will need:

- Book or video about the geography of North America from the Library List, an illustrated atlas, or the YouTube playlist for this unit
- Student atlas
- "North American Landscapes" from the Printable Pack
- Colored pencils or crayons

Bookworms

Before We Were Free by Julia Alvarez is about 12-year-old Anita who lives under a dictatorship in 1960s Dominican Republic.

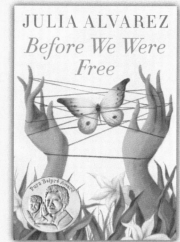

The author was a child in the Dominican Republic before immigrating to America.

For ages 12 and up.

Additional Layer

Cryptids are animals that some people believe exist but that mainstream scientists don't believe in.

Bigfoot, Chupacabra, Jersey Devil, Champy, Igopogo, Skunk Ape, and the Thuderbird are cryptids from North America.

Frida Khalo is a famous Mexican artist who is known for her folk-style self-portraits.

Diego Rivera, husband of Frida Khalo for a time, was another famous artist from Mexico. He is known for abstract portraits, landscapes, and Mexican history paintings like this one showing enslaved natives.

Writer's Workshop

Read about the badlands of South Dakota, then write a thrilling story about getting lost there.

This is a physical map of North America, showing the natural features such as mountains, lakes, and rivers. You will color it to show even more features - ice caps, grasslands, and deserts.

☻You can simplify this activity for younger children by having them color, but not label, the map as you talk through it. If they get tired, put it away to finish later in the day or week.

North American Landscapes

1. Using a student atlas as a guide, label and trace over the Arctic Circle and the Tropic of Cancer in purple. These are lines that mark the position of the sun over the earth. In the winter, the sun's rays don't reach above the Arctic Circle. In the summer, the sun is directly over the Tropic of Cancer at the solstice and goes no further north.

2. Label these rivers and color them blue: Mississippi, Missouri, Ohio, Arkansas, Rio Grande, Colorado, Mackenzie, and St. Lawrence.

3. Label and color these lakes blue: Great Lakes, Lake

Winnipeg, Great Slave Lake, Great Bear Lake, Lake Nicaragua.

4. Label and color the seas blue: Hudson Bay, Baffin Bay, Arctic Ocean, Bering Strait, Pacific Ocean, Gulf of Mexico, Caribbean Sea, Atlantic Ocean, Labrador Sea.

5. Label Greenland and color the ice cap in the middle of the island purple.

6. Label Baffin Island, Victoria Island, Aleutian Islands, Greater Antilles, and Lesser Antilles. Color these islands green.

7. Label these mountains and color them brown: Rocky Mountains, Coast Range, Sierra Nevada, Sierra Madre, Appalachian, Laurentian.

8. Label the Great Plains and color them light green.

9. Label these deserts and color them yellow: Great Basin, Sonoran, and Baja California.

10. Label the Yucatan Peninsula, Canadian Shield, and Isthmus of Panama. Color the rest of the land on the map green.

☺ ☺ ☺**EXPLORATION: Poster Map of North America**

For this activity, you will need:

- Book or video about North America from the Library List or YouTube playlist for this unit
- "North America" from the Printable Pack (This is a simple outline of the continent. Print it onto multiple sheets of paper. Your printer should have settings for "multi-page" or "poster" printing.)
- Tape
- Student atlas
- Colored crayons, pens, or pencils
- Glitter and school glue or glitter glue
- Colored paper
- Scissors
- Glue stick
- Oil pastels (optional)
- Paints and brushes (optional)

1. Read a book or watch a video about North America.

2. Tape the large North America map together into one large map. Put the tape on the back of the sheets of paper so it won't get in the way of coloring and crafting.

3. Use a student atlas and your craft supplies to add the features to North America that you want. Add rivers like

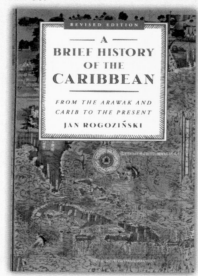

Granny's Kitchen by Sadé Smith is about a Jamaican grandmother who teaches her granddaughter about her heritage by cooking in the kitchen.

For your youngest kids, up to age 7.

Deep Thoughts

North America has a big problem with international drug trading. Drug abuse leads to poverty, under education, unemployment, domestic abuse, violence, and criminal behavior.

The white floating packages in this picture are filled with illegal drugs. They were seized by the US Coast Guard in the Caribbean Sea. Way more drugs make it to their destinations than are stopped.

If you were the leader of North America, how would you stop the drug trade and convince individuals to not use harmful substances? Or would you make drugs legal instead? Explain your reasoning.

the Mississippi, Ohio, and Mackenzie. Add mountains like Rockies and Appalachians. Add the tallest mountain: Mount McKinley. Add the Arctic Circle. Add the Great Plains and the Sonoran Desert. Include cities like Washington D.C., New York, Ottawa, Mexico City, Los Angeles, Havana, and Seattle.

4. Put your completed map of North America on the wall until the end of this unit. Review the landmarks you added regularly to memorize the important places within North America and where they are located.

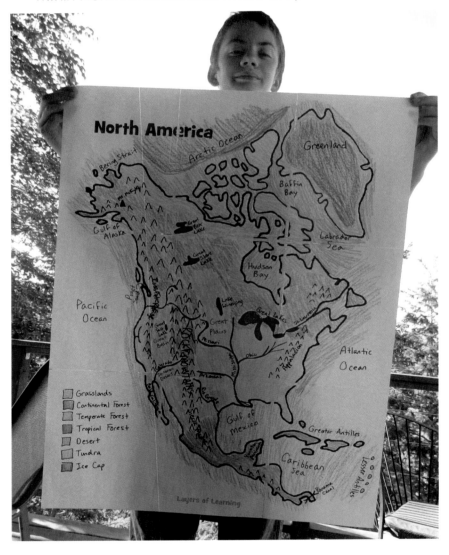

☺ ☺ ☻**EXPLORATION: North American Animal Snapshots**
For this activity, you will need:

- Book or video about North American animals from the Library List or YouTube playlist
- "North American Animal Snapshots" from the Printable Pack

- Internet to look up how-to-draws for animals
- Colored pencils or crayons
- Scissors
- Glue stick

A few species of North American animals are similar to those found in Asia and Europe, but North America has its own varieties of bears, wolves, deer, caribou, robins, mice, and other animals. Besides this, North America has many species that are completely unique, like American bison, raccoons, turkeys, and gila monsters. North America is separated from the eastern hemisphere by large bodies of water that have prevented migration of animals between the continents for a very long time.

1. Read a book or watch a video about North American animals. While you read, take note of three of your favorite animals.

2. Look up an online how-to-draw tutorial for three North American animals. Draw one each in the photo rectangles on the "North American Animal Snapshots" printable. Color the animal and the background of the reference photo.

3. Cut out your three snapshots and glue them into your World Explorer Journal, along with the title. Write the name of the animal beneath each photo.

☺ ☺ ☺ **EXPLORATION: Great Lakes**
For this activity, you will need:

- "The Great Lakes" from the Printable Pack

Los Haitises National Park in the Dominican Republic is known for its karst hills and sinkholes.

Karst is highly eroded limestone rock that forms into dome shapes.

The park is full of beautiful scenery and rare species.

Bookworms

In Darkness by Nick Lake is a powerfully impactful story of a teen boy from Haiti who is trapped in the rubble of an earthquake. While trapped, the story happens inside his head, from his long lost twin sister and the gang violence he is embroiled in, to the slave rebellion of Toussaint L'Ouverture two hundred years previously.

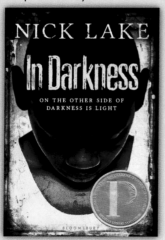

This book has disturbing violence and difficult themes. For ages 14 and up.

- Colored pencils or crayons

The Great Lakes are large, interconnected freshwater lakes in the mid-east region of North America. They are so big that they have huge rolling waves, currents, and sustained winds like the sea. They also have a large effect on the weather directly around them, mitigating the temperature and causing extra precipitation, similar to the way the ocean does for coastal regions. They were formed as the huge ice sheets covering North America retreated, leaving behind a basin. They created a shipping corridor that extends from the Great Plains in the mid-west to the St. Lawrence River and the Atlantic Ocean in the east. Because of this shipping corridor, the shores of the lakes, especially in the southern regions, are built up with a series of cities which specialize in manufacturing and food processing, and are then shipped across the world.

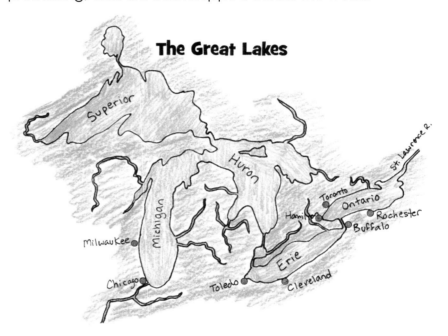

1. Label each of the Great Lakes on the map of the "The Great Lakes."

   - Lake Huron is directly in the center.
   - Ontario is furthest east.
   - Michigan runs north and south and is just west of Huron.
   - Erie is between Huron and Ontario.
   - Lake Superior is the furthest north and west.

   You can remember the names with the acronym HOMES.

2. Color the Great Lakes and their **tributaries** blue. Notice how short the tributaries are? The Great Lakes are in a

low-lying area, called a **basin**. Rivers that begin outside of the basin flow in other directions. The Great Lakes have very little new water added each year.

3. Color each of the city dots on the map red. The dots on the map are the largest cities that sit on the shores of the Great Lakes. Label each city.

   • Milwaukee and Chicago are on Lake Michigan with Milwaukee being further north.
   • Toledo and Cleveland are on Lake Erie with Toledo being further west.
   • Buffalo is on the short Niagara River between Erie and Ontario.
   • Hamilton is on the western tip of Ontario and Toronto is just east on the same shore.
   • Rochester is on the southern shore of Lake Ontario.

4. Label the St. Lawrence River, the outlet on the northeast end of Lake Ontario. This is the way to the sea.

5. Color the land around the lakes green. This area is a continental climate with hot summers and cold winters.

6. Put this map in your Layers of Learning Notebook in the Geography section.

☺ ☺ ☺ **EXPLORATION: West Indies Archipelago**

For this activity, you will need:

• Student atlas
• "West Indies Archipelago" from the Printable Pack
• Colored pencils or crayons
• Scissors
• Glue stick
• Paper
• Stapler
• Internet for how-to-draw tutorials

The West Indies is an archipelago in the Caribbean Sea. The islands are divided into three parts: the Greater Antilles, Lesser Antilles, and Lucayan Archipelago. The Greater

Memorization Station

Tributary: a river or stream that flows into a bigger river or lake

Basin: a depression or dip in the earth's surface with sides higher than the middle, sometimes basins are filled with water

Additional Layer

The Great Basin is a low-lying desert area between the Rocky Mountain and the Sierra Nevada ranges. It does not have drainage to any sea. The Great Salt Lake and the Salton Sea have accumulated salt deposits as a result.

Image by Kmusser, CC by SA 3.0

Learn more about the Great Basin, its geology, human populations, history, and ecology.

Writer's Workshop

Use the animals from the "West Indies Archipelago" booklet to write a story. The main plot is that each is trying to be dominant, but they have to learn to live together because they find out they need each other.

Bookworms

Game Seven by Paul Volponi is about young Julio who was left behind with his mother and sister when his baseball star father defected to the United States from Cuba.

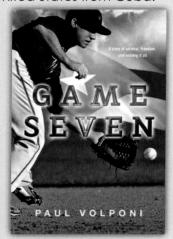

Now, Julio might not make the team because his family members are traitors. Can he join his father in America? Has his father forgotten all about him?

For ages 12 and up.

Memorization Station

Ethnic group: a large group of people who identify with one another because they have a common language, culture, and history

Migrant: a person who moves permanently to a new place

Assimilation: rejecting all or part of a native culture and adopting the culture of the host in order to fit in

Ethnicity is sometimes confused with skin color, but ethnicity is mostly about culture. Even so, people who share a culture and history are usually from the same genetic group as well.

Antilles are made of continental rock and are larger in size. The Lesser Antilles are volcanic and are small. The Lesser Antilles sit on the edge of the Caribbean and South American tectonic plates. The Lucayan Islands are coral.

1. On a map of North America or the Caribbean from your student atlas, find the West Indies. Find the Greater Antilles and Lesser Antilles. What are the seas around the islands named?

2. Color the Greater Antilles, Lesser Antilles, and Lucayan Archipelago on the "West Indies Archipelago" map, each a different color.

3. Color the seas blue.

4. Cut out the parts of the map on the dashed lines. Arrange them in the correct places on the table in front of you for practice.

5. Cut three pieces of paper in half, the short way, hamburger-style. Staple them together along one short edge to make a booklet.

6. Design a cover for the West Indies Archipelago book.

7. Think of an animal that, in your mind, represents each of the parts of the map. Use online how-to-draw tutorials to draw and color a picture of each animal, on each right facing sheet. Glue each of the parts of the map you cut out to the sheet facing the animal you drew.

8. On each page of your book, write a simile and adjective sentence like "The Greater Antilles are like a crocodile, rugged, tough, green, and patient."

9. Read your book to someone else, then add it to your classroom library.

People of North America

☺ ☺ ☺**EXPLORATION: Countries of North America**
For this activity, you will need:

- Book or video about North America from the Library List or YouTube playlist
- "Countries of North America" from the Printable Pack
- Colored pencils or crayons

North America is made up of 23 countries as well as many territories such as Greenland, Puerto Rico, and the Cayman Islands. We have divided North America into three regions: Mainland, Central America, and Caribbean.

Countries of North America

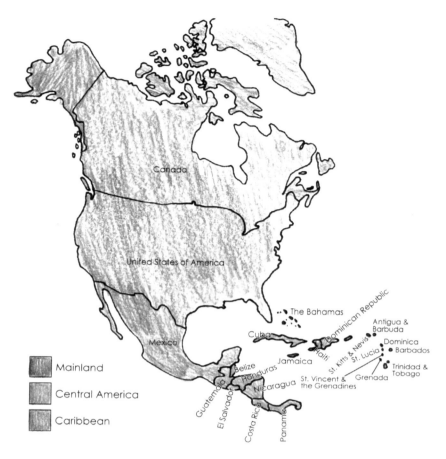

1. Mainland
2. Central America
3. Caribbean

1. Read a book or watch a video about North America.

2. Color the "Countries of North America" map by region. Use the map, above, to help you.

3. Put the map in your Layers of Learning notebook in the Geography section.

☺ ☻**EXPLORATION: North American Ethnicities**
For this activity, you will need:

- "Ethnicities of _____" from the Printable Pack
- Internet for research
- World Explorer Journal
- Colored pencils

North American people are from **ethnic groups** originating all over the world. Each ethnic group has its own culture. Sometimes these cultures live side-by-side with other ethnic groups, and sometimes the various ethnic groups mix their cultures, forming new groups. Often, when new **migrants** move to North American countries, they try to

Memorization Station

Use the blank map of North America from the Printable Pack to label, color, and learn the countries in North America.

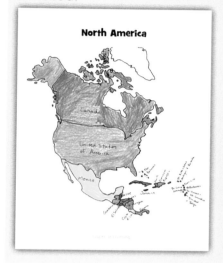

Teaching Tip

Memorizing isn't just about knowing facts and trivia. It is also brain training. In order to develop the ability to memorize, you have to memorize. In order to reason, you have to have facts to build reasoning on. Don't be afraid of asking your kids to memorize difficult things.

Deep Thoughts

Most migrants choose to live in neighborhoods with people from their native culture. For example, Chinese immigrants to American cities tended to live in "Chinatown" neighborhoods and many still do.

Why do you think people do this? Is it good or bad?

Would you live in a community of your ethnic group if you moved to a foreign country? Why?

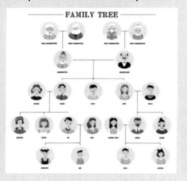

assimilate, or fit in, to their host country. This makes it easier to communicate, participate in institutions such as schools, churches, and social events, and be accepted by people in the host country. But it also means losing something of one's heritage.

1. Choose a North American country and look up "ethnicities of _____" in a search engine. You will get results about ethnicity or demographics. Read the article(s) you find about that country.

2. Different ethnicities have different histories, customs, and languages or dialects. Use the "Ethnicities of _____" chart to take notes on the different ethnicities of the country you researched.

3. In your World Explorer Journal, write a definition of ethnicity and then draw a miniature portrait of an imaginary person from each ethnicity. Consider how each person from your researched country has different experiences even though they live in the same nation. Write a sentence captioning your portraits.

☺ ☺ ☺EXPLORATION: Native Dancers of Mexico

For this activity, you will need:

- "Native Dancers" from the Printable Pack
- Internet for research
- Video tutorial of a traditional North American dance from the YouTube playlist for this unit

Even within the same country, North American people often have a specific culture they belong to. Mexico, for example, has many different traditional dances belonging to different cultures within Mexico.

1. Compare the two photographs of "Native Dancers."

2. Look at the two photos and pick out cultural differences and similarities. Notice things like skin/hair color, differences and similarities in the costumes, and people and objects in the background.

3. Online, find other similar photos of North American people dancing.

4. Discuss how cultures, even in the same country, can be different and also have similarities. Talk about how culture makes people secure and happy.

5. Use a video tutorial to learn the basics of a traditional North American dance. Make sure to locate the country it is from on a map.

☺ ☺ ☺EXPLORATION: City Skylines

For this activity, you will need:

- "City Skylines" from the Printable Pack, printed on card stock
- Student atlas
- Scissors
- Glue stick
- Colored pencils or crayons
- Internet

North Americans are more likely to live in a city than people from any other continent. Approximately 80% of everyone in North America lives in a city rather than a small town or the country. Mexico City, New York, Toronto, and Havana are some of the largest cities in North America.

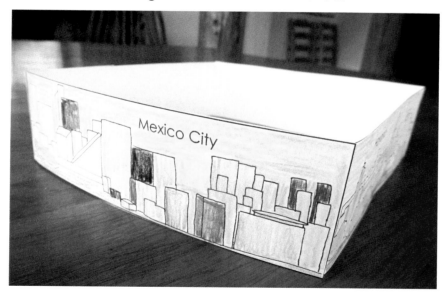

Jesse Owens is one of the most famous athletes of North America. He won four Olympic gold medals in track and field in the 1936 Olympics in Berlin.

As a black man, he performed in front of Hitler who believed that Aryan white people were a superior race. Obviously, that's not how it works.

Fabulous Fact

A cloud forest is a tropical mountain forest that has fog or low-lying cloud coverage most of the time.

The cloud forests of Costa Rica have thick moss, a dense forest canopy, and soggy soil. Because of the mild temperatures and abundant water, thousands of unique species live there.

Deep Thoughts

Would you rather live in a big city or a small town? Explain your reasoning.

This is Los Angeles, California, a city of almost 4 million people.

This is Sandpoint, Idaho, a town with a population of just under 9,000 people.

Famous Folks

In 1988, Jamaica entered a bobsled team in the Calgary Winter Olympics. They had to ask other teams for help with equipment and during their fourth run, crashed the sled.

Their story was told in the family film, Cool Runnings.

1. Use the gazetteer in the back of your student atlas to find Mexico City, New York City, Toronto, and Havana.

2. Color the buildings from the "City Skylines" sheet.

3. Cut apart the city rectangles. Then, glue them together end to end, so they form a square when you are done.

4. Look up two or more facts about each city. Write the facts as questions and answers on a sheet of paper. Play a quiz game with your city facts.

5. Display your city skylines on a shelf or table until the end of this unit.

☺ ☺ ☻**EXPLORATION: North American Foods**

For this activity, you will need:

- "North American Recipes" from the Printable Pack
- Ingredients for the recipes you choose to make
- Book or video about North America from the Library List or YouTube playlist

North Americans have brought foods from all over the world and made them their own, but there are also some foods that are uniquely from the continent. Pancakes, cheeseburgers, enchiladas, and jerked meat are four of those unique North American foods.

1. Decide which of the "North American Recipes" you would like to try and gather the ingredients.

2. Cook the food together as a group.

3. During a lull in the cooking, or once the food is done, read a book or watch a video about North America.

☺ ☻**EXPLORATION: Flag Windsocks**

For this activity, you will need:

- Construction paper
- Scissors
- Glue
- Student atlas
- Ribbon or tissue paper streamers (optional)
- String
- Hole punch

1. In your student atlas, have each child find the flags of three North American countries.

2. Design windsocks, paper cylinders made of construction paper, to look like the flags of these countries, or be inspired by the flags of these countries.

3. Glue ribbons, streamers, or paper strips to the bottom of the wind socks.

4. Punch holes around the top and hang the windsocks with string until the end of this unit.

Step 3: Show What You Know

During this unit, choose one of the assignments below to show what you have learned during the unit. Add this work to your Layers of Learning Notebook. You can also use this assignment to show your supervising teacher or your charter school as a sample of what you've been working on in your homeschool, if needed.

There are more ideas for writing assignments in the "Writer's Workshop" sidebars.

😊 😊 **Coloring or Narration Page**
For this activity, you will need:

- "North America" printable from the Printable Pack
- Writing or drawing utensils

1. Depending on the age and ability of the child, choose either the "North America" coloring sheet or the "North America" narration page from the Printable Pack.

2. Younger kids can color the coloring sheet as you review some of the things you learned about during this unit. On the bottom of the coloring page, kids can write a sentence about what

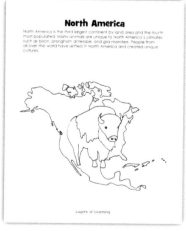

North America

North America is the third largest continent by land area and the fourth most populated. Many animals are unique to North America's climates such as bison, pronghorn antelope, and gila monsters. People from all over the world have settled in North America and created unique cultures.

Layers of Learning

Writer's Workshop

Continents don't have flags because they are not political divisions with governments, but if you were to design a North American flag, what would it look like?

Draw your flag design, color it, and then write about what the flag means.

Additional Layer

Here is a list of some famous landmarks in North America. Look them up online to see what they look like and to learn a few facts.

- Statue of Liberty
- Mount Rushmore
- Grand Canyon
- Copper Canyon
- Golden Gate Bridge
- Niagara Falls
- Petit-Champlain neighborhood
- Banff National Park
- Old Faithful Geyser
- Metropolitan Cathedral

- Great Blue Hole
- Parliament Hill
- National Mall
- Great Pyramid of Cholula
- Palenque
- Chichen Itza
- Teotihuacan
- Old San Juan
- Tortuga pirate forts
- Trunk Bay underwater trail
- Monarch Butterfly Biosphere Reserve

Unit Trivia Questions

1. If someone says "we had a super hot summer!" they are referring to the:

   a) Weather

   b) Climate

2. What is the difference between weather and climate?

   Weather is the temperature and precipitation at a particular time. Climate is a 30-year average of the weather.

3. Name the five main climate zones.

   Polar, continental, temperate, desert, tropical

4. True or false - If you live close to an ocean, your climate will be more moderate than people who live further inland.

   True. Large bodies of water moderate the climate, making it warmer in the winter and cooler in the summer.

5. The hottest climates are near which imaginary line on the globe?

   Equator

6. Name 10 of the 23 North American countries from memory.

   Answers vary

7. What are the three regions of North America?

   Mainland North America, Central America, Caribbean

8. On a blank map of North America, point out the location of these features: Rocky Mountains, Gulf of Mexico, Mississippi River, Great Lakes, Greater Antilles.

they learned. Very young children can explain their ideas orally while a parent writes for them.

3. Older kids can write about some of the concepts you learned on the narration page and color the picture as well.

4. Add this to the Geography section of your Layers of Learning Notebook.

☺ ☺ ☺ **Writer's Workshop**

For this activity, you will need:

- A computer or a piece of paper and a writing utensil

Choose from one of the ideas below or write about something else you learned during this unit. Each of these prompts corresponds with one of the units from the Layers of Learning Writer's Workshop curriculum, so you may choose to coordinate the assignment with the monthly unit you are learning about in Writer's Workshop.

- **Sentences, Paragraphs, & Narrations:** Use the "sandwich organizer" to write a paragraph about the climates of the North American continent.
- **Descriptions & Instructions:** Write 10 words that describe a North American desert. Then write a synonym and antonym for each of your words.
- **Fanciful Stories**: Write a dialogue between two different North American animals. One of them has wandered out of its climate zone and is lost.
- **Poetry:** Take a paragraph from a non-fiction book about North America and turn it into a poem by removing some of the words, using a thesaurus to find better words, and rearranging the ideas.
- **True Stories:** Learn about a famous person from North America. Write one incident from that person's life, highlighting a theme as you do.
- **Reports and Essays:** Make an illustrated fact sheet about a landmark in North America.
- **Letters:** Write a thank you to North America letter where you express gratitude for foods, customs, music, holidays, or inventions from North America.
- **Persuasive Writing:** Most North Americans drive cars more than they use public transportation. Do you think this is good or bad. Why?

☺ ☺ ☺ **North America Heads Up**

For this activity, you will need:

- "North America Heads Up" from the Printable Pack, on

card stock (one set for the whole group)
- "Countries of North America" from the Printable Pack
- Scissors

1. Cut apart the "North America Heads Up" cards. Shuffle them and place them upside down in a stack.

2. With maps visible for every player, have one player draw a card. Don't let the person look at it; just hold it on his or her forehead.

3. The player with the card must then ask the group yes or no questions until the player identifies which country card is on his or her forehead.

4. Keep playing until all the cards are gone.

5. For extra challenges, add new rules like a maximum of six questions may be asked, or the used cards are shuffled back in so they are not eliminated from the game, or no one can look at a map.

☺ ☺ ☺ Big Book of Knowledge

For this activity, you will need:

- "Big Book of Knowledge: North America" printable from the Printable Pack, printed on card stock
- Writing or drawing utensils
- Big Book of Knowledge

1. Color, draw on, or write on the Big Book of Knowledge page. Record concepts, definitions, and facts you learned during this unit. It's a record of the things you learned and hope to remember. Add the page to your Big Book of Knowledge.

2. Use your Big Book of Knowledge regularly to help you review, quiz, or create games that will help you commit the things you've learned to memory.

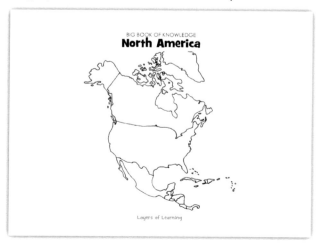

Big Book of Knowledge

The Big Book of Knowledge is a book for you, the mentor, to use as a constant review of all of the things you're learning about. You can use it to quiz your kids or prepare tests or review games. Whenever you learn something in Layers of Learning that you want your kids to remember, add it to your Big Book of Knowledge.

Assemble your Big Book of Knowledge in a binder or with binder rings. Divide it into sections for each subject.

In the Printable Pack for this unit you will find a "Big Book of Knowledge" sheet. You can add this sheet to others you collect or create yourself as you progress through the Layers of Learning curriculum. Customize the Big Book of Knowledge to your family by adding facts and topics that you enjoyed exploring as you were learning.

Visit Layers of Learning online to find more information on how to assemble and use your own Big Book of Knowledge.

You will also find cover and section pages to print along with creative games to play with your Big Book of Knowledge to keep school, even the tests, fun!

EUROPE

Europe is the second smallest continent, just a bit bigger than Oceania in land area. It is entirely in the Northern Hemisphere and lies mainly in the temperate climate zone. The climate is mild for the high latitudes because warm, moist, westerly winds from the Gulf Stream keep it warmer and wetter than similar latitudes in Asia and North America. Europe is one big peninsula surrounded by the Arctic Ocean, Atlantic Ocean, and Mediterranean Sea. Europe's wildlife has long lived side-by-side with high populations of humans, leaving few wilderness areas on the continent, except in Russia, the Carpathians, and the far north. Even so, Europe is rich in diverse animal species such as wolves, bears, foxes, hedgehogs, owls, roe deer, and wild boars.

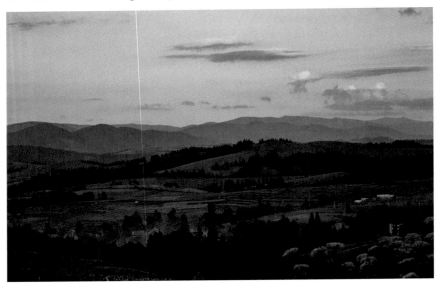

In this view of Hungary you can see farmland in the foreground and the Carpathian Mountains in the background.

Europe is diverse for such a small geographic area. There are 49 different countries with cultures as unique as those of France, Greece, Finland, and Italy. Historically, Europe has been forcible in shaping the modern world, particularly because of colonization but also due to the Christian religion which flourished in Europe. Beyond that, they were the major home stage of the two World Wars that reshaped the world's balance of power in the 20th century.

The many navigable rivers, easy access to ice-free seas, plentiful deep ports, and wealth of rainfall for agriculture have made Europe prosperous and powerful. In large part because Europe is well-watered and temperate in climate, it rose to the position it has in world affairs.

Access to clean water for drinking, plentiful water for agriculture, and navigable water for trade is essential for the flourishing of nations. Of all natural resources, water is the most vital for life. Its location and availability creates borders, prevents conquests, and inspires wars.

Step 1: Library List

Choose books from your library that go with this topic. Here's a list of some favorites and also a list of search terms so you can utilize what your library offers. Read the books with your kids and/or assign them some to read independently. It is from these books your kids will learn most of the facts they need from this unit.

Search for: rivers, lakes, water resources, Europe, Europe geography, Europe travel, European animals

☺ ☺ ☺*Geography of the World* by DK. Read "Europe" on page 78 and "Peoples of Europe" on page 80.

☺*Explore Europe* by Molly Aloian and Bobbie Kalman. This is a very simple book with few words for the younger kids.

☺*Introducing Europe* by Chris Oxlade. A basic look at some interesting facts about Europe.

☺*The Ultimate Book of Water* by Anne-Sophie Baumann. Learn about the water cycle, lakes, rivers, energy production with water, where Earth got its water, where the water is located, water in dry places, and more. This is a book with cute illustrations, pop-ups, flaps, and pull-outs.

☺*What Is A River?* by Monika Vaicenavičiene. Child-like illustrations and lyrical text describes how rivers connect people, lead to places, support cities, and so much more.

☺*River Stories* by Timothy Knapman. Each river highlighted in the book has true stories, folk tales, or history told about it. This underlines how important rivers are to people, travel, culture, and history.

☺ ☺*Great Rivers of the World* by Volker Mehnert. Illustrations, details, and text full of fascinating facts about the most important rivers around the world.

☺ ☺*The Seven Continents: Europe* by Joana Costa Knufinke. Learn about the landscape, animals, and people with lots of full-color photos and maps paired with simple paragraphs.

☺ ☺*Water: A Resource Our World Depends On* by Ian Graham. From why ice floats to where the water is located and how to use this resource responsibly, this is a solid non-

Family School Levels

The colored smilies in this unit help you choose the correct levels of books and activities for your child.

☺ = Ages 6-9
☺ = Ages 10-13
☺ = Ages 14-18

On the Web

For videos, web pages, games, and more to add to this unit, visit the People & Planet Resources at Layers-of-Learning.com.

You will find a link to video playlists, web links, and more.

Bookworms

If you're looking for a family read-aloud, we'd like to suggest this one.

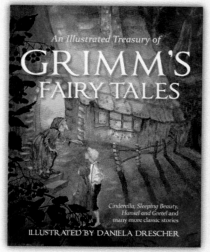

Grimm's Fairy Tales by The Brothers Grimm and Daniela Drescher (illustrator) is an uncensored original version of the tales. These classic European tales are considered Great Books, childhood staples because they teach caution, bravery, persistence, sacrifice, and grace in a magical way.

Famous Folks

German geographer Alexander von Humbodt traveled the world while creating ways to research and define the distribution of species, air, and water.

He is considered one of the fathers of geography.

Additional Layer

Water is important enough that countries have gone to war many times over access to sea ports or access to freshwater sources.

Learn more about the Russia-Ukraine War that began in 2022 and its connection to the Crimean Peninsula, the North Crimean Canal that feeds water to the peninsula, and the Russian ports on the Black Sea.

This is the North Crimean Canal, empty of water, in 2019. Photo by Rumlin, CC by SA 3.0.

fiction book about the science and geography of water.

😊 😊 *One Well: The Story of Water on Earth* by Rochelle Strauss. Playful full-page illustrations are paired with snippets of text that discuss where Earth's water comes from, how it is all connected, and how we need to care for it.

😊 😊 *The Rhine: Europe's River Highway* by Gary G. Miller. This is a book highlighting one of the most important rivers in Europe. Readers see how important rivers are for human civilizations.

😊 😊 *One Animal a Day: A Journey Across Europe* by Laure Ondoua. The reader "travels" to different European countries and sees one animal in each place.

😊 *Every Last Drop* by Michelle Mulder. This book is about the struggle to obtain clean drinking water that people all over the planet deal with every day.

😊 😊 *Draw Europe* by Kristin J. Draeger. The author teaches kids to draw the map of Europe from memory in tiny bite-sized steps.

😊 😊 *Lonely Planet's Where to Go When Europe* by Lonely Planet. This is intended to help you plan a trip, but it is also amazing to browse through and see the beautiful places, festivals, and people of Europe.

😊 😊 *The Atlas of Water: Mapping the World's Most Critical Resource* by Maggie Black. This book is full of images, maps, graphs, and charts accompanied by text that explains where Earth's water is, who has access to it, and how it is scarce in some places.

😊 *For the Love of Europe* by Rick Steves. The author is a long time travel writer and this book is an anthology of his best stories of traveling in Europe. Each story is short and can be read independently in any order.

😊 *The Struggle for Europe* by William I. Hitchcock. This is the modern history of Europe from the end of World War II to the early 2000s, when the book was written. It gives an excellent synopsis of European politics and social condition in the modern world.

😊 *Epic Continent: Adventures in the Great Stories of Europe* by Nicholas Jubber. The author links the epic tales of Europe such as *Beowulf* and *Roland* to the character of the European people and the path their history has followed as he travels across the continent from one epic setting to the next.

😊 *Into the Carpathians: A Journey Through the Heart and*

History of Central and Eastern Europe (Part 1: The Eastern Mountains) by Alan E. Sparks. The story of the author hiking through the Carpathian Mountains is interspersed with stories about the history and culture of the area.

☺*Water 4.0* by David Sedlak. This book explains the history of human water systems from the Roman aqueducts to modern plumbing and sewers. It takes a look at the future of water and what we need to do better with a limited resource.

☺*Water: The Epic Struggle for Wealth, Power, and Civilization* by Steven Solomon. Both a history of water and a book about the politics of water in today's world, this book explains why cities are where they are, how crucial water is to national prosperity, and how, in the future, water may become a major power struggle for the world.

Step 2: Explore

Choose a few hands-on Explorations from this section to work on as a family. They should be appealing activities that will create mental hooks so your kids remember the information in the unit. Save the rest of the Explorations for the next time you do this unit in four years when your kids are older. You can also read the sidebars together and explore some little rabbit trails.

This unit includes printables. See the introduction for instructions on retrieving your Printable Pack.

Water

Water is a big deal. It is essential to human life, both for drinking and for agriculture to produce food. Furthermore, it is also crucial for transportation and economic success. Understanding where water comes from, how it is used, and how people obtain it, and sometimes fight over it, is an important part of understanding how the world works.

☺ ☺ ☺**EXPLORATION: Hydrosphere**
For this activity, you will need:

- Book or video about the hydrosphere or the water on Earth from the Library List and YouTube playlist for this unit
- Pitcher or beaker that can measure in liters
- 4 small containers that can hold water
- Water
- Index cards
- Graduated cylinder

On the Web

Because Europe is so far north, its size is skewed on most maps. Visit "The True Size Of" online to compare Europe or specific European nations to places you are familiar with. How big is Europe compared to the United States, Australia, or India?

Alaska compared to Europe.

Deep Thoughts

Bottled water is big business across the world, but it's also an industry under fire.

Discuss why people might choose bottled water over tap water.

Where does the water come from for bottled water? Does it affect local ecosystems?

How is bottled water used in emergency situations?

What happens to the bottles once they are empty?

Is bottled water a scam? How does marketing change perceptions about the safety of tap water versus bottled water?

Hydrosphere: all of the water on earth

Hydro is Greek for water and sphere is Greek for globe or ball.

In this image, the volume of the world's water is compared to the volume of the whole planet. The biggest water ball represents all of the water on earth. The little ball of water represents the freshwater. The itty, bitty ball represents the water in rivers and lakes.

Renewable resource: a natural material used by humans that replenishes itself quickly after use

Water, timber, food, fibers, sunlight, wind, and air are renewable resources. Even renewable resources can be depleted by overuse or pollution. But if they are used responsibly, we don't need to worry about them running out.

Additional Layer

Water is necessary for life, but it can also be destructive.

Find out how water can cause natural disasters in Layers of Learning *Earth & Space: Weather.*

- Dropper
- "Freshwater Distribution in the Hydrosphere" from the Printable Pack
- Colored pencils or crayons

The **hydrosphere** is all of the water on earth, including oceans, rivers, lakes, glaciers, ice caps, groundwater, and water in the air. The total amount of water on Earth doesn't change, but the water is constantly moving by means of gravity, evaporation, wind, and currents. Humans use about .03% of the Earth's supply of water. But when we use the water, it isn't used up; it goes back into the water cycle after we drink, bathe, spray it on our crops, or use it in our factories. This makes water a **renewable resource**. But water, especially the freshwater needed by living things, is not equally available across the planet. Some places have too much and others don't have enough.

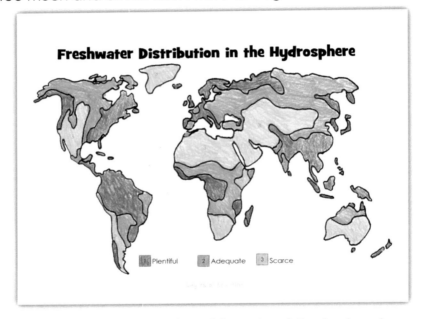

Freshwater Distribution in the Hydrosphere

1. Plentiful   2. Adequate   3. Scarce

1. Read a book or watch a video about the hydrosphere, Earth's water.

2. Discuss where you think water can be found on Earth. Make index card labels for the five places we find water: ocean, rivers & lakes, groundwater, atmosphere, ice caps & glaciers.

3. Measure 1 liter of water. Out of the 1 liter, remove 2 ml, 1ml, 2 drops, and 1 drop each into the four small containers.

4. The water in the five containers represents all of the water on earth. Try to match the index card labels you made with the containers of water.

Ocean: large 1-liter container

Ice caps & glaciers: 2 ml
Groundwater: 1 ml
Atmosphere: 2 drops
Rivers & Lakes: 1 drop

5. Discuss the amount of water on Earth. What surprised you and what did you already suspect?

6. Color the "Freshwater Distribution in the Hydrosphere" map by numbers. Put this map in your Layers of Learning Notebook in the Geography section.

☺ ☺ ☺ EXPLORATION: Saltwater & Freshwater

For this activity, you will need:

- Video about saltwater and freshwater
- Student atlas
- Timer
- World Explorer Journal
- Colored pencils or crayons

Water is very good at dissolving things, including salts that are found in the earth's crust. As water falls on the land and travels through the rocks and soil, it dissolves and carries the salts with it. Over time, salts build up in the water until the water is too salty for people to drink. Places where water collects, like oceans and lakes without an outlet, become **saltwater**. Places where water is flowing and moving have much less dissolved salt and we call this **freshwater**.

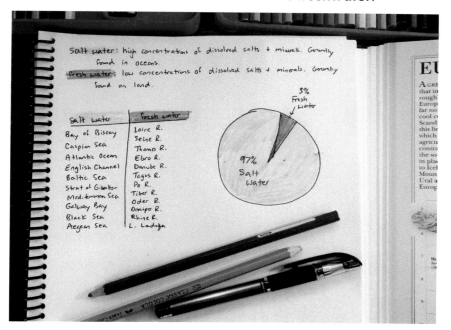

1. Watch a video about saltwater and freshwater.

2. In your World Explorer Journal, write down definitions for

Additional Layer

The most frequent natural disasters in Europe are floods. In July 2021, flash floods caught communities in Germany and Belgium by surprise and 165 people died.

Devastation from natural disasters is partly simply nature and outside of human control, but part of it is infrastructure, like dams or drainage and sewer systems.

Learn more about how water is controlled and directed by people.

Memorization Station

Saltwater: contains high concentrations of dissolved salts and minerals

Freshwater: contains less than 1% dissolved salts and includes lakes and streams

Deep Thoughts

Who owns the water? Unlike land, water is flowing and moving from one place to another.

In most places, governments own the water and they allow their citizens to use it according to the law.

If you own a piece of land and a stream runs through your land, who should own that stream? What about rainwater that falls on your land or groundwater you get from a well?

Here is a poem by Robert Louis Stevenson about rivers.

Looking Glass River

Smooth it glides upon its travel,
Here a wimple, there a gleam--
O the clean gravel!
O the smooth stream!

Sailing blossoms, silver fishes,
Pave pools as clear as air--
How a child wishes
To live down there!

Read it and talk about the picture the poem makes in your mind. There are four more stanzas you can look up online as well.

Memorization Station

Watershed: a region where all of the water eventually runs into one river that drains into the sea, also called drainage basins

River mouth: the point where a river drains into the sea

Tributary: a river or stream that flows into a bigger river or lake

Source: the place where a river or stream begins

Mountain divide: the boundary between two watersheds

saltwater and freshwater.

3. Use a map of Europe from a student atlas to find bodies of water that are freshwater (rivers and lakes) and bodies of water that are saltwater (oceans and seas). Set a timer for ten minutes. Make two lists in your World Explorer Journal.

4. Draw a pie chart in your World Explorer Journal that shows that 97% of the water on Earth is saltwater and 3% is freshwater.

😊 😊 😊 **EXPLORATION: Watersheds & Drainage Basins**

For this activity, you will need:

- Sheet of plastic - tarp, shower curtain, tablecloth, etc
- Small objects to place under the plastic sheet to make mountains and hills or bumpy outdoor ground
- Water in 2-4 spray bottles or a hose with a spray nozzle
- Food coloring
- Paper
- Student atlas
- "Danube Watershed" from the Printable Pack
- Colored pencils or crayons

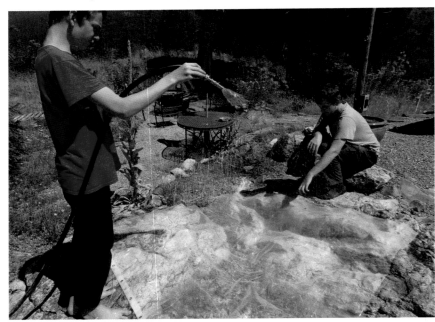

A **watershed,** or drainage basin, is an area where the rainwater that falls drains off into a single outlet into the sea. A watershed can be small or it can cover half of a continent. Every **river mouth** that pours into the sea is the end point of a watershed. If you follow that river and all of its **tributaries** back to their **sources** and then draw a boundary line around the whole system, that is the watershed. Since water flows downhill with gravity, mountains or high land separates one watershed from the next. Where the mountains are highest, you can draw a line that shows which direction the water will flow. This line is called the **mountain divide**.

1. Build a watershed with plastic draped over random objects. You will probably want to do this outside so water doesn't get everywhere.

2. Put water with a few drops of blue food coloring into spray bottles or just use a hose outside.

3. Spray water from spray bottles onto the plastic, representing rainfall, and watch the paths the water takes as it travels over the landscape. Can you identify a river, lake, tributary, source, river mouth, and mountain divide?

4. Draw a map of your landscape with its mountains, rivers, and divides marked and labeled.

5. Find the Danube River on a map of Europe from your student atlas.

6. Color the map of the "Danube Watershed." Start by labeling the Black Sea and the Adriatic Sea. Then, label the Carpathians, Alps, Dinaric Alps, and Baltic Mountains and draw mountains surrounding the Danube watershed. The mountains or highlands surround the watershed.

Danube Watershed

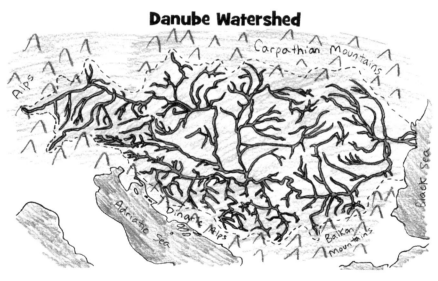

7. Starting with the mouth of the Danube, color the rivers. Then, color the land inside the Danube watershed green.

8. Add the map to the Geography section of your Layers of Learning Notebook.

Deep Thoughts

"Water, water everywhere, nor any drop to drink" is a line from Samuel Taylor Coleridge's poem, *The Rime of the Ancient Mariner*.

In the poem, a sailor is dying of thirst at sea, surrounded by water that he could not drink.

Discuss this line, what you think it means literally and metaphorically.

Are you surrounded by plentiful things, but that you cannot have?

Teaching Tip

Taking a lesson outside is a change of pace which can result in better attention, reduced stress, a more memorable lesson, and sunlight and fresh air in young bodies. Any lesson can be taken outside, even if its just the deck or yard.

Fabulous Fact

Europe rarely has problems with water scarcity. In fact, most of Europe does not have irrigation systems for farmland. When they do a have a dry year, the crops can be stunted.

In this picture, you can see that the barley in this field is barely tall enough to be harvested. A drought stunted the growth of the plants.

☺ ☻ EXPLORATION: Rivers

For this activity, you will need:

- Poster board
- Markers, colored pencils, or crayons
- Book or video about rivers
- A nearby river to travel to (optional)

Rivers are streams of water that carry rain and snow melt from higher elevations down to the sea. Sometimes, the river water collects in a depression of the land and forms a lake. Rivers and lakes are important to people for many reasons.

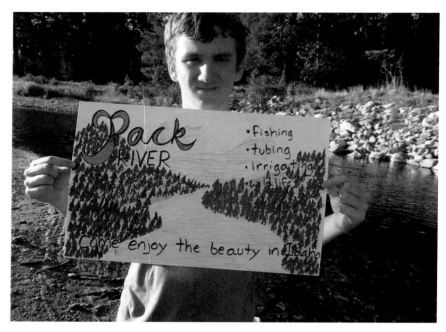

1. If you are near enough, travel to a river or lake and do this lesson on the bank or shore.

2. Read a book or watch a video about rivers and lakes.

3. Discuss:

   a. Which rivers and lakes are nearest to where we live? (You may want to look at them on a map)

   b. How do people use our river (lake)?

   c. Are all rivers (lakes) used the same way or are there other ways people can use rivers (lakes)?

4. On a sheet of poster board, make an advertisement for a nearby river or lake as though it were a tourist attraction or entertainment venue. Make your poster colorful and share it with your group.

5. Display your poster on a wall until the end of this unit.

☺ ☺ EXPEDITION: Clean Water Sources

For this activity, you will need:

- A nearby body of water
- Water from your tap
- pH indicator papers
- Thermometer
- Clear glass or plastic jar
- 2 petri dishes with nutrient agar

There is plenty of freshwater in the world, but most of it isn't safe for humans to drink. Water is often full of dangerous bacteria that makes people sick and can kill them. In addition, much of the surface water has been polluted by people. Safe drinking water comes from wells, which have clean water filtered through the soil and rocks, and from water that has been filtered and cleaned by city systems before people drink it. In wealthy nations, there are water systems with pipes that bring clean, safe water to homes. But people in poorer nations often have no plumbing systems, no water treatment plants, and no nearby wells. They have to get their water from rivers and streams, filter it themselves, and then treat it by boiling before they can drink it. Many thousands of people die each year from diseases caused from drinking contaminated water.

1. Go to a nearby body of water. Take the temperature of the water and record it. Bacteria and parasites grow best in warmer water.

2. Next, dip a pH paper into the water and compare its color to the key on the package. pH between 5.5 and 8 is normal. Anything outside that range indicates that human or natural pollution is a problem in that water.

Fabulous Fact

There are two forms of water scarcity. One is physical water scarcity. There simply isn't much water because it is a desert or arid place.

The second kind of water scarcity is economic. Water is there, but the people are too poor to build wells, pipes, water pumps, or to clean dirty water with water treatment plants.

On the map above, the dark blue areas suffer from economic water scarcity. The lighter blue areas have physical water scarcity, and the green areas have plenty of water.

Bookworms

The Water Princess by Susan Verde is a picture book story from the childhood of model Georgie Badel.

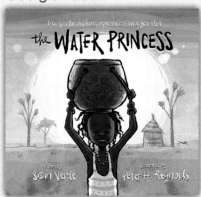

Her village didn't have clean water and this story highlights the struggle that so many people across the world have in obtaining water.

Expedition

Visit a water treatment plant where you live.

Before water is sent through pipes to people's homes, it is treated with filtration and chemicals such as chlorine to kill bacteria and parasites that may be in the water.

After waste water leaves homes and businesses, it is filtered and cleaned again before being put back in the environment.

Think of at least one good question for the guide before you go.

Bookworms

Crime Travelers: Brainwashed by Paul Aertker is the first in a series about orphan kids who are being trained to take on a child trafficking company.

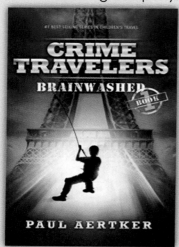

In the first book, they zoom around Paris, defeating bad guys. In the second book, it's off to Rome. In the third, they fight evil in Spain.

Action-packed story telling, awesome settings, and quirky characters make this a page turner.

For ages 10 and up.

3. Fill a clear jar with water from the river. Make sure it isn't an area you where you have stirred up the bottom. Hold the jar in front of someone else's face. How easily can you see through the water and see his or her face? Is it clear, cloudy, or opaque? Clear water lets sunlight through to plants in the water and it indicates that there is less sediment pollution and often less bacterial growth, all of which can cause cloudy water.

4. Smear a few drops of water from the river across a nutrient agar petri dish. Let it sit for several days in a warm place and then observe how many bacterial colonies have grown. The more bacteria, the less safe it is to drink.

5. Repeat all of the water tests with tap water from your house. Make sure to let the tap water run for 2 minutes on cold before you begin sampling and testing. You don't want to test the old water that has been sitting in your house pipes.

6. In your World Explorer Journal, write down a summary of what you discovered about surface water compared to treated tap water.

🙂 🙂 EXPLORATION: People Need Water

WARNING: This activity uses a hot iron. Ironing should be done by an adult.

For this activity, you will need:

- Videos about how things are made
- Waxed paper
- Blue crayons
- Pencil sharpeners
- Iron
- Tape
- Permanent marker

People use water for transportation, to mark borders between countries, as an ingredient or wash in industry, for drinking and washing, to flush away sewage, for recreation, to water agricultural crops and animals, and for energy production. Humans can't survive without adequate freshwater, and our economic prosperity also depends on it.

1. Discuss the ways people use water.

   a. What do you use water for throughout your day?

   b. What does your household use water for?

   c. What do you think farmers use water for?

   d. Where do we get our electricity? Do you know if water is used to make our electricity?

   e. Do the clothes we wear need water to make them?

2. Watch some videos that show how things are made. Keep an eye out for water being used.

3. Peel blue crayons in various shades.

4. Lay a sheet of waxed paper on a surface and sharpen crayons directly onto the waxed paper. Spread the crayon shavings evenly and then lay a second sheet of waxed paper over the crayon shavings.

5. Run an iron on a low setting across the waxed paper. This will melt the crayon shavings.

6. Give it a moment to cool, then cut raindrop shapes out of the waxed paper. Write a word on each raindrop for ways water is used.

7. Tape the raindrops up in a window to make sun catchers.

European Landscapes

😊 😊 😊 **EXPLORATION: Charm Map of Europe**
For this activity, you will need:

- Poster board
- Colored pencils, crayons, markers, or paints
- "Europe's Charms" from the Printable Pack, printed on card stock
- Glue stick
- Internet
- Scissors

1. Freehand draw a map of Europe on a piece of poster board. Color the map of Europe to show mountains, rivers, and other geographical features.

Fabulous Fact

Not counting transportation and recreation, which don't use up water, by far, the most water is used for energy production. After that, agriculture and industry are the biggies. Household use of water is only about 7% or less of the total water usage in most countries.

Fabulous Fact

The exact borders of Europe and which countries ought to be included is up for debate.

We include Georgia, Azerbaijan, and Armenia with Europe because, geologically, they are in the Caucasus Mountains, which are considered European, and because the people of those countries consider themselves European.

Russia, because of its history and cultural ties, we include with Europe, though it did appear on the map in the Asia unit as well.

Turkey, on the other hand, has a central Asian background and culture and is primarily located on the Asian continent, so we consider it an Asian country.

Cyprus is closer geographically to Asia, but culturally it is closer to Europe and the people consider themselves European, so we place it with Europe.

Kosovo acts de facto as a country and so we consider it one even though it is not recognized officially around the world.

Feel free to join the lively debate about how many countries are in Europe.

Famous Folks

Ancient people defined the eastern edge of Europe at the Don River, which it remained until Swedish geographer Philip Johan von Strahlenberg suggested in 1730 that the Ural Mountains would be a better divider.

This portrait of the geographer was drawn by himself on a map he made.

Fabulous Fact

Europe is named after Europa, a Phoenician mythological princess who was abducted by Zeus who had taken the form of a white bull.

The Greeks themselves were the first to apply the name to the continent.

2. Print out "Europe's Charms" on card stock. Cut them out.

3. Glue the charms to the map near their locations.

4. Look up any of the cool places you have never heard of before.

5. Display on the wall until the end of this unit.

☺ ☺ ☺EXPLORATION: Poster Map of Europe

For this activity, you will need:

- Book or video about Europe from the Library List or YouTube playlist
- "Europe" from the Printable Pack (Print using "poster" or "multi-page" settings on your printer.)
- Tape
- Student atlas
- Glitter or glitter glue
- Scissors
- Colored crayons, pastels, pencils, markers, or paints

1. Read a book or watch a video about Europe.

2. Tape the Europe map together into one large map. Put the tape on the back of the papers so it won't get in the way of coloring and labeling.

3. Use a student atlas and label the features of Europe that you want to. Remember mountains, rivers, peninsulas, islands, seas, and plains.

4. Add major cities like London, Paris, Athens, and Moscow.

5. Draw the Arctic Circle on your map.

6. Hang your completed map of Europe on a wall until the

end of this unit.

☺ ☺ ☺EXPLORATION: European Landscapes

For this activity, you will need:

- "European Landscapes" from the Printable Pack
- Colored pencils or crayons
- Student atlas
- Book or video about Europe from the Library List or YouTube playlist

This map shows the physical features of Europe such as rivers, mountains, and seas. If you have young children, they can color, but not label, the map to make it easier.

European Landscapes

Fabulous Fact

Perućica is a rainforest in Europe and one of the last remaining untouched forests as well.

Photo by 00cska00, CC by SA 3.0.

It is in Bosnia and Herzegovina on the southern border of Montenegro.

Additional Layer

Europe sits on the enormous Eurasian plate. The southern border of the plate is right through the middle of the Mediterranean, which explains all the volcanoes in southern Italy and the Alps mountains at the top of the boot.

Image by Alataristarion, CC by SA 4.0.

The Caucuses Mountains and Iceland are also scenes of volcanic activity.

Learn more about the geology of Europe, including the Alpide Belt System that extends from Spain clear to Indonesia, along the margins of plates.

Writer's Workshop

The Volga River is the longest river in Europe and the center of Russian history and civilization. It flows into the Caspian Sea Basin. The Volga has long served as a trade route between Finland and the Scandinavian countries and Russia and the Persians.

There is a Russian folk song about the barge handlers who used to work along the river called *The Song of the Volga Boatmen*. This is the first stanza translated into English:

Yo, heave ho!
Yo, heave ho!
Once more, once again, still once more!
Yo, heave ho!
Yo, heave ho!
Once more, once again, still once more!

Write a second stanza for the song. Make sure it keeps the "Yo, heave ho!" and sounds like a bunch of strong bargemen.

Fabulous Fact

The Faroe Islands are an archipelago north of Britain. They are part of Denmark but govern themselves.

1. Use a student atlas to label these rivers on the "European Landscapes" map: Ebro, Loire, Thames, Rhine, Ehone, Po, Danube, Elbe, Vistula, Dneiper, Don, Volga. Color the rivers blue.

2. Draw a dashed line finishing the coast of the Black Sea and the outline of Turkey. Label Asia in Turkey and in Russia.

3. Label these seas: Mediterranean, Black, Caspian, Adriatic, Aegean, Bay of Biscay, English Channel, North, Baltic, Gulf of Bothnia, Norwegian, Barents, Atlantic Ocean. Color the seas blue.

4. Label the Iberian, Scandinavian, Jutland, Crimean, and Kola Peninsulas.

5. Label the North European Plain, Massif Central, Pripet Marshes, and Central Russian Upland.

6. Label these mountains and color them brown: Pyrenees, Alps, Dinaric Alps, Balkans, Carpathians, Urals, Apennines, Caucasus.

7. Color the rest of the land green.

8. Read a book or watch a video about Europe.

9. Put the map in the Geography section of your Layers of Learning Notebook.

☺ ☺ ☺**EXPLORATION: Landform Search**
For this activity, you will need:

- "European Landforms" and "European Landscapes" from the Printable Pack
- Student atlas
- Colored pencils

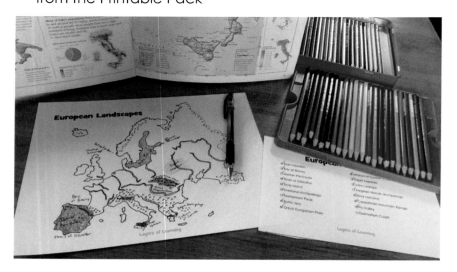

1. Use the index or gazetteer in the back of a student

atlas to find each of the landforms on the "European Landforms" check list.

2. Color and label each landform on the "European Landscapes" map. (You may have already colored this map if you did the European Landscapes Exploration. You can add to it or use the printable again.)

3. Put the map in your Layers of Learning Notebook in the Geography section.

☺ ☺ ☺ **EXPLORATION: Rhine River**
For this activity, you will need:

- Globe or World Map
- Video about the Rhine River from the YouTube playlist
- "Rhine River" from the Printable Pack
- Colored pencils or crayons
- Scissors
- Glue stick
- World Explorer Journal

The Rhine River is one of the most important rivers in Europe. It has many cities, large and small, along its banks, including Rotterdam, Dusseldorf, and Cologne. It is used for shipping, with river barges being able to navigate far upstream. It also has factories and power production plants along its banks. In addition, the river provides water for irrigating vineyards and other crops. It forms a major transportation corridor but also acts as a barrier. Castles from the Middle Ages dot its banks in strategic locations.

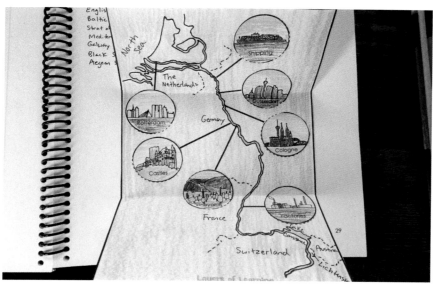

1. Find Europe on a globe or world map. Then, find the Rhine River in Europe. Which countries does it pass through? Where does the river have its source and

Writer's Workshop

The Alps follow the curving border of northern Italy and then extend east into Austria. Species like the ibex, Apollo butterfly, and golden eagles live high on the mountain sides.

This is an ibex in Switzerland.

Pick two animals from the Alps. Which one would you rather be? Write about it.

Additional Layer

The saiga antelope lives in the foothills of the Carpathian Mountains and the steppes of Eastern Europe and Central Asia.

Image by Andrey Giljov, CC by SA 4.0.

The species is critically endangered because they are hunted for use in Chinese medicine and because their range is declining due to desertification. In 1990, Russia established the Chornye Zemli Nature Reserve in order to protect the saiga.

Learn more about nature reserves and how well they work at helping species recover.

which body of water does it empty into?

2. Watch a video about the Rhine River.

3. Label the North Sea in the upper left of the "Rhine River" map. Color the North Sea and the River blue. Label Lake Constance in the lower right of the map.

4. Label each of the countries that borders the Rhine. Starting on the west bank of the river, from the north to the south, are The Netherlands, Germany, France, and Switzerland. On the east bank of the river, from north to south, are The Netherlands, Germany, Austria, Lichtenstein, and Switzerland.

5. Color the land green, then, color each of the round pictures.

6. Cut out the map, the title, and the round pictures.

7. Glue the round pictures to their spots on the map as follows:

   1. Shipping
   2. Dusseldorf
   3. Cologne
   4. Factories
   5. Rotterdam
   6. Castles
   7. Vineyards

8. Fold the map into thirds. Glue the center section down to a page in your World Explorer Journal. With the map folded, glue the title to the front.

☺ ☺ EXPLORATION: Wildlife Spotter

For this activity, you will need:

- Toilet paper rolls
- Paint or markers
- Craft supplies like glitter, sequins, feathers, and so on
- "European Wildlife" from the Printable Pack
- Scissors
- Glue stick
- World Explorer Journal

1. Ahead of time, cut apart the "European Wildlife" cards, fold them in half on the dashed lines so the facts are on the back, and place around your home or yard.

2. Decorate a toilet paper tube with paint, glitter, markers, sequins, and other craft supplies to make a spyglass.

3. Use your spyglass to seek and find the European wildlife that are hidden around your home. Read the facts about the animals as you go.

4. Choose one or more "European Wildlife" cards to glue

into your World Explorer Journal.

☺ ☺EXPLORATION: Features of Europe Necklace

For this activity, you will need:

- Book or video about Europe from the Library List or YouTube playlist
- "Europe Necklace" from the Printable Pack, printed on card stock
- Colored pencils or crayons
- Scissors
- String or yarn
- Beads or pasta with holes
- Hole punch
- Internet (optional)

1. Read a book or watch a video about Europe.

2. Color the "Europe Necklace" charms. Cut them out and hole punch them on the dot. While you work, look up

Bookworms

The Children of Noisy Village by Astrid Lindgren takes place in a Swedish village.

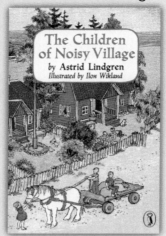

The book is episodic, with each chapter being its own short story. Charming and laugh-out-loud funny.

For ages 8 and up, or read aloud to younger kids.

Memorization Station

Start memorizing the countries of Europe. We have included a blank map of the countries so you can practice filling them in from memory or as a quiz.

Writer's Workshop

Write an argument for whether you think Georgia, Azerbaijan, and Armenia should be included in Europe or in Asia. Be convincing.

information and talk about each of the landmarks.

3. Thread beads or pasta onto a string alternating with the paper charms. Cut the string so it is long enough to go over a child's head when tied.

4. Name each of the charms on your necklace and tell one fact you learned about it.

People of Europe

☺ ☺ ☺ EXPLORATION: European Countries

For this activity, you will need:

- Book or video about Europe from the Library List or YouTube playlist
- "European Countries" from the Printable Pack
- Colored pencils or crayons

There are 49 countries in Europe. For convenience, we have divided Europe into five regions - Western Europe, Eastern Europe, Nordic Countries, Central Europe, and Southern Europe. Regions are useful for discussing areas of the world that encompass more than one country. Regions are arbitrary; there are no accepted geographical regions that everyone agrees on.

1. Read a book or watch a video about European countries.

2. Color the "European Countries" map by region.

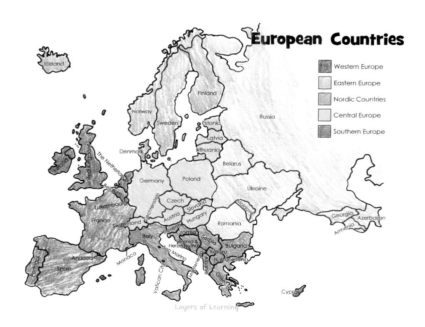

Western Europe	Eastern Europe	Nordic Countries
• Ireland • Great Britain • The Netherlands • Belgium • France • Spain • Portugal • Andorra • Luxembourg • Monaco	• Russia • Belarus • Ukraine • Moldova • Romania • Georgia • Armenia • Azerbaijan	• Iceland • Norway • Sweden • Finland • Denmark
Central Europe	**Southern Europe**	

• Estonia
• Latvia
• Lithuania
• Poland
• Germany
• Czech Republic
• Slovakia
• Switzerland
• Lichtenstein
• Austria
• Hungary
	• Italy
	• Vatican City
	• San Marino
	• Slovenia
	• Croatia
	• Bosnia &
	  Herzegovina
	• Montenegro
	• Albania
		• Greece
		• North
		  Macedonia
		• Kosovo
		• Serbia
		• Bulgaria
		• Cyprus
		• Malta

3. Put the map in your Layers of Learning Notebook in the Geography section.

☺ ☺ ☺EXPLORATION: Grand Tour of Europe's Art

For this activity, you will need:

• Videos about the Parthenon, Louvre, and Uffizi Gallery from the YouTube playlist for this unit
• Student Atlas
• "Grand Tour of Europe's Art" from the Printable Pack
• Scissors
• Stapler
• Glue stick
• World Explorer Journal

A grand tour was a European tradition during the 18th and 19th centuries. Young people who were completing their education would travel for several years to see the art and culture of Europe. They traveled to visit ruins and museums of art. Europe has some of the most prolific, varied, and technically superior art in the world.

1. Watch three videos of European artworks to take your own Grand Tour. One should be a visit to the Parthenon, one a visit to the Louvre, and one a visit to the Uffizi Gallery in Florence. Be aware that anytime you are touring a lot of art, you could potentially see nudes. Please preview if you are concerned.

Fabulous Fact

Many countries in Europe have joined an organization called the European Union.

This is a map of the countries that are part of the European Union. Image by Sredina, CC by SA 4.0.

The biggest benefit is that they share one currency, the Euro, making it easy to trade. The EU also helps countries come to agreements about fisheries, agriculture, and regional development. It also has defense agreements and many of its citizens can travel freely between member states.

This is a treaty and trade organization, not a single government.

Learn more about the European Union and how it works. What problems does it have?

Deep Thoughts

Do you think there could ever be a United States of Europe?

Europe is smaller than the the U.S.A., but it is divided into many countries. Why do you think Europe remained divided while the United States established itself as one nation? What are the benefits of each way?

On the Web

The Louvre art museum in Paris, France is the most popular attraction in all of Europe and the most popular museum in the world.

The building began its life as a fortified castle. Later, it was turned into a larger and more sumptuous palace. Then, during the French Revolution, the government declared it would be a national museum.

Today it contains more than 380,000 objects.

You can visit the Louvre online and see some of the exhibits and gardens.

Bookworms

The Wall: Growing Up Behind the Iron Curtain by famous children's author Peter Sis is the true story of the author's childhood in Czechoslovakia when it was communist.

For ages 8 and up.

2. Find Athens, where the Parthenon is located, on a map of Europe from your student atlas. Then find Paris, the location of the Louvre. Finally, find Florence, Italy, the location of the Uffizi Gallery.

3. Europeans created many kinds of art, but the big three are painting, sculpture, and architecture. Fill these three types of art in on the spaces on the cover of the "Grand Tour of Europe's Art."

4. Cut the booklet apart and then staple the pages on the left side. Glue the booklet into your World Explorer Journal and then read it.

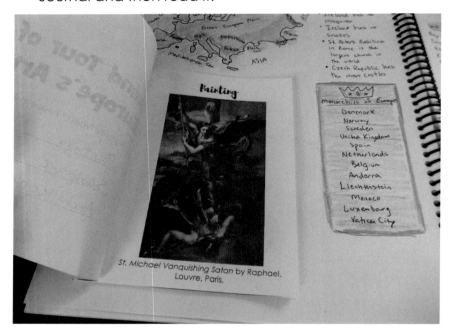

☺ ☺ ☺ EXPLORATION: European Food

For this activity, you will need:

- "European Recipes" from the Printable Pack
- Ingredients for recipes you decide on
- Cooking utensils and a kitchen
- Travel video of Europe from the YouTube playlist for this unit

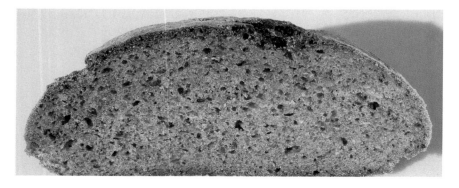

1. Choose some or all of the European recipes you want to try and make them together.

2. While you eat, watch a travel video about Europe.

☺ ☺EXPLORATION: Formula 1 Racing

For this activity, you will need:

- Video clip of a Formula 1 race from the YouTube playlist for this unit
- "Formula 1 Racing Car" from the Printable Pack, printed onto white or colorful card stock
- Markers or crayons
- Clear tape
- School glue
- Stapler
- Sidewalk chalk or masking tape

Europeans invented cars and Europe is the home of many car racing events, including the Formula 1 Grand Prix Championship which first started in the 1920s. Grand Prix events are held all over the world now in places like Japan, Canada, Australia, Brazil, and Italy. Formula 1 racing cars, crews, and drivers are expensive, so they are funded or sponsored by big companies like Ferrari, BMW, Ford, Toyota, Aston Martin, and Renault. Races are held on tracks or circuits of varying designs that can include sharp turns and hills. All racers begin with a warm up lap and then cars line up in a grid according to their qualifying times. They start at a signal from a light and then complete the number of laps required in the race. The first one across the finish line wins.

1. Watch a video of a Formula 1 race.

2. Cut off the bottom half of the "Formula 1 Racing Car" paper. Roll it into a long tube. This will become the body

Fabulous Fact

The world cup is an international soccer tournament begun in 1930 and held every four years.

Italy, Germany, France, England, and Spain are European countries which have won the world cup.

Famous Folks

Lewis Hamilton is a famous Formula 1 race car driver from the UK.

Photo by Morio, CC by SA 4.0.

He has won seven World Drivers' Championship titles and holds the record for the most wins ever (103). He started racing go-karts at the age of 10.

This is Lewis Hamilton in his race car. Photo by Malcolm grima83, CC by SA 4.0.

Fabulous Fact

There are more than 200 languages spoken in Europe. The five most common are Russian, French, English, Italian, and German.

Bookworms

Babushka's Doll by Patricia Polacco is about a little girl who wants everything right now. When she plays with her grandmother's doll she gets a taste of her own medicine.

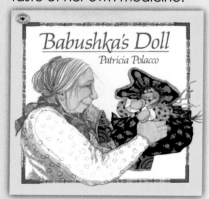

This author writes picture books based on eastern European folklore.

For ages 4 to 8.

Memorization Station

Folk music: simple songs that are often anonymous and passed down orally among ordinary people

of your car, with the seam at the bottom. Unroll it and use markers or crayons to add words and designs.

3. Decorate the front and rear wings, the driver's helmet, and the tires. Cut out the pieces.

4. Tape the body of the car into a long tube. Staple one end of the tube into a wedge.

5. Glue the front, longer, wing on top of the stapled end. Then, glue the shorter rear wing to the opposite end of the car.

6. Glue the driver's helmet to the middle of the car body. Then, glue on the four wheels.

7. Make a circuit for your car with sidewalk chalk outside or with masking tape inside.

☺ ☺ ☺EXPLORATION: European Folk Music

For this activity, you will need:

- World Explorer Journal
- Videos of folk songs from the YouTube playlist for this unit
- Scissors
- Glue stick
- World map or globe
- "Danny Boy" from the Printable Pack

Folk music includes songs that were transmitted orally and with an unknown composer. The songs were created by ordinary people singing lullabies to their babies, having fun with friends over a drink, or working together over a harvest. They are usually easy to sing, catchy tunes that tell stories.

Each region of Europe has its own style of folk music.

1. Write the definition of folk music down in your World Explorer Journal.

2. Listen to some folk songs from different countries of Europe. Find the countries the songs are from on a world map or globe.

3. Play "Danny Boy" while you read the lyrics. Find Ireland on a map or globe.

4. Teach any word definitions, phrases, or context that the children do not know. Then, learn to sing it. Sing the song while you all work on a chore together. How many times do you get through the song before your chore is done?

5. Cut out and then glue the lyrics for the Danny Boy into your World Explorer Journal.

☺ ☺ ☺**EXPLORATION: Europe is Diverse**

For this activity, you will need:

- Poster board
- Markers or crayons
- Internet or books for research

The countries of Europe each have unique cultures, languages, histories, and traditions. For example, Finland and Greece are very different places with entirely different cultures, Likewise, Portugal and Bulgaria are very unique from each other. Even though Europe is a small continent, it has a mosaic of peoples.

1. Choose two European countries and learn about them online or from books from your library.

2. Draw a line right down the middle of a poster board. Put one country on each side.

3. Draw or print a flag from each country. Draw or print a locator map of the country, so you can see where it is in Europe.

4. Compare and contrast the two countries by writing down facts about the type of government, the currency, the language, typical homes, national foods, and landscapes.

5. Present your poster to an audience. Explain the things you compared (the things the two nations had in common) and the things you contrasted (the things that are different between the two countries).

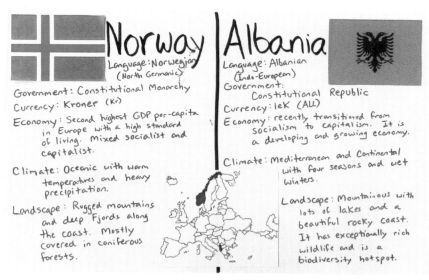

☺ ☺**EXPLORATION: Wealth Distribution in Europe Map**

For this activity, you will need:

Additional Layer

These Russian girls are playing the bells to accompany a song during a festival.

Bells, horns, guitars, fiddles, and pipes are all common instruments in European folk music. Learn more about European instruments.

You can learn more about folk music in the *Folk Art* unit from the Colonial Period Arts course.

Additional Layer

The British Museum in London has over 8 million different objects in its collection, of which only about 1% are on display at any given time.

It is a collection of the development of human history across the whole world, made possible by Britain's colonial empire.

Many of these pieces are from ancient cultures.

You can learn more about ancient art in *Art Beginnings: Ancient Art Around the World*.

- "Wealth Distribution in Europe" from the Printable Pack
- Colored Pencils

Fabulous Fact

San Marino was founded in AD 301 by Saint Marinus, a Christian holy man and stone mason who founded a monastery on Monte Titano.

A village grew up around the monastery and has been independently ruled since its founding, making it the oldest country in Europe.

Memorization Station

Wealth distribution: the way that money and other assets are divided among people

Median wealth: the amount of monetary assets that divides people exactly into two groups

Fabulous Fact

The biggest cities in Europe are London, Moscow, and Paris. Each of these cities has over 10 million inhabitants. Cities that are larger than 10 million people are known as "mega-cities."

This is Moscow, Russia. It is home to 12.4 million people.

Wealth Distribution in Europe
Based on the median wealth of all households.

Legend:
- > €30,000
- €15,000 - €30,000
- €5,000 - €15,000
- < €5,000

Layers of Learning

Wealth distribution maps can help you understand which countries have more money than others. Once you know which countries are rich and which ones are poor, you can look at what the rich countries are doing differently from the poor ones. Things like education, free market principles, the rule of law, natural resources, and cultural attitudes about work and spending can all have an effect on the wealth of a nation.

The map in this Exploration shows the **median wealth**. Median means that half of the people have more wealth and half have less. Wealth means everything a person owns such as the money in their bank accounts, the value of their home or other real estate, and the value of investments.

1. Discuss the definitions of median wealth and wealth distribution.

2. People are happier when wealth is distributed more evenly among all groups in a society. Why do you think that is?

   a. What do you think causes wide wealth gaps between the rich and poor? Consider human nature, laws, national ethics, and crime.

   b. Should wide gaps in wealth be fixed by governments or not? Why? How?

3. Color the "Wealth Distribution in Europe" map and discuss why you think the map looks the way it does.

4. Put the map in the Geography section of your Layers of Learning Notebook.

Step 3: Show What You Know

During this unit, choose one of the assignments below to show what you have learned during the unit. Add this work to your Layers of Learning Notebook. You can also use this assignment to show your supervising teacher or your charter school as a sample of what you've been working on in your homeschool, if needed.

There are more ideas for writing assignments in the "Writer's Workshop" sidebars.

☺ ☺ Coloring or Narration Page

For this activity, you will need:

- "Europe" printable from the Printable Pack
- Writing or drawing utensils

1. Depending on the age and ability of the child, choose either the "Europe" coloring sheet or the "Europe" narration page from the Printable Pack.

2. Younger kids can color the coloring sheet as you review some of the things you learned about during this unit. On the bottom of the coloring page, kids can write a sentence about what they learned. Very young children can explain their ideas orally while a parent writes for them.

Europe

Europe is the second smallest continent, but in spite of its small size it has many interesting landscapes and cultures. Europe has high glacier covered mountains, vast green plains, wet and stormy coasts, and sun drenched beaches. In Europe you can visit art museums and see some of the greatest paintings and sculptures in the world, visit an ancient historical ruin, or enjoy a folk festival with music and dancing.

Layers of Learning

3. Older kids can write about some of the concepts you learned on the narration page and color the picture as well.

4. Add this to the Geography section of your Layers of Learning Notebook.

☺ ☺ ☺ Writer's Workshop

For this activity, you will need:

- A computer or a piece of paper and a writing utensil

Choose from one of the ideas below or write about

Additional Layer

The main form of transportation in The Netherlands is the bicycle. No one wears helmets, but because they have worked to keep bicycles and cars separate, it is also the safest place to cycle.

Learn more about making a bike-friendly city. Do you feel like bicycles are a practical form of transportation where you live? Why or why not?

Writer's Workshop

Pick five countries in Europe. Pretend you visited each of them. Write about what you ate on your trip.

Deep Thoughts

Europeans colonized huge parts of the world from 1600 to 1900. Their descendants now live in Oceania, Asia, Africa, and the Americas.

Photo by Nagihuin, CC by SA 4.0

Consider the way mass migrations like this affect the land that is colonized, the colonizers, and those left behind.

Unit Trivia Questions

1. All of the water on Earth, including saltwater and freshwater, is called the _____.

   Hydrosphere

2. True or false - A watershed and a drainage basin are two words for the same thing.

   True

3. Name five rivers in Europe from memory and describe their location.

   Danube (southeast Europe), Rhine (West Germany), Volga (Western Russia), Seine (Central France), Thames (Southern England) Answers vary

4. What are the two main types of water shortages that people experience?

   Economic water shortage where there is water, but it isn't clean or available. And physical water shortage where there physically isn't enough water, such as in a desert.

5. Which mountains create the dividing line between Europe and Asia?

   Urals and Caucasus

6. Which one of these countries is not in Europe?

   a) Albania

   b) Latvia

   c) Andorra

   d) Ecuador

7. Name as many peninsulas in Europe as you can. One point for each peninsula.

   Answers vary. Iberian, Scandinavian, Jutland, Balkan, Italian, Crimean, Kola

something else you learned during this unit. Each of these prompts corresponds with one of the units from the Layers of Learning Writer's Workshop curriculum, so you may choose to coordinate the assignment with the monthly unit you are learning about in Writer's Workshop.

- **Sentences, Paragraphs, & Narrations:** Write a paragraph about the things people need water for.
- **Descriptions & Instructions:** Write a description of a place in Europe you would like to visit. Then, go back and circle five weak words. Use a thesaurus to replace those words with better ones.
- **Fanciful Stories:** Pretend Europe is a person. Write a character description including favorite foods, religious behavior, lifestyle, ethics, and so on.
- **Poetry:** Find a description of Europe in a book or encyclopedia. Edit the words out to make it into a free verse poem about the continent.
- **True Stories:** If you have ever been to a foreign country in Europe, write about it. If you haven't, pick a European country and write about why you would like to visit.
- **Reports and Essays:** Compare and contrast Europe's physical geography with Africa's.
- **Letters:** Think of something that came from Europe and write a thank you note to Europe for it.
- **Persuasive Writing:** Make an advertisement for Europe. It could be a poster, video, brochure, or website.

☺ ☺ ☻ **Blank Map of Europe Challenge**
For this activity, you will need:

- "Europe" from the Printable Pack
- Colored pencils or crayons

1. Decide how many things, places, or landmarks you expect your kids to remember from this unit. For young kids it might be 10 items, for middle grades perhaps 20, and for high schoolers 30. That number becomes the points available for this quiz.

2. From memory, label, mark, and color landmarks or places on the blank "Europe" map. These could be countries with outlines drawn, mountain ranges, rivers, or man-made attractions like the Eiffel Tower. Draw and label each in the correct location.

3. Give one point for each item added to the map in the correct spot. Give bonus points for extra items beyond the goal number.

☺ ☺ ☺ Show & Tell

For this activity, you will need:

- Projects or papers you completed during this unit

1. Have each child choose her or his best or favorite work from this unit. Ask the child to think about what made it the best or favorite.

2. Have each child show off her or his work in front of the group. The child should explain what the project was about, what was learned, and why it was the best.

3. The audience should clap and then ask thoughtful questions.

4. Give points for presentation, being a good audience, and asking a good question.

☺ ☺ ☺ Big Book of Knowledge

For this activity, you will need:

- "Big Book of Knowledge: Europe" printable from the Printable Pack, printed on card stock
- Writing or drawing utensils
- Big Book of Knowledge

1. Color, draw on, or write on the Big Book of Knowledge page. Record concepts, definitions, and facts you learned during this unit. It's a record of the things you learned and hope to remember. Add the page to your Big Book of Knowledge.

2. Use your Big Book of Knowledge regularly to help you review, quiz, or create games that will help you commit the things you've learned to memory.

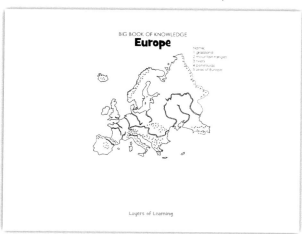

Big Book of Knowledge

The Big Book of Knowledge is a book for you, the mentor, to use as a constant review of all of the things you're learning about. You can use it to quiz your kids or prepare tests or review games. Whenever you learn something in Layers of Learning that you want your kids to remember, add it to your Big Book of Knowledge.

Assemble your Big Book of Knowledge in a binder or with binder rings. Divide it into sections for each subject.

In the Printable Pack for this unit you will find a "Big Book of Knowledge" sheet. You can add this sheet to others you collect or create yourself as you progress through the Layers of Learning curriculum. Customize the Big Book of Knowledge to your family by adding facts and topics that you enjoyed exploring as you were learning.

Visit Layers of Learning online to find more information on how to assemble and use your own Big Book of Knowledge.

You will also find cover and section pages to print along with creative games to play with your Big Book of Knowledge to keep school, even the tests, fun!

POLAR REGIONS

The regions above the Arctic and below the Antarctic Circles get much less sunlight than regions closer to the equator. The North and South Poles of the planet never get direct sunlight. This means the top and bottom of the world stay cold and frozen year round.

At the bottom of the world is a continent called Antarctica. It is surrounded by the Southern Ocean. Most of Antarctica is covered by a permanent ice cap. In spite of this, there are animals on land and in the sea that thrive on the continent. People live there too, although they are mostly scientists and those who support them. No one lives there permanently or is native to Antarctica.

Antarctica is a continent with volcanoes, mountain ranges, valleys, lakes, and lots of ice.

At the top of the world is an ocean called the Arctic Ocean that is nearly surrounded by land. There is a permanent ice sheet that expands in the winter and shrinks in the summer but never entirely goes away. The Arctic is a little warmer than the Antarctic because it is ocean rather than land. The Arctic region does have permanent populations of people who have lived in the cold region since ancient times.

The biomes of both Antarctica and the Arctic are called polar biomes. Before we learn about the poles, we'll also take a look at the other biomes on our earth. Besides polar, there are four other major biomes - forest, grassland, desert, and aquatic. These biomes are places with dominant plant and animal life based on each type of climate. Biomes are a way to classify zones of life.

Step 1: Library List

Choose books from your library that go with this topic. Here's a list of some favorites and also a list of search terms so you can utilize what your library offers. Read the books with your kids and/or assign them some to read independently. It is from these books your kids will learn most of the facts they need from this unit.

Search for: Biomes, Antarctica, Arctic, Polar regions,

☺ ☺ ☺*Geography of the World* by DK. Read "The Arctic" and "The Antarctic" on pages 266-269.

☺ ☺ ☺*DK Eyewitness Videos: Arctic & Antarctic.*

☺ ☺ ☺*Disney Nature: Penguins.* An exceptional documentary video your family will enjoy.

☺*What Is a Biome?* by Bobbie Kalman. A very simple and colorful picture book for young children that introduces the idea of biomes.

☺*Tour the Tundra* by Laura Perdew. This is an illustrated picture book that introduces children to the animals and plants that live in the tundra as well as on the ice caps. Look for the other four biome books in the series as well.

☺*Antarctica* by Rebecca Hirsch. With full-color, full-page photos and just a few big words on each page, this is for your youngest learners.

☺*The Seven Continents: Antarctica* by Karen Kellaher. Learn about the geography, animals, plants, and history of the frozen continent. This book has lots of full-color photos and maps. There are also hefty, but simple, paragraphs.

☺*Antarctica: A Continent of Wonder* by Mario Cuesta Hernando. A picture book with charming illustrations that takes you on a trip to Antarctica.

☺*Antarctica* by Helen Cowcher. This is a picture book story of a year with a colony of emperor penguins in Antarctica.

☺*You Wouldn't Want to be a Polar Explorer* by Jen Green. Learn all about the explorers who were part of Ernest Shackleton's expedition to Antarctica.

☺*Polar Bears* by Gail Gibbons. Learn how polar bears live and thrive in a hostile Arctic climate.

☺*Penguin Chick* by Betty Tatham and Helen K. Davie. Part

On the Web

For videos, web pages, games, and more to add to this unit, visit the People & Planet Resources at Layers-of-Learning.com.

You will find a link to video playlists, web links, and more.

Bookworms

If you're looking for a family read-aloud, we'd like to suggest this one.

SHIPWRECK AT THE BOTTOM OF THE WORLD

Shipwreck at the Bottom of the World by Jennifer Armstrong is the true story of Ernest Shackleton's ill-fated attempt to reach the South Pole. You can feel the bone-aching cold, the gut-gnawing hunger, and the edge of despair as you root for this team of explorers to survive, a much greater feat than merely reaching the end of the earth.

of the Let's Read and Find Out series.

☺ ☺*Beastly Biomes* by Carly Allen-Fletcher. An illustrated picture book with text that explains how certain animals can live only in certain biomes.

☺ ☺*Amazing Biome Projects You Can Build Yourself* by Donna Latham. Each chapter is about a different type of biome, the animals, and plants that live there. At the end of the chapter are several hands-on projects to try.

☺ ☺*A Walk in the Tundra* by Rebecca L. Johnson. Colorful photos and ample text explain the animals, plants, seasons, and location of the tundra biome. This book is part of the "Biomes of North America" series, which includes nine titles.

☺ ☺*Tundra Biomes Around the World* by Phillip Simpson. Full-color photos and text describe the weather and wildlife of the tundra biomes. This is part of a series of five books about biomes around the world.

☺ ☺*Where Is Antarctica?* by Sarah Fabiny. This is a chapter book with paragraphs and black and white illustrations. It is filled with tidbits about the continent, from explorers and the history to animals and volcanoes.

☺ ☺*Can You Survive Antarctica? An Interactive Survival Adventure* by Rachael Hanel. The reader makes decisions that change the outcome as you move through the story. This book includes real scenarios from Antarctic exploration.

☺*Biomes: Discover the Earth's Ecosystems With Environmental Science Activities for Kids* by Donna Latham. Explains what and where biomes are and how they are interconnected. It also goes into detail on each of the nine defined biomes and includes hands-on activities.

☺*Antarctica: An Intimate Portrait of a Mysterious Continent* by Gabrielle Walker. The author visited Antarctica, the touristy parts and the scientific stations, and interviewed people. This book is an overview of Antarctica, and also a look at the people who live and work there.

☺*Antarctic Atlas* by Peter Fretwell. The author is a professional cartographer and research scientist who has worked in and with Antarctica for decades. This book is map after map of concepts about Antarctica with plain explanations. You will see maps of the whole continent, maps of glaciers, maps of penguin colonies, and so much more.

☺*The Polar Regions: An Environmental History* by Adrian Howkins. This book looks at the history of the Arctic and Antarctica, including exploration, myths, settlements,

Deep Thoughts

Biomes are difficult to classify and map because, in reality, there is gradual change from one biome to another.

There are also many variations in biomes. For example, Canada and Brazil both have vast forests, but the forests are so different, they don't share a single species in common. Are they both "forest" biomes or should we be more specific?

How specific is specific enough? Is a cloud forest different enough from other tropical forests that it should be its own biome? The answer is arbitrary.

Some people say there are five biomes, others insist there are seven or nine or twenty-six. There is no consensus.

What criteria do you think should be used to classify biomes?

Additional Layer

Sometimes we imagine that the polar lands are bleak and barren because they are cold. The truth is, they are thriving biomes. Over 7,500 species have been recorded in the Antarctic and over 5,550 species have been recorded in the Arctic. There are over 200 species that are found in both. Learn more about the plant and animal life that thrives at our world's poles.

An Arctic Starflower

scientific pursuits, and economic exploitation. For good readers and those really interested in the poles.

Step 2: Explore

Choose a few hands-on Explorations from this section to work on as a family. They should be appealing activities that will create mental hooks so your kids remember the information in the unit. Save the rest of the Explorations for the next time you do this unit in four years when your kids are older. You can also read the sidebars together and explore some little rabbit trails.

This unit includes printables. See the introduction for instructions on retrieving your Printable Pack.

Biomes

Biomes are large zones defined by the major vegetation, wildlife, and climate. In this unit, we will learn about the five major biomes and their subtypes. They are desert, forest, polar, grassland, and aquatic. Forests can be divided into three groups: tropical, temperate, and boreal. Polar can be divided into two groups: tundra and ice cap. There are two types of grasslands: temperate and tropical. And finally, there are two types of aquatic biomes: freshwater and saltwater.

☺ ☺ ☺ EXPLORATION: Biomes on the Map

For this activity, you will need:

- Book or video about biomes from the Library List or YouTube playlist for this unit
- "Biomes" from the Printable Pack
- Colored pencils or crayons
- World Explorer Journal

There are five major types of biomes and nine subtypes. The major biomes are polar, forest, grassland, desert, and aquatic. The subtypes are tropical forest, temperate forest, boreal forest, tropical grassland, temperate grassland, tundra, ice cap, freshwater, and saltwater. This map shows the subtypes and deserts.

1. Read a book or watch a video about biomes.

2. Write the definition of biomes in your World Explorer Journal and list the ten types of biomes. (With younger kids, you can list just the five major types of biomes: polar, forest, grassland, desert, aquatic).

Memorization Station

Memorize the definition of biomes and the major types of biomes.

Biomes: geographical regions with dominant plant and animal populations due to the climate

Here are the major types of biomes:

Polar
    Tundra
    Ice Cap

Forest
    Tropical forest
    Temperate forest
    Boreal forest

Grassland
    Tropical grassland
    Temperate grassland

Desert

Aquatic
    Freshwater
    Saltwater

Additional Layer

Cut colored squares out of paper and label each with a biome name. Then, glue the top edge of each paper square to a page in your World Explorer Journal to make flaps that can be opened. Under each flap, write facts about each of the biomes.

Fabulous Fact

Antarctica is a desert. It gets less than 10 inches of precipitation a year. But since it is always cold, the snow stays year after year, not melting off in the summer.

Bookworms

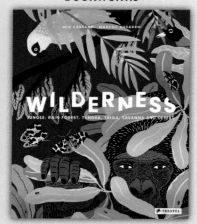

Wilderness by Mia Cassany and Marcos Navarro takes young readers on an illustrated tour of some of the world's most amazing nature reserves in tundra, forest, rainforest, grassland, and desert biomes. Just a few words and gorgeous pictures.

For ages 6 to 9.

3. Color the "biomes" map by number.

4. Put the map in your Layers of Learning Notebook in the Geography section.

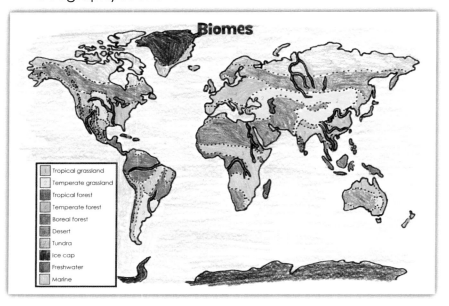

☺ ☺ ☺EXPLORATION: Desert Biomes

For this activity, you will need:

- Book or video about deserts, Arizona coral snake, and kangaroo rat from the Library List or YouTube playlist
- Colored paper
- Scissors
- Glue stick
- Markers
- Crayons
- World Explorer Journal

Deserts are dry and often experience wide temperature swings between hot and cold in a single day. Animals and plants that live in deserts have to be able to live with low water supplies and extreme temperatures. Arizona coral snakes and kangaroo rats are two such animals. They are also predator and prey.

1. Read a book or watch a video about deserts.

2. You may also want to watch a video about the Arizona coral snake and the kangaroo rat.

3. Make a paper chain Arizona coral snake from 1½ inch (4 cm) wide strips of paper. The snake's head is black and then the pattern is yellow, black, yellow, red, repeating. There are copycat snakes that look similar but have a different pattern. Add a forked tongue and draw on eyes with a white crayon.

4. Make a little paper chain kangaroo rat from two shorter

strips of orange or brown paper (half the length, but the same width as the snake papers). Add ears, a tail and draw on eyes and a nose.

5. Discuss the environment these animals live in and how the animals are specific to their environment. They wouldn't thrive on the grasslands or in the forest.

6. Draw a picture of a desert biome in your World Explorer Journal and add a caption about what the desert environment is like.

😊 😊 😊EXPLORATION: 3 Types of Forest Biome

For this activity, you will need:

- Book or video about forest biomes from the Library List or YouTube playlist
- "3 Types of Forest Biome" from the Printable Pack
- Scissors
- Crayons or colored pencils
- Glue stick
- World Explorer Journal

Forest is a major type of biome where large trees are the dominant vegetation, but there are such big differences between forests in different climates that we separate them into three sub-biomes.

- **Tropical rainforests** can be found in zones near the equator where it is hot year round, lots of rain falls regularly, and there is abundant sunlight.
- **Temperate forests** are in the mid-latitudes in places with plenty of precipitation and definite seasons of warm or

Memorization Station

Desert: land with sparse vegetation that gets less than 10 inches (25 cm) of rain per year

Forest: an area where large trees are the dominant vegetation

Tropical rainforest: a region of dense plant growth near the equator with heavy rainfall for at least half the year

Temperate forest: a zone of mixed deciduous and evergreen trees where there are cool or cold winters and warm or hot summers

Boreal forest: (taiga) a region of mostly coniferous trees in the high latitudes or in mountains with very cold winters and warm or hot summers

Additional Layer

The boreal forest is the largest land biome, covering almost one third of the land on Earth. This type of forest is only in northern latitudes because there is no land in the boreal zone in the Southern Hemisphere.

Find out what economic uses the Great Northern Forests have.

Fabulous Fact

Warmer and wetter biomes have more species and are more densely inhabited by plants and animals than colder, drier biomes.

The most abundant biomes on Earth are in warm, coral waters and hot rainforests.

The Magic Tree House: Polar Bears Past Bedtime by Mary Pope Osborne, along with its companion book, *Polar Bears and the Arctic*, would make great read-aloud books during this unit. It's a great story coupled with learning a lot of cool facts about the Arctic.

Ice! Poems About Polar Life by Douglas Florian is filled with funny poems. As you read the poems, you will also learn about polar animals, adaptation, biomes, and global warming.

Ages 6 to 10.

hot summers and cool or cold winters.

- **Boreal forests** are in the far north or high in the mountains where it is very cold in the winter and rainfall is adequate.

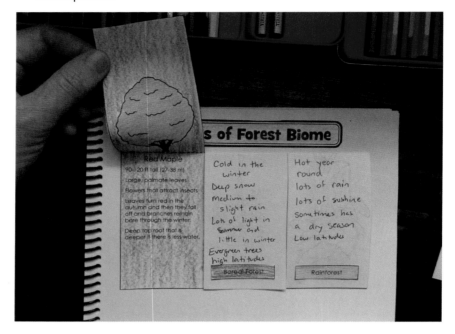

1. Read a book or watch a video about the three types of forest biomes. Pay attention to what makes them different from one another. Discuss:

   a. If you were suddenly plopped into the middle of a forest, could you tell which type of forest you were in?

   b. What clues could you look for?

2. Color the three trees from the "3 Types of Forest Biome" page. Read the descriptions of each tree.

3. Cut out the title, the large rectangle with the three trees, and the word tags at the bottom of the page. Cut on all of the solid lines.

4. Glue the title to a page in your World Explorer Journal. Then, glue the bottom part of the three trees rectangle to the page, folding the top over so it makes three flaps. Glue the correct word tag to the top of each flap, matching the biome to the tree that is in that biome.

   Answers: Red Maple = Temperate Forest, Scotch Pine = Boreal Forest, Kapok = Rainforest

5. On the front of each flap, write down the characteristics of each type of biome.

☺ ☺ ☺**EXPLORATION: Tundra Tree Line**

For this activity, you will need:

- Book or video about tundra from the Library List or YouTube playlist
- Art paper
- Green, light green, gray paint
- Sponge or foam paint brush
- Paper
- Colored pencils or crayons
- Scissors or glue

As you travel north through the boreal forest, the trees get smaller, stunted, and sparse. Eventually, they peter out to nothing; only small willows, grasses, and lichens cover the rocks and frozen soil of the **tundra**. The point where the trees stop is called the tree line. It marks the end of the zone where trees can survive.

1. Press a sponge into dark green paint and then onto a piece of art paper from the bottom of the page to about halfway up the page.

2. Then, press a sponge into gray paint and dab the top portion of the page. Over the top of the gray, dab on some light green spots. The dark green is the boreal forest and the gray and light green is the tundra.

3. Read a book or watch a video about the tundra. Pay attention to specific animals and plants that live in the tundra.

4. On another piece of paper, draw some animals and plants that live in the tundra. Color them and then cut them out. Glue them to your tree line painting.

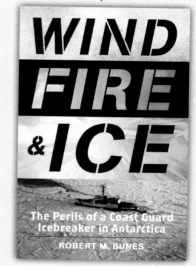
Memorization Station

Tundra: a zone too cold for trees and where the ground remains frozen under the surface year round

Grassland: A zone that is too dry for many trees and the dominant vegetation is grasses

Deep Thoughts

Discuss what you think American naturalist Aldo Leopold meant when he said:

"What a thousand acres of Silphiums looked like when they tickled the bellies of the buffalo is a question never again to be answered, and perhaps not even asked."

5. Once your painting is dry, label the tundra, boreal forest, and tree line. Display it on your wall until the end of this unit.

Additional Layer

Grasslands go by many different names depending on where you live.

In North America, they are known as prairies. Argentinians call them the pampas. People in Africa have the savanna and the veld. Australians have the Downs. And the people of Central Asia and China call them steppes.

This boy is riding a horse on the Mongolian steppe.

Each of the grasslands around the world has unique characteristics. Make a poster highlighting at least four different grasslands and the differences between them.

Fabulous Fact

Terrestrial biomes are defined by the temperature and the amount of water, but aquatic biomes are mostly defined by the amount of salt in the water and the amount of available nutrients.

Oceans are divided into zones based on the sunlight, which directly affects the amount of nutrients.

Estuaries and mangroves are zones where freshwater and saltwater mingle to make a unique environment.

☺ ☺ ☺EXPLORATION: Grasslands

WARNING: This activiy uses a hot glue gun. Be careful!

For this activity, you will need:

- *Bringing the Rain to Kapiti Plain* by Verna Aardema (You can view this being read aloud on YouTube as well.)
- *If You're Not From the Prairie* by David Bouchard (You can view this being read aloud on YouTube as well.)
- Grass seed
- Nylon stockings
- Potting soil
- Cup or jar
- Wiggly eyes, felt, and other decorations, as desired
- Hot glue gun

Grasslands are dry enough that trees don't grow well but not so dry that they are deserts. Grass is the dominant vegetation. But tropical grasslands are very different from temperate grasslands.

1. Read *Bringing the Rain to Kapiti Plain* and then *If You're Not From the Prairie*. Discuss the differences between a tropical grassland and a temperate grassland.

2. Put grass seed in the toe of a knee-high nylon stocking.

3. Put a shovel full of potting soil in on top of the grass seed, and tie a knot to hold the seed and soil in a little ball.

4. Now, soak the ball in a bowl of water for two to three minutes.

5. Fill a jar with water and put the ball on top of the jar, with the end of the nylon hanging down into the water. This will draw water up and keep your grass head moist.

6. Glue on face pieces made of felt, wiggly eyes, or any craft supplies you like. Use hot glue or another non-water soluble glue.

7. In about 10 days, you will have green grass hair. Anytime the water in the jar gets low, pull the head out to pour in

a little more water. You can trim it as much or as little as you like, depending upon your preferred hairstyle.

😊 😊 😊 **EXPLORATION: Aquatic**
For this activity, you will need:

- Book or video about aquatic biomes from the Library List or YouTube playlist
- World Explorer Journal
- Large white board and pens (optional)
- Globe or world map
- Large transparent jar with a lid
- Rocks, cleaned
- Shells (optional)
- Green yarn
- Scissors
- Small plastic ocean or freshwater toys (optional)
- Small sticks
- "Saltwater Life" and "Freshwater Life" from the Printable Pack
- Crayons or colored pencils
- Tape

The **aquatic** biome is the largest on the planet. It occurs at every latitude and has the most species of animals and plants. The aquatic biome can be broadly separated into **saltwater** and **freshwater** sub-biomes. Each of these biomes includes the animals and plants that live in the water all of the time and those that live on or near the water in such a way that it is indispensable to them, like ducks or frogs, for example.

Memorization Station

Aquatic: relating to water

Saltwater: contains high concentrations of dissolved salts and minerals

Freshwater: contains less than 1% dissolved salts and includes lakes and streams

Writer's Workshop

People have made homes in every biome on Earth, except aquatic. If people wanted to live under the sea, what would they need to do? Write about your ideas for an underwater city.

Additional Layer

Aquatic biomes can be further broken down.

Saltwater biomes include estuaries, mangroves, coral reefs, continental shelves, deep sea, and others.

Freshwater biomes include rivers, lakes, and wetlands.

This is a kelp forest from a continental shelf biome.

Learn more about a specific aquatic biome and where it is located.

By international treaty, countries can claim up to 12 nautical miles from their coast. Anyone can sail in these waters, but they can't fish, gather natural resources, or conduct military operations inside another country's ocean territories.

This map shows the maritime boundary between the US and Russia.

Learn more about maritime boundaries and the disputes these ambiguous lines on a map sometimes cause.

Bookworms

Fighting to Survive the Polar Regions: Terrifying True Stories by Michael Burgan tells six stories of harrowing Arctic and Antarctic explorers.

For ages 10 and up.

1. Read a book or watch a video about aquatic biomes.

2. Draw a Venn diagram in your World Explorer Journal. Label one side saltwater and the other freshwater. Write down characteristics and animals and plants from each as you discuss them together. It is helpful if a large Venn diagram is drawn on a whiteboard or sheet of paper where all the children can see and copy the information.

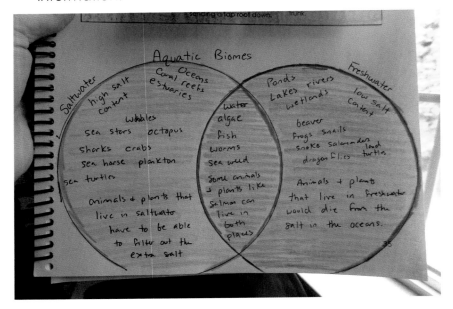

3. On a globe or world map, identify and name the five oceans: Pacific, Atlantic, Indian, Arctic, and Southern. See if your kids can do it from memory. Have older kids name as many seas as possible as you point to them. These are all saltwater biomes.

4. Name some rivers and lakes on your home continent. Can you name and find any from the other continents? These are all freshwater biomes.

5. Make an aquatic biome in a jar. Choose between saltwater or freshwater. Put some clean rocks in the bottom.

6. For a saltwater biome, add green yarn strands (seaweed), shells, and any plastic sea creatures you might have. Fill the jar with water and screw the lid on tight. Color the "Saltwater Life" from the printable, cut out the pictures, and tape the ones you want to the outside of the jar.

7. For a freshwater biome, pick apart green yarn strands to make thin mermaid grass strands. Then add a couple of sticks and any plastic freshwater creatures you might have. Fill the jar with water and screw the lid on tight.

Color the "Freshwater Life" from the printable, cut out the pictures, and tape the ones you want to the outside of the jar.

8. The round title can be taped to the lid of the jar. Display your jar until the end of this unit.

Antarctica

☺ ☺ ☺**EXPLORATION: Map of Antarctica**
For this activity, you will need:

• Book or video about Antarctica from the Library List or YouTube playlist
• Globe
• "Antarctica" from the Printable Pack
• Colored pencils or crayons

Antarctica is the fifth largest continent, almost twice as big as Australia. Most of the continent is covered by a permanent ice cap and parts of the sea around the continent are also covered with permanent ice. In addition, the sea ice around the continent expands each winter and contracts each summer. It is also a mountainous continent with volcanoes, massive ranges, and high plateaus.

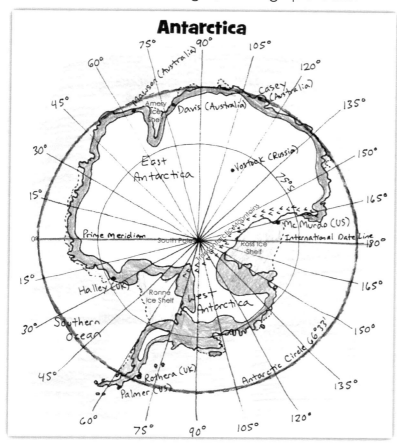

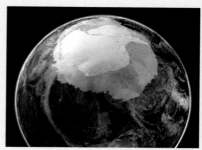

Fabulous Fact

The coldest temperature ever recorded was in Antarctica at Vostok Station. It was -128.56 °F (-89.2 °C)!

This is Vostok. It is a Russian station located in the middle of the East Antarctic Ice Sheet, miles and miles from the sea and more than 11,000 feet in elevation.

1. Read a book or watch a video about Antarctica.

2. Find Antarctica on a globe. Notice how far it is from other land. Compare the size of it to other continents. The post of your globe goes through the geographic south pole, the point where the earth turns on its axis.

3. On the "Antarctica" map, label the longitude lines in increments of 15°, starting with 0°, which is already marked for you. On this map, the numbers clockwise from 0 are east and the numbers counter-clockwise from 0 are west.

4. Trace over the Prime Meridian, at 0°, and the International Date Line, at 180°, in red. Label the part above the red line "East Antarctica" and the part below the red line "West Antarctica."

5. Label the dashed circle surrounding the continent "Antarctic Circle 66°33' " and trace it in dark blue. Label the other line of latitude 75°S.

6. Label these research stations. The dots are on the map and these are the coordinates for each one.

    *   McMurdo (US) 77°S 166°E
    *   Vostok (Russia) 78°S 106°E
    *   Casey (Australia) 66°S 110°E
    *   Rothera (UK) 66°S 68°W
    *   Mawson (Australia) 67°S 62°E
    *   Palmer (US) 64°S 64°W
    *   Davis (Australia) 68°S 77°E
    *   Halley (UK) 75°S 26°W

7. Color the exposed, non-icy, land around the edges of Antarctica brown. This land is mostly ice and snow-free in the summer months but is usually covered in snow and ice in the winter.

8. Label the Southern Ocean and color it light blue.

9. Color the ice shelves light purple. They are around the edges of Antarctica and separated by a dashed line from the sea.

    These are permanent ice shelves of freshwater that flow off the continent and are permanently attached to the land as the ice floats on the water. It is constantly added to by the glaciers moving from the land and also melts every year in the summer along the edges. In some places, the ice shelves are growing overall and, in other places, they are shrinking. Overall, the total amount of ice shelf seems to be decreasing.

    The white space left in the middle of the continent is the

permanent ice cap, a sheet of ice an average of 1.25 miles thick (2 kilometers). This ice cap is increasing in thickness and overall size, even as the edges melt.

☺ ☺ ☺ EXPLORATION: Antarctic Explorer Game

For this activity, you will need:

- Book or video about Antarctica and Antarctic explorers from the Library List or YouTube playlist
- "Antarctic Explorer" from the Printable Pack (If desired, print on multiple sheets of paper with "multi" or "poster" settings on your printer for a larger game board. We used 2x2 size.)
- Colored pencils, crayons, or markers
- Game pieces
- Index cards
- Other supplies as determined

Antarctic exploration is dangerous. Antarctica is cold, frozen, rugged, and extremely remote. Sea ice traps ships or punches holes through their sides, sinking their crews. High winds flip aircraft. Blizzards halt all travel. Avalanches bury acres of land at a time. The cold freezes runners of sleds and snow machines. Crevasses open up under explorers' feet. There is almost no food and absolutely no shelter.

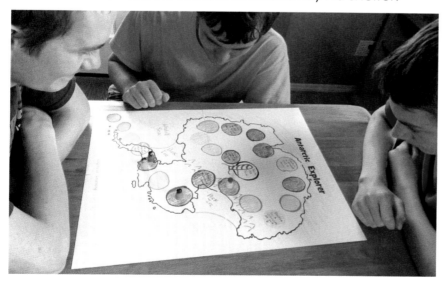

1. Read a book or watch a video about Antarctica and/ or Antarctic explorers. While you learn, watch for trivia facts you can use in a game.

2. Color the "Antarctic Explorer" map, making it into a game board. If you printed it on multiple sheets of paper, then tape them together.

3. Have everyone write trivia questions from your learning on index cards with the answers. The more questions you

Famous Folks

The first expedition to reach the South Pole was led by Norwegian Roald Amundsen in December of 1911.

Here is the team with their tent and a flag planted at the South Pole.

Since then, the ice sheet has moved and snow has fallen, so the tent and flag are now buried under approximately 56 feet of ice a mile from where they began.

Fabulous Fact

The Antarctic Treaty was signed in Washington DC in 1959 by twelve countries. Since then, 42 more countries have signed the treaty. It states that Antarctica is to be used for peaceful purposes only, that science conducted in Antarctica should be made freely available to all, and that no country can claim territory in Antarctica.

The flags of the 12 original countries that signed the Antarctic Treaty are flown at the ceremonial South Pole.

create, the better the game will be.

4. Agree on the rules for your game.

5. Play your Antarctic Explorers trivia game.

EXPLORATION: Temperature Difference

For this activity, you will need:

- "Temperature Difference" from the Printable Pack
- Colored pencils or crayons
- Internet
- Video comparing the Arctic to the Antarctic from the YouTube playlist for this unit

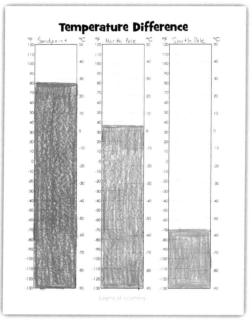

The sun hits the poles at a steep angle, meaning the sun's heat is spread out and weaker as you approach the poles. Also, the poles don't get any sun during the winter months. This makes the poles colder than lower latitudes. Still, the poles have seasons just like the rest of the earth. It is warmer in the summer and colder in the winter. When it is summer in the Arctic, it is winter in the Antarctic. The Arctic is water surrounded by land and the Antarctic is land surrounded by water. Water collects and slowly releases back heat from the sun, so the Arctic is warmer, on average, than the Antarctic. The two places are very different in spite of both being on the ends of the earth and receiving the same amount of sunlight.

1. Online, look up today's high temperature at the North Pole (or Alert, Canada), the South Pole, and your hometown.

2. Label the three columns on the "Temperature Differences" paper after the North Pole, South Pole, and your town. Color the thermometers to match the temperatures in each place.

3. Label the paper with the date.

4. As you work, talk about why the poles are colder than other places on Earth and why the South Pole is colder than the North Pole.

The Transantarctic Mountains stretch across most of the continent and divide Antarctica into east and west regions.

This is one of the longest mountain ranges on Earth. Some of the peaks and dry valleys in the mountains are among the few ice-free areas of Antarctica.

Learn more about the geological and biological history of these mountains.

Famous Folks

Antarctica was first discovered in 1820 by Russian explorers, Fabian Gottlieb von Bellingshausen and Mikhail Lazarev, who circumnavigated Antarctica.

Writer's Workshop

Imagine you were to accidentally stumble upon a continent not yet discovered. Write about where it is, how you found it, what it looks like, and what you will name it.

5. Watch a video comparing the Arctic to the Antarctic.

6. Put your "Temperature Difference" paper in the Geography section of your Layers of Learning Notebook.

😊 😊 EXPLORATION: Antarctic Scientist

For this activity, you will need:

- Internet
- Paper and pencil
- Card stock
- Colored pencils or crayons or markers

Most of the people in Antarctica are scientists or the people who support the scientists, like cooks, pilots, and repair staff. There are about 74 scientific stations in Antarctica. Some of them operate year round and others are staffed only in the summer. They are run by China, Sweden, Russia, Ukraine, Norway, Japan, United Kingdom, New Zealand, Australia, South Africa, Belgium, Argentina, the United States, and many other countries.

1. You are a scientist. Make plans for your upcoming expedition to Palmer Station in Antarctica. You will need to:

   - Plan how to get there.
   - Decide what supplies you will need.
   - Determine what scientific research you'd like to do while there.

2. Planning how to get there might be tricky. You can't fly into Palmer without a ski-equipped plane, so you'll probably need to take a boat from Punta Arenas, Chile. Plan out and map your air travel from your hometown to Punta Arenas, and then map your ship travel aboard the Laurence M. Gould ship that sails to Palmer Station.

3. Refer to the USAP Participant Guide at www.usap.gov to help you decide what you will pack for your trip. It's a guide put together by the United States Antarctic Program to help people prepare for a scientific expedition there. You are only allowed to take two 70-pound packs with you to Antarctica, so you won't be able to take everything. Refer to the lists from the guide and make your own "to-pack" list.

4. Write the approximate weight of each item and then add up your items to make sure you are within the weight limit (the backpack itself could weigh up to 5 pounds without anything in it!).

Additional Layer

Learn more about the Aurora Borealis and the Aurora Australis, the northern and southern lights, and what causes these light shows in the sky at each of the poles.

Fabulous Fact

Lake Vostok is one of several hundred liquid lakes under the Antarctic ice. The pressure under a mile of ice is great enough that water can remain liquid at very cold temperatures. The ice above Lake Vostok is about 2 miles (3.7 km) deep. In 2012, Russian scientists drilled through the ice to the liquid water to study it.

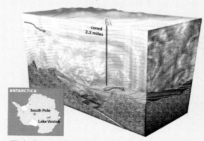

This is a diagram of Lake Vostok, the ice above it, and the core drilling that was done.

Today, scientists are arguing over whether anything could be alive down there. If it were, it would almost certainly be bacteria or other microscopic organisms.

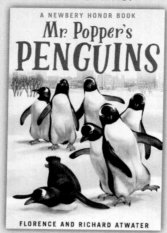
Deep Thoughts

About 4,000 people live in Antarctica during the summer and about 1,000 during the winter.

The super isolated Vostok Station has just 13 inhabitants through the long Antarctic winter.

Would you be willing to spend a winter cooped up with work colleagues inside a tiny research station in the sub-zero temperatures and darkness? Why or why not?

Compare wintering at Vostok Station to spending 6 months on a space station or in a submarine. Which would be hardest for you?

5. Once you arrive, you've got to have a research plan. Palmer Station is situated right near several penguin colonies, so a lot of the research there centers around Antarctic wildlife and marine biology. You may want to read the Wikipedia article about Palmer Station for more ideas about what you could research. Here are a few topics to consider: ozone changes, climatology, glaciology, astronomy, marine ecosystems, and marine biology. Write down your research topic and some questions you want to answer while you're there.

6. Now, put together all your plans and bind them into your own Antarctic travel plan book using card stock for covers. Add it to your home library.

☺ ☺EXPLORATION: Penguin Ice Portrait

For this activity, you will need:

- Small cups or ice cube tray
- Water
- Food coloring
- Craft sticks
- Freezer
- Art paper or card stock
- Black paint
- Potato
- Knife
- Cutting board
- Orange and white card stock
- Scissors
- Googly eyes
- Book or video about penguins from the Library List or YouTube playlist

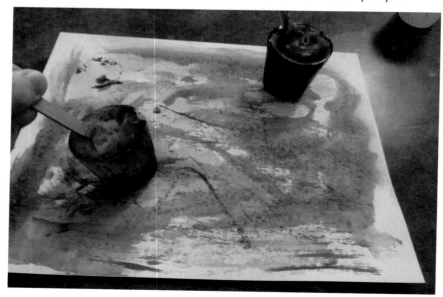

1. Ahead of time, put water in small cups or an ice cube tray with shades of blue and purple food coloring. Stand a craft stick up in each cup. Freeze solid for four hours or more.

2. Use the frozen colored ice to paint on a piece of art

paper until the paper is covered to make a watery icy scene.

3. Read a book or watch a video about penguins.

4. Cut a potato in half the long way to make one flat oval side. Dip the potato in black paint, making sure to get lots of paint. Press the potato onto the watery icy background. Lift it off, leaving paint behind.

5. Cut a round oval or circle piece from the white card stock, a bit smaller than your potato oval. Cut two small oval and one small triangle out of orange card stock. These will become feet and a beak.

6. Stick the white oval, googly eyes, orange feet and orange beak to the wet black paint to make a penguin. Paint black wings on your penguin if you want.

Arctic Circle

☺ ☺ ☺ **EXPLORATION: Mapping the Arctic**

For this activity, you will need:

- Book or video about the Arctic
- Globe
- Student atlas
- Colored pencils or crayons
- "The Arctic" from the Printable Pack

1. Read a book or watch a video about the Arctic.

2. Find the Arctic on a globe. Compare it to the Antarctic.

3. Color each of the city dots red. These are a few of the towns that are north of the Arctic Circle.

Fabulous Fact

The word Arctic literally means "of the bear." That means Antarctic literally means "opposite the bear." It's fitting then, that polar bears live in the Arctic but there are no bears in Antarctica.

Deep Thoughts

The Arctic is not as easy to define as Antarctica. Where exactly is the edge of the Arctic? Is it the Arctic Circle? Is it the tree line? Is it defined by places with cold temperatures?

The red line on this map shows the Arctic isotherm. Places north of the line have July average temperatures below 50 °F (10 °C). Some people define the Arctic as everything north of this line.

What do you think defines the Arctic? When you think of the Arctic, where do you include?

Fabulous Fact

This composite satellite image of the Arctic was taken in June of 2010. You can see that gray-blue sea ice is covering most of the Arctic Ocean. Greenland's ice cap is bright white.

Bookworms

The Three Snow Bears by Jan Brett is a remix of Goldilocks and the Three Bears, set in the Arctic.

This is an adorable picture book from a favorite children's illustrator.

Writer's Workshop

In the middle of a sheet of paper, write down your favorite Arctic animal. Surround it with reasons you like it. Then, turn your ideas into a paragraph convincing someone that it is the best animal.

4. Color the Arctic Circle in dark blue.

5. Use a student atlas to label the rivers, islands, seas, and other features that you would like to add to your map.

6. Color the ocean and rivers light blue. Leave the ice (surrounded by a thin line on the map) white for the sea ice. This is the ice that is still there at the height of summer. In the winter, the ice expands beyond the Arctic Circle.

7. Color the land light brown, leaving the ice cap on Greenland white.

8. Add the map to the Geography section of your Layers of Learning Notebook.

The Arctic

☺ ☺ ☺**EXPLORATION: Arctic Animal Facts**

For this activity, you will need:

- Library trip
- Internet
- World Explorer Journal
- Book or website about an Arctic animal

1. Go to the library and find a book about an animal that lives in the Arctic Circle. Polar bears, Arctic tern, Arctic fox, Arctic hare, walrus, reindeer, musk ox, wolverine,

and puffin are all Arctic animals.

2. Bring your book home and read it.

3. Find a how-to-draw online and draw a picture of your animal in your World Explorer Journal.

4. Write facts about your animal near your drawing. What makes your animal able to survive in the cold environment?

EXPLORATION: Arctic Ice Floe

For this activity, you will need:

- Books or video about the Arctic from the Library List or YouTube playlist
- Long roll of paper, like freezer paper or butcher paper
- Scissors
- Masking tape

In the Arctic, most of the ice is sea ice. It is floating on the surface of the sea and it is made of saltwater. This floating sea ice is called a **floe**. Often, many floes are packed close together. Animals like walruses and polar bears climb onto ice floes while they are resting or waiting while hunting. The ice floes allow the animals to stay far out at sea where their prey is and still have a place to rest.

1. Read a book or watch a video about the Arctic. Pay attention while you learn so you can ask and answer questions for a game.

2. Cut up pieces of white paper into large "ice floes." Place them on the floor, close enough that you can step or

Memorization Station

Floe: frozen block of saltwater that is floating freely on the surface

Walrus and pup sitting on an ice floe in the Chukchi Sea.

Fabulous Fact

The position of the Arctic and Antarctic Circles is not constant. The tilt of the earth on its axis changes cyclically over a 41,000 year period. At the moment, the Arctic and Antarctic Circles are both moving closer to the poles as the tilt of the Earth decreases.

The Arctic and Antarctic Circles are defined by the sun never clearing the horizon during mid-winter and never setting during mid-summer. That means the poles are getting slightly more sun every year as time goes on.

The island of Grimsey has a stone ball it moves 48 feet (14.5 meters) north every year to mark the changing location of the Arctic Circle.

Grimsey's stone Arctic Circle marker. Photo by Andrii Gladii, CC by SA 4.0.

In 1908, Frederick A. Cook claimed to have reached the North Pole. Since it is at sea, there is no way to mark the achievement with a flag or marker. A year later, Matthew Peary claimed to have reached the North Pole.

Peary disputed Cook's claim, calling him a fraud who never made it to the North Pole at all. Peary was backed by the New York Times and the National Geographic Society. He has generally, but never officially, been credited as the first to reach the North Pole. But was he?

This is a photograph of Peary's team at the North Pole in 1909.

Read an article online about each man and then discuss who you think was actually the first to the North Pole.

Fabulous Fact

Polar bears are carnivores that mostly eat seals they hunt from the pack ice.

Their skin is actually black and their hairs are hollow and translucent. The clear hair reflects the light.

jump from one to the other across the "sea." Set them up so that you can travel from one side of the room to the other. You may need to tape them down with masking tape.

3. Take turns asking each other questions from the books or videos about the Arctic. Each time the player answers correctly, he or she gets to move to a new ice floe. If you make it across the "sea," you win.

☺☺EXPLORATION: Polar Bears
For this activity, you will need:

- Book or video about polar bears from the Library List or YouTube playlist
- Blue card stock
- White paint
- Cotton balls
- Black felt or black card stock
- School glue or craft glue
- Googly eyes
- Scissors
- Fork

Polar bears live in the Arctic, including in Canada, Alaska, Russia, and Greenland, as well as on the sea ice of the Arctic Ocean. They have thick layers of fat under their skin to keep them warm. Short guard hairs underneath the longer fur provide a thick winter coat which is partially shed during the warm summer months. Their feet are large and have short, sharp claws that grip the ice. Polar bears are excellent swimmers, sometimes swimming for days at a time to reach their destinations.

They are classified as marine mammals because so much of their lives are spent on the Arctic Ocean. Some of that time is spent swimming, but the sea ice they walk on is also classified as ocean. They are the only bear species to be classified as a marine animal.

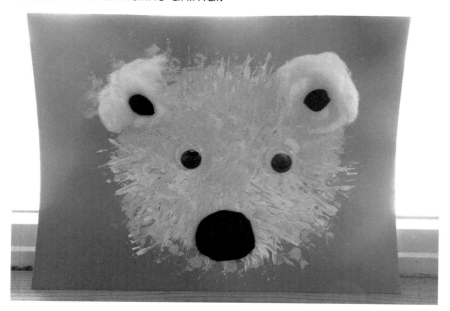

1. Read a book or watch a video about polar bears.

2. Squirt some white paint in the center of a sheet of blue card stock paper. Use a cotton ball to dab the paint around the paper to make a round polar bear head. Use a fork and a bit more paint around the edges of the white painted space to make shaggy hairs.

3. Glue wiggly eyes to the middle of the face.

4. Cut a large circle out of black felt and glue it to the bottom of the circle as a nose. Then, tease apart a cotton ball, divide it in half, and glue it to the top left and right of the circle to be ears. Glue small black felt circles to the center of the ears.

5. While the painting is drying, write a narration about polar bears on a sheet of paper. Glue your polar bear narration to the back of the polar bear picture you made.

6. Share your art and your report with an audience, then display it on the wall until the end of this unit.

People of the Arctic

Nobody really lives south of the Antarctic Circle, but scientists have permanent bases there and ecotourists visit Antarctica in the summer months. There's even a marathon held in Antarctica every year. However, people really do live above the Arctic Circle in the north. Some of these

On the Web

Visit Polar Bears International online to see their web tracker.

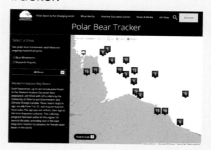

Some polar bears have been fitted with collars that track the movements of the bears. It helps researchers understand polar bear habitats, movements, and changes in their patterns.

Additional Layer

People of the Arctic in North America really did and do build igloos as shelters during travel or while on hunting trips.

Read a book or watch a video to learn more about igloos.

Then, if you have snow, go outside and build your own igloo or snow fort.

Famous Folks

Suersaq, aka Hans Hendrik, was an Arctic explorer from Greenland. He joined his first expedition at the age of 18 as an expert hunter, kayaker, and dog sled handler. Suersaq did it for the money and for the adventure, not to be first or reach an imaginary line on the globe.

After he married Maqu, he always took her and his children on expeditions with him. One time, they were stranded on sea ice for six months with a newborn baby until a whaler rescued them.

Suersaq's skills saved the expeditions he was on over and over as he tracked the trails of lost men, found food for starving men, and built igloos to shelter freezing men.

Writer's Workshop

In history, a primary source is from someone who was there at the *time*. In geography, a primary source is from someone who was in the *place*. Write a primary source description of a place you live in or have visited.

groups include the Inuit of North America, the Sami of Scandinavia, and the Yugyt and Nenet of Siberia. In the past, these people were all nomadic, living largely off the sea. Today, many of them have moved into towns in the far north. How do people survive in places that are so cold year round?

🙂 🙂 **EXPLORATION: Diorama of People in the Far North**

For this activity, you will need:

- Book or video about the Inuit, Sami, Yugyt, Yupik, or Nenets people
- Shoe box
- White spray paint
- Cotton balls
- Paper and other craft supplies

1. Choose one of the groups of people who live in the far north and read a book or watch a video about them.

2. Spray paint a shoe box, inside and out, white.

3. Create a diorama that showcases their lifestyle and environment. Show a home, a survival technique, a modern town, a hunting camp, or a group working together. You can also add things that live or exist within their habitat.

4. Present your diorama to a group, explain what you learned, and tell how the people are the same as you and how they are different.

5. Display your project until the end of this unit.

☺ ☺ ☺**EXPLORATION: Inukshuk**

WARNING: This activiy uses a hot glue gun. Be careful!

For this activity, you will need:

- Video about inukshuk from the YouTube playlist
- Rocks, smaller than a fist and cleaned
- Cardboard
- Hot glue and glue gun
- World Explorer Journal

The Inuit of Canada and Greenland build stone cairns, or inuksuit (plural form), that traditionally were used for navigation or as markers of hunting trails or food caches. They were also built in long avenues that the people could herd caribou through, funneling them into a dead end against a hillside where the animals could be killed for their meat and hides. Today they are symbols of Inuit culture. The word inukshuk means "one who looks like a person" and the cairns are often, though not always, vaguely person-shaped with arms and a head and sometimes legs.

1. Watch a video about inukshuk.

2. Discuss: why would the Inuit use stacked stones as markers in the Arctic?

3. Build an inukshuk out of rocks. Glue it to a cardboard base with hot glue. Young kids should have help from an older sibling or adult.

4. Show your inukshuk off to an audience and explain who made them and why.

5. Display your inukshuk until the end of this unit. Add an illustration and entry in your World Explorer of your project.

On the Web

Frozen Planet, a 2011 BBC documentary, is about the Arctic and Antarctic environments.

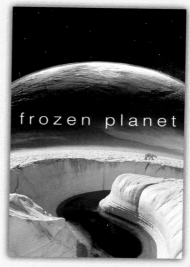

You can rent it from online streaming services including YouTube, Prime Video, and Netflix.

Watch it with the whole family in the evening with some snacks and blankets.

Additional Layer

In 1958, the USS Nautilus, the world's first nuclear-powered submarine, was ordered to travel across the Arctic Ocean under the North Pole.

It was a difficult journey because compasses don't work at the North Pole and there was a risk that the sub could become lost and be stuck under the pack ice.

Learn more about the historic voyage.

Arctic people across the north have hunted and herded caribou or reindeer throughout history.

Learn more about these animals and the people who depend on them.

Greenland's southern coast is green in summer. The land is covered with grass, ferns, and flowers. Learn more.

The biggest city in the Arctic is Murmansk, Russia, established in 1916 as a port. Because of the warm North Atlantic Current, the port is ice free all year. During the Cold War, the population grew but has been in steep decline since 1990.

☺ ☺ ☺ EXPLORATION: Arctic Lifestyle

For this activity, you will need:

- Book or video about the Arctic
- Internet to access Google Earth
- World Explorer Journal

1. Read a book or watch a video about people who live above the Arctic Circle.

2. As a group, make a list of the things the people do because of their Arctic biome. Think about homes, food, clothing, occupation, social customs, and leisure time.

3. Go to Google Earth and explore the Arctic. Look for towns in the Arctic. Observe road and transportation systems as well as the buildings.

4. In your World Explorer Journal, write a definition for "Arctic" and a paragraph about the things people do to survive and enjoy their Arctic homeland.

☺ ☺ ☺ EXPLORATION: Map of Arctic People

For this activity, you will need:

- "Arctic People" from the Printable Pack
- Colored pencils
- Scissors
- Glue stick
- Internet

The Inuit, Yupik, Sami, Nenets, Yakut, and Scandinavians are just a few of the people groups who live in the Arctic. These people have learned how to keep warm, how to find food, and how to endure the long dark winters. They have joyful, colorful lives with songs, stories, close family ties, and a strong sense of community, at least partly fostered by their difficult environment.

1. On the "Arctic People" map, color in the city dots with red.

2. Choose one or more of the cities or settlements and look up information about it online or watch a video. Pay attention to the things the people in the town have to do to protect against the cold. Look for at least one way they make their world brighter and more fun.

3. Label Greenland, Russia, Canada, Alaska USA, Finland, Sweden, Norway, and Iceland on the map. Use a student atlas if you need help. Color each country a different color.

4. Label the dot in the center "North Pole." This is the

geographic North Pole, around which the planet rotates.

5. Label the Arctic Ocean and any other seas you would like to, then color the water light blue.

6. Color each of the pictures of people at the bottom of the page. Then, cut them out. Glue the Yupik into square 1, the Sami into square 2, the Nenets into square 3, the Inuit into square 4, the Yakut into square 5, and the Scandinavians into square 6. They are on the map in roughly the area where they live.

7. Do a bit of online research about each of these groups as you add them to your map to learn more about them. Try to spot similarities between the groups as well as a few things that make them unique.

8. Share your map and what you learned.

9. Put the map into your Layers of Learning Notebook in the Geography section.

Arctic People

An Inuit man with a narwhal head and tusk. In his hand, he holds the harpoon he shot the whale with.

Both of these whales spend their whole lives in Arctic waters.

Find out more about these whales.

Step 3: Show What You Know

During this unit, choose one of the assignments below to show what you have learned during the unit. Add this work to your Layers of Learning Notebook. You can also use this assignment to show your supervising teacher or your charter school as a sample of what you've been working on in your homeschool, if needed.

Famous Folks

Learn more about one of these famous polar explorers:

- Sir James Clark Ross
- Sir Ernest Shackleton
- Fridtjof Nansen
- Robert Peary
- Sir John Franklin
- Erik the Red
- Sir Edmund Hillary
- Richard Weber

Unit Trivia Questions

1. Name the five major biomes.

   Polar, forest, grassland, desert, and aquatic

2. What is the literal meaning of the word Arctic?

   Of the bear

3. Who was the first person we know of to reach the South Pole?

   Roald Amundsen of Norway

4. Which is colder on average - the North Pole or the South Pole?

   The South Pole

5. What is the only bear species that is classified as a marine mammal?

   Polar bear

6. Which kind of forests are in the far north or high in the mountains where it is very cold in the winter and rainfall is adequate?

   a) Tropical rainforests

   b) Temperate forests

   c) Boreal forest

7. True or false - There are days in the Arctic when the sun doesn't set.

   True. This also happens in Antarctica.

8. Which of the following species would you NOT find in the Arctic?

   a) Polar bears

   b) Penguins

   c) Snowy owls

   d) Seals

There are more ideas for writing assignments in the "Writer's Workshop" sidebars.

😊 😊 **Coloring or Narration Page**

For this activity, you will need:

- "Polar Regions" printable from the Printable Pack
- Writing or drawing utensils

1. Depending on the age and ability of the child, choose either the "Polar Regions" coloring sheet or the "Polar Regions" narration page from the Printable Pack.

2. Younger kids can color the coloring sheet as you review some of the things you learned about during this unit. On the bottom of the coloring page, kids can write a sentence about what they learned. Very young children can explain their ideas orally while a parent writes for them.

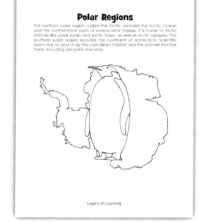

3. Older kids can write about some of the concepts you learned on the narration page and color the picture as well.

4. Add this to the Geography section of your Layers of Learning Notebook.

😊 😊 😊 **Poles Comparison Lapbook**

For this activity, you will need:

- Card stock
- "Arctic" and "Antarctica" clip art printable (optional)
- Glue, scissors, crayons, or other art supplies
- File folder or hole punch (optional)

1. Create a lapbook with one page about the Arctic and the facing page about Antarctica, comparing the two. You can draw pictures, write facts, or glue in clip art from the Printable Pack. Design your pages however you'd like to show the comparison between the two polar regions of the earth.

2. Glue each page into a file folder to create a lapbook, or hole punch the pages so they create a spread inside the Geography section of your Layers of Learning Notebook.

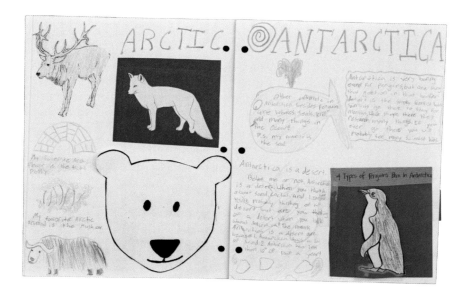

☺ ☺ ☺**Big Book of Knowledge**
For this activity, you will need:

- "Big Book of Knowledge: Polar Regions" printable from the Printable Pack, printed on card stock
- Writing or drawing utensils
- Big Book of Knowledge

1. Color, draw on, or write on the Big Book of Knowledge page. Record concepts, definitions, and facts you learned during this unit. It's a record of the things you learned and hope to remember. Add the page to your Big Book of Knowledge.

2. Use your Big Book of Knowledge regularly to help you review, quiz, or create games that will help you commit the things you've learned to memory.

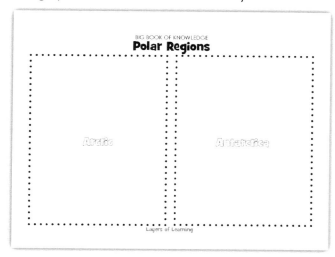

Big Book of Knowledge

The Big Book of Knowledge is a book for you, the mentor, to use as a constant review of all of the things you're learning about. You can use it to quiz your kids or prepare tests or review games. Whenever you learn something in Layers of Learning that you want your kids to remember, add it to your Big Book of Knowledge.

Assemble your Big Book of Knowledge in a binder or with binder rings. Divide it into sections for each subject.

In the Printable Pack for this unit you will find a "Big Book of Knowledge" sheet. You can add this sheet to others you collect or create yourself as you progress through the Layers of Learning curriculum. Customize the Big Book of Knowledge to your family by adding facts and topics that you enjoyed exploring as you were learning.

Visit Layers of Learning online to find more information on how to assemble and use your own Big Book of Knowledge.

You will also find cover and section pages to print along with creative games to play with your Big Book of Knowledge to keep school, even the tests, fun!

OCEANS

Oceans cover approximately 71% of the earth's surface. They are essential to all life on Earth as they are the source of most of the oxygen, most of the carbon dioxide, all of the water, much of the food, and a pleasant global climate. They are also the place where, by far, most living things on Earth find a home. We have probably only discovered a tiny fraction of the species that live in the oceans.

There is really just one big ocean on the earth but, for convenience, people divide the water into geographical regions of oceans, bays, gulfs, and seas. The five biggest divisions are the Pacific Ocean, Atlantic Ocean, Indian Ocean, Southern Ocean, and Arctic Ocean. They are all connected to each other. Under the surface, there are plains, valleys, mountains, volcanoes, canyons, cliffs, and deep rifts. Most of the ocean is unexplored territory, and human beings are only at the beginning of understanding the intricacies and wonder of the oceans.

The oceans are also a source of many of the things that people use to survive and make life pleasant. Fish, salt, copper, nickle, sand, gravel, oil, and natural gas are all important resources that come from the ocean. Everything that people use originally comes from the earth. Plastic, paper, gasoline, furniture, clothing, and food are all made from things harvested on Earth. We call the products we harvest from the earth natural resources. Their distribution on land and in the sea affects human prosperity and well-being across the world. The way we harvest them also affects human well-being.

Step 1: Library List

Choose books from your library that go with this topic. Here's a list of some favorites and also a list of search terms so you can utilize what your library offers. Read the books with your kids and/or assign them some to read independently. It is from these books your kids will learn most of the facts they need from this unit.

Search for: natural resources, oceans, coastlines, ocean animals, marine life

☺ ☺ ☺*Geography of the World* from DK. During this unit, read pages 76-77, 202-203, and 264-265. You'll learn a bit about some of our Earth's oceans.

☺ ☺ ☺*DK Student Atlas*. During this unit, read the small section about oceans on page 17.

☺ ☺ ☺*Ocean!* from DK and Smithsonian. This fat, illustrated encyclopedia includes topics such as how the oceans formed, ocean currents, tides, food chains, Sargasso Sea, kelp forests, horseshoe crabs, shipwrecks, mangrove forests, sea ice, orca whales, oil rigs, silt fishing, and dozens more.

☺ ☺ ☺*Ocean: A Visual Encyclopedia* from DK and Smithsonian. Lots of visuals accompanied by the sweet spot of text.

☺ ☺ ☺*Bill Nye the Science Guy Ocean Exploration*. This is an excellent video for your whole family to watch about oceans. Also look for *Ocean Life* and *Oceanography*.

☺*How Deep Is the Ocean?* by Kathleen Weidner Zoehfeld. Fun illustrations and simple text about the creatures, the water pressure, and the darkness of the deep ocean.

☺*Our Natural Resources* by Jennifer Overend Prior. This is a basic look at what natural resources are, how people use them, and how people should use them wisely.

☺*Ocean Animals For Kids: A Junior Scientist's Guide to Whales, Sharks, and Other Marine Life* by Bethanie and Josh Hestermann. This book has chapters on the ocean, marine mammals and seabirds, fish, marine reptiles, and marine invertebrates. Colorful pictures and fairly hefty text.

☺*The Magic School Bus On the Ocean Floor* by Joanna Cole. This is part of the original series, which means it is charming with Bruce Degan's illustrations and absolutely packed with information while still being entertaining. Learn about hot water vents, coral reefs, and animals.

Family School Levels

The colored smilies in this unit help you choose the correct levels of books and activities for your child.

☺ = Ages 6-9
☺ = Ages 10-13
☺ = Ages 14-18

On the Web

For videos, web pages, games, and more to add to this unit, visit the People & Planet Resources at Layers-of-Learning.com.

You will find a link to video playlists, web links, and more.

Bookworms

If you're looking for a family read-aloud, we'd like to suggest this one.

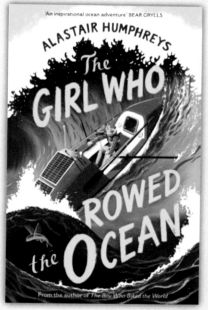

The Girl Who Rowed the Ocean by Alastair Humphreys is about Lucy, a girl who decides to cross the Atlantic in a rowboat. Will she survive the storms, seasickness, loneliness, and close encounters with danger?

Memorization Station

Natural resources: materials that people harvest from the earth

☺ *Coral Reefs* by Kristin Rattini. A National Geographic Reader with beautiful illustrations.

☺ ☺ *Explore Natural Resources!* by Anita Yasuda. This book has chapters on air, water, soil, minerals, energy, and conservation. It is filled with cute black and white illustrations and hands-on projects.

☺ ☺ *Finding Out About Coal, Oil, and Natural Gas* by Matt Doeden. Explains why we use these fuels for energy, where they come from, and how harvesting and using these resources affects the environment.

☺ ☺ *Atlas of Ocean Adventures* by Emily Hawkins. Divided into sections by ocean, this book has two-page spreads that each highlight a different ocean animal.

☺ *Marine Resources* by John Parritano. This book explores which natural resources are found in the oceans and how people are not being careful about using them. This is part of the "North American Natural Resources" series.

☺ *Ultimate Ocean-pedia* by National Geographic Kids. This book is excellent because it covers everything from the size and breadth of the oceans to the life that lives in them.

☺ *Ocean: The Definitive Visual Guide* by DK. This covers everything about the oceans from the chemistry of sea water and surface currents to bacteria and sea grass. Visual, informative, and highly browsable.

☺ *Soundings: The Story of the Remarkable Woman Who Mapped the Ocean Floor* by Hali Felt. This is a biography of Maria Tharp, who took all the data scientists had been collecting and analyzed it and drew maps of what the ocean floor really looked like.

☺ *The Deep* by Claire Nouvian. Combining photos with essays by renowned marine scientists, this book explores life and ecology of the deep, dark parts of the ocean.

Step 2: Explore

Choose hands-on Explorations from this section to work on as a family. They should be appealing activities that will create mental hooks so your kids remember the information in the unit. Save the rest of the Explorations for the next time you do this unit in four years when your kids are older. You can also read the sidebars together and explore some little rabbit trails.

This unit includes printables. See the introduction for instructions on retrieving your Printable Pack.

Natural Resources

☺ ☺ ☺**EXPLORATION: Natural Resources 4 in a Row**

For this activity, you will need:

- "Natural Resources" and "Natural Resources 4 in a Row" from the Printable Pack
- Colored pencils or crayons
- Scissors
- Markers like coins, beans, or tokens
- World Explorer Journal

Everything we use comes from the earth, and we use nearly everything the earth provides. Food, lumber, paper, plastics, metals, fuel, and clothing all come from the earth. We call the things the earth provides **natural resources**.

1. Color the "Natural Resources" pictures. As you color, discuss these things:

   a. What is a natural resource?

   b. How do we use each of these natural resources? What things are made from each of these? (If you don't know, look them up online.)

2. Cut apart the natural resource cards.

3. Place natural resources on a "Natural Resources 4 in a Row" game board.

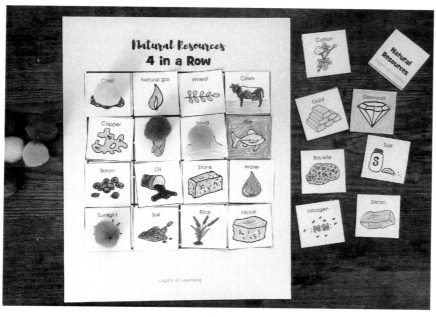

4. The mentor then calls out a natural resource. If it is on the game board, cover it with a marker. The first person to get 4 in a row wins.

Additional Layer

This unit is full of topics that are easy to find in the children's nonfiction section of the library. Take your kids to the library and let them find their own books about oceans and ocean animals to explore. Once your kids have found some books that interest them, give them a chance to put on the teacher's hat. They will learn about their topic and then teach everyone else what they learned.

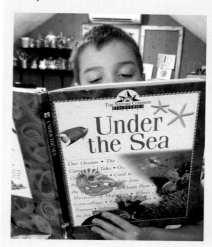

Additional Layer

Draw a line down the center of a piece of poster board or a white board, creating two columns. At the top of one, write, "Natural" and at the top of the other, write "Man-made." Take turns drawing or writing resources that belong in one of the two columns.

Natural	Manmade
sand wood water	concrete plastic
salt	soap paper
cotton	polyester
coal organic oils	light bulb
iron	nylon
silk	glass
fish flowers	synthetic rubber

Renewable resource: a natural material used by humans that replenishes itself quickly after use

Non-renewable resource: a resource that cannot be readily replaced by natural means at a pace fast enough to keep up with consumption

Flow resource: a resource that will always exist but that moves because of the natural physical environment and is not always available in all places at all times

Fabulous Fact

Water is considered a renewable resource, but running water is a flow resource. We can harness energy from running water in hydroelectric dams or using waterwheels.

Deep Thoughts

What can you do in your home to help conserve non-renewable resources and renew those resources that are renewable?

Do you turn off lights when you aren't using them? Do you recycle? What things do you do as a family and what could you be better at doing?

5. To make the game harder, require the player to name something the natural resource is used for before covering it on the board. Play as many times as you would like.

6. Write the definition of a natural resource in the middle of a page of your World Explorer Journal. Glue some or all of the natural resource cards around the definition.

☺ ☺ ☻EXPLORATION: Renewable, Non-Renewable, & Flow

For this activity, you will need:

- Videos about renewable and non-renewable resources from this unit's YouTube playlist
- "Three Types of Natural Resources" from the Printable Pack
- Drawing or coloring utensils

Natural resources can be divided into three groups: renewable resources, non-renewable resources, and flow resources.

Renewable resources are those that can be replaced relatively quickly. Timber, animals, plants, and water are all renewable. They can be renewed if we use them responsibly. There are lots of animal and plant species that are now extinct because we weren't responsible. Think of a forest. If we cut down all of the trees, no new trees will grow there. However, if we use selective harvesting and just cut down some of them, the existing trees will continue to grow new trees. We can also help the process along by planting new seedling trees. Using our renewable resources responsibly means we will continue to have those resources in the future.

Some resources cannot be replaced once they are used. Coal, oil, and natural gas are three commonly used **non-renewable resources**. We can't just get more coal once we use it up. When it's gone, it's gone. Fossil fuels, minerals, metals, and other materials that are mined from the earth are also non-renewable. We rely on many of these things, but once they're gone, they're gone.

Flow resources are resources that are inexhaustible. We can't run out of them, but they can only be used when they're available. We can use solar energy when the sun is shining but we can't collect it at nighttime. We can harness power from the wind but not on a calm day. If we can store flow resources, we may be able to use them at other times. If I collect energy using solar panels, I can store it and use it at night even after the sun has set. Running water, wind, and sunlight are all flow resources.

1. Watch videos about resources to learn about the differences between renewable, non-renewable, and flow resources.

2. Fill in the boxes on the "Three Types of Natural Resources" printable with examples of each kind of resource. You can write words or draw pictures of each. Here are a few to get you started:

   Renewable = Tree, fish, water, flowers, bears, lions, mushrooms, any plants or animals

   Non-renewable = coal, oil, petroleum, natural gas, metal ores, steel, diamonds, minerals

   Flow = solar power (solar panel), wind (windmill), running water (hydroelectric dam or waterwheel)

3. Add the chart to the Geography section of your Layers of Learning Notebook.

☺ ☻EXPLORATION: How Is It Made?

For this activity, you will need:

- Any item from your home
- Internet
- PowerPoint or other digital slideshow program

Sometimes we take things for granted so much that we don't even think about where they actually come from or how they are made.

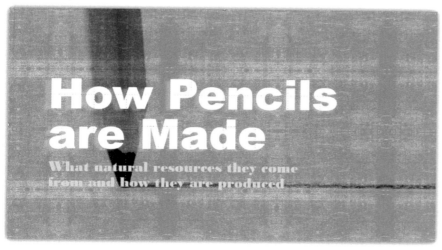

1. Pick any object from your home. Research online how it is made. What natural resources are used in the object and in the process of making the object?

2. Create a simple slideshow presentation that has several slides that include these details:

Bookworms

Gail Gibbons has written lots of great books about oceans. Here are a few to look for:

Memorization Station

Ocean: a continuous body of saltwater that is contained in an enormous basin on Earth's surface

On the Web

You can find tons of fun ocean crafts and activities online. Look for ocean animal puppets, dot-to-dots, puzzles, greeting cards, sun catchers, painting projects, and more. Spend an afternoon just crafting together and enjoying an ocean movie playing in the background.

Writer's Workshop

After learning about oil and off-shore drilling, do a quick write and answer these questions:

- Would you want to live or work on an oil rig?
- Why or why not?
- Have you ever thought about the people who get our oil when your family is heating your home or buying fuel or oil for your car?

- A description of the item with a picture of it
- A list of the natural resources used to make the item
- A step-by-step description of how it is made

3. Make sure to add a title slide and add fun transitions, clear fonts, and colorful elements to your presentation.

4. Present your slideshow to an audience and explain how your item is made and what natural resources were used to make it.

☺ ☺ ☺ EXPLORATION: Resources From the Ocean

For this activity, you will need:

- Magazines
- Internet
- Poster board or piece of card stock
- Scissors
- Glue
- Markers

Humans collect an impressive range of natural resources from the **ocean**. These resources are vital to our economy and well being. From fish for eating to kelp for toothpaste, we depend on the oceans for a whole lot of the things we use in our lives. Ice cream, salad dressing, cancer fighting drugs, shampoo, lotion, salt, sponges, many beauty products, and lots more items wouldn't exist without the ingredients they include that come from the oceans.

1. Do a bit of research online and find out what things you use that have ingredients that come from the oceans.

2. Make a collage poster showing some of the resources we obtain from the ocean. You can draw pictures, cut

them from magazines, or find images from the internet to print out.

3. Present your poster to an audience and describe each thing you included and what it uses that comes from the ocean.

☺ ☺EXPLORATION: Off-Shore Drilling
For this activity, you will need:

- Video from this unit's YouTube playlist about off-shore drilling
- Internet

The crust under the oceans is much thinner than the continental crust, making it an ideal site for drilling for gas and oil. Known reserves of oil and gas have been found along nearly every coast of every continent all over the world. Oil and gas also naturally leak from vents in the ocean floor all the time.

Giant oil rigs with huge drills can be found off the shores of many continents. They use huge drills to extract oil from underneath the ground.

1. Watch a video about how off-shore oil drilling works and see the process in action.

2. Search online for at least two articles about off-shore oil drilling. Read one about the pros of off-shore drilling and one about the cons. You might search for "benefits of off-shore drilling" and "dangers of off-shore drilling."

3. Write a narration about some of the benefits and dangers of off-shore drilling. Include one paragraph about the benefits, one paragraph about the dangers, and a final paragraph about your opinion of off-shore drilling.

Oceans, Bays, & Seas

☺ ☺ ☺EXPLORATION: Map of the Oceans
For this activity, you will need:

- "Earth's Oceans" from the Printable Pack (or the smaller version found within the World Explorer Journal)
- Book or video about oceans from the Library List or YouTube playlist
- Atlas (optional)
- Colored pencils or crayons
- Black pen for labeling

Additional Layer
Use the blank "Earth's Oceans" map from the Printable Pack and show the known off-shore oil deposits and major areas of drilling in the ocean.

This map shows the known petroleum resources in the world. Each of the numbers is in billions of barrels. Use it to help you complete your map or look up "oil deposits map" online.

Search online and find out how many offshore drilling rigs there are that drill in these areas currently.

Memorization Station
Memorize the names and locations of each of the earth's oceans. This little song, sung to the tune of "Frère Jacques" can help you:

There are five,
There are five,
Oceans, oceans.
Pacific and Atlantic
Indian and Arctic
Southern too,
Southern too.

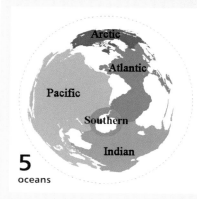

Bookworms

The Ocean Calls by Tina Cho is a picture book about a child who wants to be just like her grandmother. Grandmother is a haenyo diver who gathers treasures from the sea floor.

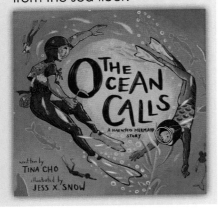

Famous Folks

Jacques Cousteau was a French oceanographer who invented the first Aqua-Lung, an open circuit SCUBA. Using it, he produced some amazing underwater documentaries and brought the underwater world of the ocean to many who had never been able to personally explore it before.

There are five oceans on earth: Pacific, Atlantic, Arctic, Indian, and Southern. The oceans all run together, of course, and the boundaries are somewhat arbitrary. Defining and naming different oceans makes it easier to talk about where something is and to categorize places.

Oceans cover about 71% of the earth's surface. The oceans provide over half of the oxygen we breathe, most of which comes from tiny plants like phytoplankton, kelp, and algal plankton. Amazingly, about 94% of all of life on Earth has the ocean as its home, including around a million different species of animals. The biggest living structure on Earth, the Great Barrier Reef, is also found within the ocean. In addition, the oceans help us regulate our climate, so without them, life on land could never be the same.

Earth's Oceans

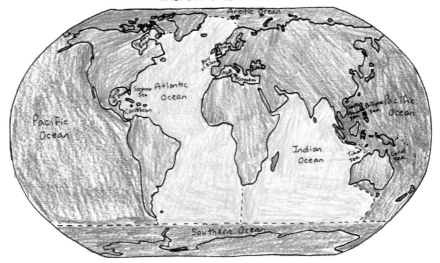

1. Read a book or watch a video about the oceans.

2. Label each of the five oceans on the "Earth's Oceans" map. Try to do it from memory, but use an atlas if you need to. You can use the small map in your World Explorer Journal or the larger map from the Printable Pack.

3. Kids 10 and up can also label five seas, gulfs, or bays. Teens 14 and up can label ten additional seas, gulfs, or bays.

4. Color the oceans each a different shade of blue.

5. Color the land light brown.

6. Put the map in your Layers of Learning Notebook in the Geography section.

☺ ☺ ☺ EXPLORATION: Ocean in a Bottle

For this activity, you will need:

- Transparent bottle with a narrow neck and a lid (a 2-liter soda bottle works well)
- Funnel
- Water
- Blue food coloring
- Mineral spirits (often found in the painting section of a grocery or home improvement store) or baby oil (found in the baby section of stores)
- Hot glue gun and hot glue (optional)
- Books or video about the waves or the ocean from the Library List or YouTube playlist

The oceans of the earth are not still. Energy is constantly passing through the oceans. The **waves** we see in the ocean are actually moving energy, not water that is traveling long distances. Most ocean waves are caused by wind that is blowing across the surface of the water. Severe weather, like hurricanes, can cause **storm surges** that are deeper waves that intensify near land. Some waves are also caused by geologic events, like underwater volcanoes, earthquakes, or landslides. Events like these can create huge waves called **tsunamis**. Another cause of ocean waves is the gravitational pull of both the sun and the moon. These waves are called **tides**. With all of these forces acting on them, oceans are never completely still.

1. First, fill the bottle halfway with water. Add a few drops of blue food coloring and swirl it around until it mixes.

2. Using a funnel, add mineral spirits up to the top of the bottle. Put the lid on tightly. (You may want to put a little hot glue around the rim if you're worried about it leaking.)

3. Rock the bottle on its side gently to create a wave that goes back and forth.

Writer's Workshop

Write shape poems about oceans. Select a specific item, like a starfish, a seashell, a whale, a shark, or the waves and make your words follow the path of each item's outline as you describe it in the poem. You can even create several of them in one big ocean scene with lots of shape poems.

Memorization Station

Waves: a raised movement of water rolling across the surface of the sea

Storm surge: the abnormal rise of water generated by a storm, over and above the normal tides

Tsunami: a long high sea wave caused by an earthquake, underwater landslide, or another disturbance under the surface of the water

Tide: the rising and falling of the sea due to the gravitational pull of the sun and moon, usually twice in each lunar day at a particular place

Fabulous Facts

- Water covers 71 percent of the world's surface.
- If you could weigh ocean water, it would weigh 1.45 trillion tons!!
- There are over one million species of known marine animals and many more yet to be discovered. Some scientists guess there may be as many as nine million more we haven't discovered yet!
- The ocean floor is covered with ridges, mountain ranges, and canyons.
- The blue whale is the largest mammal on the earth and has a heart the size of a Volkswagen Beetle.
- The Great Barrier Reef is 1,243 miles and is the largest living structure on Earth. You can see it from space.
- The ocean is like a treasure chest. It contains not only valuable minerals, but also minerals (like salt, magnesium, and gold), fish and other marine life that we eat, and oil that we depend on for fuel.

Fabulous Fact

The Bay of Fundy is a funnel-shaped inlet between Nova Scotia and New Brunswick, Canada. It is surrounded by tall cliffs that direct the rising tide waters into two narrow channels. Because of the way the waters are channeled into narrow areas, the bay experiences the highest tides in the world, about 16.5 meters or 53 feet.

4. Read a book or watch a video about the ocean or waves. Put your ocean in a bottle on display throughout this unit.

☺ ☺ EXPLORATION: Tides

For this activity, you will need:

- Video about tides from the YouTube playlist for this unit
- "Tides" printable from the Printable Pack
- Scissors
- Glue stick
- Thin markers
- World Explorer Journal

Tides are the overall rising and falling of sea levels at the shore. They are caused by a combination of the gravitational pull of the moon and the sun and the rotation of the earth. Most places have two high and two low tides in a day, but some places have only one set of tides. Some places have very dramatic tides, while others vary by only a few feet. The shape of the shoreline and the topography of the sea bed near the shore are the largest factors in determining how dramatic the tide in a certain place will be. Tides in a particular place can be higher or lower at certain seasons of the year depending on the positions of the sun and moon. Forecasting the time and amplitude of tides is a complicated science.

1. Watch videos about what causes the tides. There is no one simple thing that is the cause of our tides, but the moon plays the biggest role.

2. Cut out the two pictures of Earth, including the water surrounding it, from the "Tides" printable. Can you identify which one shows what the water on Earth would be like without a moon? Which one shows the changing tidal water levels because we do have a moon? Glue each one into your World Explorer Journal and label which one depicts an Earth with no moon and which one shows our Earth's water bulge with a moon.

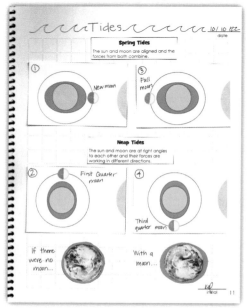

3. As the moon orbits

around the earth, we see only the parts of it that are illuminated by the sun. Cut out the two descriptions and the four diagrams of Earth and color in the moon on each orbit, making the part facing the sun yellow (because it is lit up by the sun) and the part away from the sun dark. Label each moon phase according to what we would see on Earth when the moon is in each position.

4. Sort the four diagrams by description. There are two spring tides shown and two neap tides. Talk about what you see in the diagrams as you glue them to a page of your World Explorer Journal.

☺ ☺ ☺EXPLORATION: Sea Trade Routes
For this activity, you will need:

- "Sea Trade Routes" from the Printable Pack
- Colored pencils
- Video about ocean trade routes from the YouTube playlist

The oceans have been instrumental to trade since ancient times. Today, huge ocean container ships, tankers, and barges sail the sea lanes of the world, carrying on trade between countries. Certain areas of the oceans have been designated as shipping lanes in order to reduce accidents between ships at sea. The shipping lanes are chosen as direct paths between two points but also because of prevailing currents and winds and to avoid dangerous shoals and reefs.

Sea Trade Routes

1. Color the main shipping routes on the printable "Sea Trade Routes" map. The thicker lines indicate greater volumes of sea trade.

2. Color the oceans blue.

Additional Layer

When oil spills happen within our oceans, they leave disastrous messes that are difficult to clean up and can harm plant and animal life in the area they spilled.

Surprisingly, more oil reaches the oceans each year in little bits from leaking automobiles and similar things than has ever spilled off of an oil tanker. When tankers leak, it looks dramatic because it's all in one place, but there are bits of oil being dripped in from other sources far more.

Even more interesting is that oil naturally escapes from vents in the ocean floor in far greater quantities than any disaster and more than all the man-made sources. Look up the numbers and create a graph showing where the oil in the oceans comes from.

Additional Layer

Learn about salinity and properties of sea water. You can also explore why saltwater fish can't live in freshwater and vice versa.

3. Name the oceans from memory.

4. Watch a video about ocean trade routes.

5. Put the "Sea Trade Routes" map in the Geography section of the your Layers of Learning Notebook.

☺ ☺ ☺**EXPLORATION: Ocean Currents**
For this activity, you will need:

- "Ocean Currents" and answers from the Printable Pack
- Colored pencils
- Video about ocean currents from the YouTube playlist

Ocean currents are the flow of water around the globe. Some of the currents within the oceans are right at the surface while others are deep under the sea. Currents on the surface are often caused by the prevailing winds, which are caused, in turn, by the rotation of the earth. Deep sea currents are caused by differences in the salinity and temperature of the water in the ocean. Surface water tends to be more saline than deeper

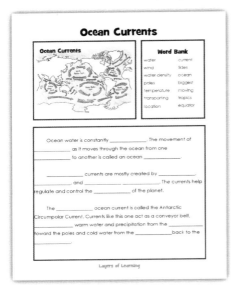

water because water that evaporates from the surface leaves behind salt. Sea surface temperatures as well as temperature differences between the equator and poles also cause water to flow in currents. Besides this, the effect of tides as well as the shape of continental shorelines also have an effect on currents.

The currents create giant loops. In the Northern Hemisphere, the loops travel clockwise. In the Southern Hemisphere, they travel counterclockwise. As the earth rotates, air is pushed from the equator to each pole, creating the circular movement of air. The currents help regulate the temperatures throughout our globe, so they are actually more useful than most people realize.

1. Watch a video about ocean currents from this unit's YouTube playlist.

2. Fill in the "Ocean Currents" printable.

3. Add your page to the Geography section of your Layers of Learning Notebook.

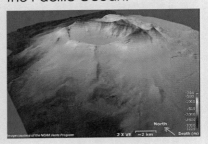

Ocean Floor & Coast

☺ ☺ ☺**EXPLORATION: The Ocean Floor**

For this activity, you will need:

- World Explorer Journal
- Crayons, colored pencils, or markers
- Book or video about the Ocean Floor (We highly recommend *The Magic School Bus on the Ocean Floor*.)
- "The Ocean Floor" from the Printable Pack
- Fine-tipped black pen
- Watercolor paints, brushes, and a water cup

The ocean floor is covered with mountains, valleys, plains, and other features similar to the land surfaces of the continents. The ocean floor's features, like the continental features, are a result of tectonic processes from deep inside the earth.

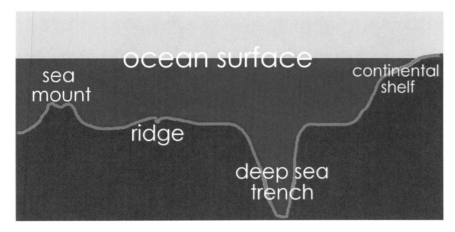

Ocean trenches are places in the earth's crust where one crustal plate is sinking under another. Where they meet, a deep crease is formed. The oceanic trenches are the deepest places on Earth. The deepest point we know of is called Challenger Deep and is in the Mariana Trench in the Pacific Ocean.

Continental shelves are where the continental plates rise from the deeper, thinner oceanic plates. The shelves are where human activity is mostly concentrated and where the fish we like to eat are mostly found. This is much shallower, warmer water. Along the edge of every continent is a continental shelf.

Ocean ridges are long, raised areas where two oceanic plates are pulling away from each other. In the center where they divide, magma wells up, creating new land.

Sea mounts are formed where hot spots under the ocean crust make undersea volcanoes or where ridges are pushed

---

Additional Layer

Not only did we not know until recently what was on the sea floor, we really didn't care. But the advent of both cross-oceanic telegraph cables and submarine warfare meant humans had an interest. Learn about the laying of the first trans-Atlantic cable and the myriad of experimentation and trial and error that had to be performed before it was possible.

Memorization Station

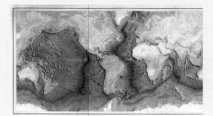

Ocean current: the continuous, predictable, directional movement of seawater caused by gravity, wind, and water density

Ocean trench: a long, narrow, deep depression in the ocean floor

Continental shelf: the area of seabed around a large landmass where the sea is relatively shallow compared with the open ocean

Ocean ridge: an elevated region or continuous chain of mountains on an ocean floor

Sea mount: an underwater mountain formed by volcanic activity that does not reach to the water's surface

Bookworms

The Girl Who Built an Ocean: An Artist, an Argonaut, and the True Story of the World's First Aquarium by Jess Keating is about Jeanne Villepreaux-Power, the first person to build an aquarium.

This is a picture book for ages 4 to 8.

Fabulous Fact

Sea mounts are some of the least understood, under mapped, and dangerous formations on the sea floor. They have caused many shipwrecks and submarine collisions. They often rest just below the surface, invisible to ships because they haven't quite emerged from the water's surface.

In addition, when there are underwater landslides, they have the potential to create huge tsunami waves.

up high enough to form mountain ranges. When they have grown enough, they form islands. The Hawaiian Islands are examples of hot spot sea mounts.

1. Start by drawing a diagram of each of the terms from this exploration in your World Explorer Journal. You can use the picture from this Exploration as an example. Older kids can also write the definitions of each of the terms.

2. Use watercolor paints to fill in "The Ocean Floor" printable. Use one color for the mountains, ridges, and higher elevation areas, marked with an upward V. Use another color for the basins, trenches, and low elevation areas found under the sea, marked with a downward V.

3. While the paint is drying, read a book, watch a video, or explore websites about the ocean floor together.

The Ocean Floor

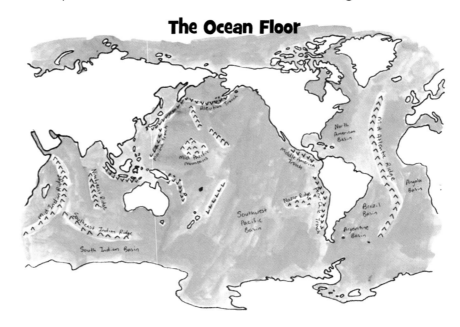

4. Label some of the major mountain ranges and trenches that can be found under the sea. Here is a list to add:

- Mariana Trench
- Aleutian Trench
- Tonga Trench
- Middle America Trench
- Peru-Chile Trench
- Puerto Rico Trench
- Mid-Atlantic Ridge
- Southwest Indian Ridge
- Mid-Indian Ridge
- Louisville Ridge
- Emperor Sea Mounts
- Mid-Pacific Mountains
- Nazca Ridge
- Ring of Fire

5. Add any other details you discover from books, websites, and videos you watch about the ocean floor.

6. Add the map to the Geography section of your Layers of Learning Notebook.

☺ ☺ ☺ **EXPLORATION: Coastal Formations**
For this activity, you will need:

- Book or video on coastal formations
- "Coastal Formations" from the Printable Pack
- Colored pencils or crayons
- Scissors
- Glue stick
- World Explorer Journal

The ocean waves pound the shore relentlessly, wearing it away and changing the shape of the land. This results in interesting and unique formations along coastlines including **sea caves**, **blowholes**, **faults**, sand or pebble **beaches**, **arches**, **stacks**, and **stumps**.

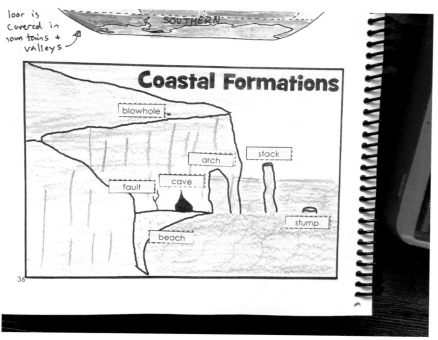

1. Read a book or watch a video about coastal formations. Take note of how the ocean waves create the formations found along coasts.

2. Color the "Coastal Formations" picture.

3. Cut out the word tags from the "Coastal Formations" printable. Glue each one in the correct places on the worksheet.

4. Cut out the rectangle on the solid lines and then glue the "Coastal Formations" into your World Explorer Journal.

5. Show your "Coastal Formations" picture to an audience and explain how each one is formed.

Memorization Station

Sea cave: a large hole formed in a cliff when waves erode the rock

Blowhole: when a sea cave grows into a vertical shaft leading to the land above

Fault: a crack in the earth between two rocks

Beach: a pebbly or sandy shore

Arch: natural bridge made of stone that is created when water wears away the underside of a rock

Stack: a column of rock standing in the sea, remaining after cliffs erode

Stump: a rock that juts just above the surface of the sea, formed when a tall sea stack erodes away

Writer's Workshop

Pretend you have spent the afternoon scuba diving on a coral reef. You don't want to forget one bit of the experience. Write about all that you saw and did as a simulated journal entry.

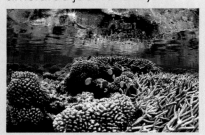

Expedition

If you have the chance, go to a rocky shore and explore the tide pools, the area of the shore which is underwater during the high tide and exposed at low tide. Tide pools are filled with interesting sea life.

Fabulous Fact

The largest mammal in the world lives in the ocean biome - the blue whale.

☺ ☺ ☺ **EXPLORATION: Sea and Coast Crossword Puzzle**

For this activity, you will need:

- "Sea & Coast Crossword Puzzle" from the Printable Pack

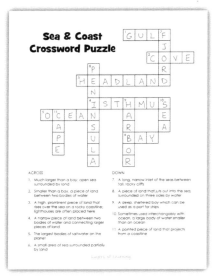

1. Use the clues to fill out the crossword puzzle as you learn the definitions of sea and coast features. You can work together as a family or give each person their own puzzle to solve.

2. Use a map or an atlas to find an example of each of these sea and coast formations.

3. Add it to the Geography section of your Layers of Learning Notebook.

   Across: (1) gulf (2) cove (3) headland (4) isthmus (5) ocean (6) bay

   Down: (7) fjord (8) peninsula (9) harbor (10) sea (11) cape

☺ ☺ **EXPLORATION: Ocean and Coastal Features**

For this activity, you will need:

- Large bowl
- 4 cups flour
- 1 1/2 cups water
- 4 cups sand
- 2 Tbsp. white glue
- Basin or plastic tote with water
- World Explorer Journal
- Crayons, colored pencils, or markers
- Internet

You can create your own ocean floor with coastal features using a batch of homemade sand dough.

1. In a large bowl, mix 4 cups of flour and 1 1/2 cups water together. Use your hands to knead it. It will be really sticky!

2. Add 4 cups of sand and continue to fold and knead it together.

3. Add 2 Tbsp. white glue to help your dough stick together a bit better. (You can adjust the consistency of your

dough by adding more flour, sand, or water as needed.)

4. Shape your dough into formations like valleys and sea arches in the ocean floor. You can also use the dough to shape other features. Here is a list of a few ideas you could look up online, learn about, and shape using your sand dough:

- Seafloor formations like valleys, sea arches, sea caves, stacks, stumps, ridges, and more.
- Island formations like archipelagos, atolls, barrier reefs, cays, deserted islands, or fringing reefs.
- Coastal features like capes, straits, bays, harbors, gulfs, or headlands.

5. Optionally, you can fill a basin with water and place your formations into the "ocean."

6. Take turns showing off your sculpted formations and see if others can identify what you made. You can practice naming them and learning the names.

7. Draw a picture of each of the formations you made in your World Explorer Journal and label them.

☺ ☺ EXPLORATION: Lighthouses

For this activity, you will need:

- Tall plastic container, like a yogurt carton or large cup
- Small plastic container, like a small yogurt cup
- Construction paper
- Glue
- Acrylic paints, brushes, and a water cup

A lighthouse is a tower or building that is built along the ocean's shore. They are usually located in places with rocky, dangerous shorelines, like **headlands**. They have shining lights at the top of the tower that act as a beacon

Additional Layer

People use coral reefs for recreation and fishing around the world. The economic value of the reefs is about $375 billion per year in U.S. dollars. Even though coral reefs have huge economic value, they are endangered in many parts of the world. Ocean pollution, over harvesting of tropical fish and coral, careless behavior of divers and shipping, plus natural phenomenon kill off huge swaths of reefs.

Memorization Station

Headland: a narrow piece of land that projects from a coastline into the sea

Writer's Workshop

Watch a movie that features a lighthouse like *Pete's Dragon* or *Captain January*.

After viewing, write a review of the movie. What did you like, not like, or think of the acting or story?

Writer's Workshop

Writer's Workshop

Make a list of some jobs people do that are related to the ocean. It could be anything from a lifeguard to a marine biologist or cruise ship captain.

Memorization Station

Lighthouses are often found atop headlands. Here's a little song to help you remember what a headland is. (To the tune of "Oh, My Darlin' Clementine")

I'm a headland, I'm a headland, I'm a headland, yes I am. Sitting high above the ocean, I'm a headland, yes I am.

Got a lighthouse, got a lighthouse, got a lighthouse right here. Right here I've got a lighthouse, got a lighthouse right here.

See for miles, see for miles, see for miles from the top. See for miles, see for miles, see for miles from the top.

I'm a headland, I'm a headland, I'm a headland yes I am. Sitting high above the ocean, I'm a headland, yes I am.

to help ships navigate and avoid dangerous coastlines, rocks, and reefs. They also mark the entrances to harbors.

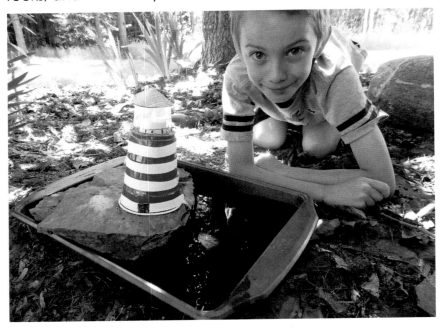

1. Make a model lighthouse. Use a tall plastic container, like a cottage cheese container as the base. Turn it upside down and cover it with construction paper or paint it. Look up some real lighthouses to see how they are designed and which colors to use.

2. Turn a small yogurt container upside down and glue it to the top to be the light. Paint or cover it in paper as well.

3. Discuss lighthouses.

    a. Why do you think a lighthouse would be placed on a headland or promontory of a rocky coast?

    b. The number of lighthouses has steadily decreased in recent years. Can you think of reasons they aren't being used as much anymore?

        (GPS and other electronic navigation systems have largely replaced them.)

    c. Lighthouse keepers are people who keep the lights burning at the top of the lighthouse. They often live inside of the lighthouse itself. Would you want that to be your job? Why or why not?

    d. Imagine your home at night if you had no lights at all. What would it be like? Can you imagine sailing the ocean at night without being able to see anything? Can you think of any reasons the boats couldn't accomplish the same thing as a lighthouse by just shining their own light around them at the water?

Ocean Life

☺ ☺ ☺**EXPLORATION: Ocean Zones**

For this activity, you will need:

- "Ocean Zones" from the Printable Pack, printed on blue paper
- Card stock
- Scissors
- Glue
- Markers
- World Explorer Journal
- Internet or books about ocean zones

Additional Layer
Look up some pictures of historic lighthouses online.

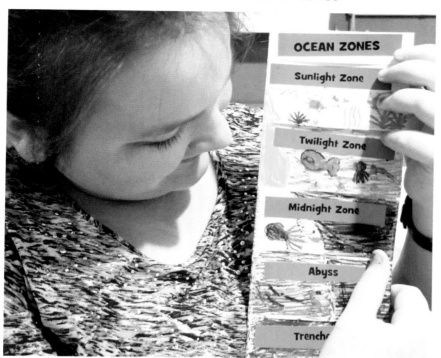

The ocean water column is made up of five different zones. Near the surface is the sunlight zone. As you get deeper and deeper, you pass through the twilight zone, the midnight zones, the abyss, and then the trenches. Because you are descending further under the surface, each zone gets deeper, darker, colder, and more full of pressure than the ones before. The plants and animals that live in the world's oceans have specific needs. You won't see the same species living in the sunlight zone that live in the trenches.

1. Cut out each "Ocean Zones" title.

2. Fold a sheet of card stock in half, the long way, hot dog-style, then draw a slope of land that travels steeply downward along the cover of your booklet, showing the depth of each zone.

3. Draw horizontal lines across the cover, dividing the

Fabulous Fact

The majority of the planet is covered by oceans, so it's not really surprising that a majority of life on Earth is aquatic. About 94% of animals live under the water.

Bookworms

Read about a hermit crab's life in a fascinating story called *Pagoo* by Holling C. Holling.

Fabulous Fact

There is about one cup of salt for every gallon of water in the ocean. If you'd like, you can add a cup of salt to a gallon of water in your kitchen to see what that's like. After you've added the salt, stir it in with a spoon and watch it dissolve.

Can you think of a way to get the salt back out of the water?

(Let it evaporate.)

How does this apply to the water cycle?

Memorization Station

Reef: a ridge of jagged rock, coral, or sand just above or below the surface of the sea

---

booklet cover into the title section and the zones.

4. Use markers to make each zone look darker than the one before as you travel downward.

5. Draw animals that live in each zone.

6. Cut the cover along each zone so you have flaps that open. Attach the titles of each zone to the booklet cover.

7. Inside of each section, write a little about each zone. Use the internet or books to research information.

8. Glue the back of your booklet directly on to the page of your World Explorer Journal, keeping the flaps free.

☺ ☺ EXPLORATION: Reef Diorama

For this activity, you will need:

- Book or video about coral reefs from the Library List or YouTube playlist
- World Explorer Journal
- Shoe box
- Colorful craft paints, brushes, and a water cup
- Sponges or sponge brushes
- Drawing paper and pens
- Ocean animal stickers, shells, or other decor (optional)
- Construction paper
- Scissors
- Glue
- Internet

A **reef** is a rock, sandbar, or biotic growth that is shallow enough for it to be a danger to ships. The type of reef most people think of is a coral reef, made up of tiny sea creatures which grow in colonies until they form huge structures. Coral reefs only thrive in warm, shallow waters, but other types of reefs can be found anywhere in the oceans.

1. Read or watch a video about coral reefs and take notes in your World Explorer Journal about some things you learned. You can also draw some illustrations to accompany your notes.

2. Make a coral reef diorama in a shoe box. Begin by painting the interior background of the shoe box blue. Paint the interior lower part of the back and the "floor" of the shoe box orange, yellow, green, and purple tones using a sponge for texture.

3. Finally, add in drawings of marine animals that are found near coral reefs. You can draw your own or use

ocean animal stickers. You can also add any plants, shells, or other things you might see at a reef.

4. Use an online world map to find and learn about each of these locations where some of the larger coral reefs on Earth are found:

- Great Barrier Reef
- Mesoamerican Barrier Reef System
- New Caledonia Barrier Reef
- Andros Bahamas Barrier Reef
- Red Sea fringing reefs
- Pulley Ridge
- Maldives reef system
- Raja Ampat Islands reefs

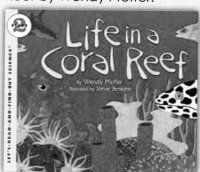
☺ ☺ EXPLORATION: An Ocean of Fish

For this activity, you will need:

- Book or video about fish
- World Explorer Journal
- Crayons, colored pencils, or markers
- White paper plates
- Scissors
- Tempera or acrylic paints, brushes, and a water cup
- Glue
- Wiggly eyes

1. Read a book about fish together. If possible, specifically read about saltwater fish that live in the ocean.

2. Draw some of the fish you read about and write some facts you learned about fish in your World Explorer Journal.

3. Use paper plates to craft some of your own colorful fish. Cut fins and a tail out of extra paper plates and attach them with glue. Paint each of your fish.

Famous Folks

Marie Tharp was an American geologist and marine cartographer who mapped the ocean floor. Her detailed underwater topography led to greater understanding about plate tectonics and continental drift.

This is Marie Tharp with some colleagues on the research vessel USNS Kane in 1968.

Additional Layer

Choose any ten marine animals to learn more about. Explore books, videos, and websites to learn about what makes them unique.

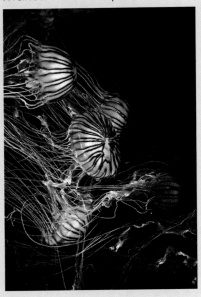

4. Once the paint has dried on your fish, glue on wiggly eyes. Hang your fish up to display them during this unit, and share a few of your favorite interesting facts you learned with a group. Describe one characteristic that makes fish unique from many other animals.

☺ ☺ ☺ **EXPLORATION: An Ocean of Information**

For this activity, you will need:

- Books about the ocean
- Large sheet of blue butcher paper or blue poster board
- "An Ocean of Information" from the Printable Pack,

printed several times onto several colors of card stock
- Scissors
- Glue sticks
- Markers

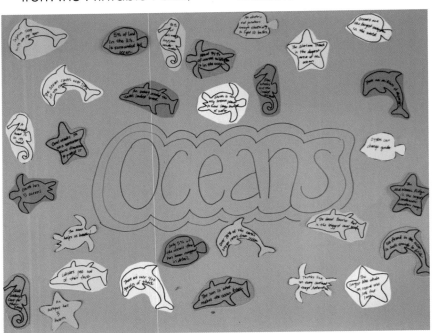

1. Start with a large piece of blue butcher paper attached to a wall or a large piece of blue poster board. Make as many copies of the printable as you'd like on a variety of brightly colored papers.

2. Work together to cut out the ocean animals. Have everyone write as many ocean facts as they can, one fact per ocean animal from the printable.

3. Read the facts you've all written out loud as you glue each one to your mural.

☺ ☺ ☺ EXPLORATION: Marine Animal Report

For this activity, you will need:

- Visit to the library
- Internet
- Computer or paper and pencils

Fish aren't the only animals that live in the ocean. Lots of animals, including mammals, rely on the sea.

1. Have each child choose a marine animal that is not a fish. Compile a list of questions or information to find out about the animal.

2. Head to the library to find books about their animals on their reading levels. Learn how to search for and locate the books you need using your library's computer system. A librarian may be able to help you if you need it. Either at the library or at home, read your book and take notes on the things you learn.

3. Go online and do a bit more research. Search on reputable sites, like National Geographic and other educational sites. Take more notes about your animal and write down some interesting facts.

4. Depending on their age and abilities, outline the length and expectations, then have them write animal reports about their chosen marine animals. One paragraph per grade is a good rule of thumb. Younger kids may need someone to act as scribe for them. You can also include

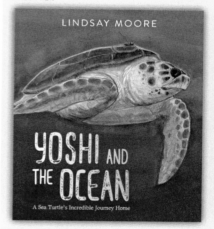

Read Eric Carle's *Mister Seahorse*.

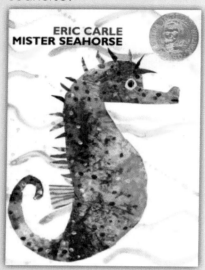

Discuss:

- How and why some species use camouflage
- The species of fish that have their fathers care for them instead of their mothers

You might enjoy *A House for Hermit Crab*, also by Eric Carle.

visuals on your report. Here are a few ideas for the types of information you can include:

- A description of which animal group it belongs to (mammal, fish, invertebrate, etc.)
- A drawing of your animal
- A photograph of your animal
- A list, graph, or chart about lifespan, diet, or predators
- A labeled diagram of body parts
- Special features like camouflage, defense mechanisms, or other special features or abilities
- A scene that shows the animal's habitat
- Any interesting facts you discovered

5. Present your final report to an audience and then add it to the Geography section of your Layers of Learning Notebook.

☺ ☺ ☺ EXPEDITION: Aquarium

For this activity, you will need:

- An aquarium destination

1. Take an expedition to an aquarium to see lots of marine life, both plant and animal.

2. Take time to observe the animals, read about them, and become more acquainted with the life that fills our oceans. If you can't get to an aquarium, at least go to a pet store to see some saltwater fish. Find out what is required to care for marine fish.

☺ ☺ ☺ EXPEDITION: A Trip to the Sea

For this activity, you will need:

- An ocean destination

1. Take a trip to the ocean to see it firsthand. Do this toward the end of your unit so the kids will have all that information fresh in their heads when they see it in real life.

2. Make a point to visit some places along the sea that help them understand the things you've learned, like tide pools, a harbor, and so on. Identify and review the concepts you learned.

Step 3: Show What You Know

During this unit, choose one of the assignments below to show what you have learned during the unit. Add this work to your Layers of Learning Notebook. You can also use this assignment to show your supervising teacher or your charter school as a sample of what you've been working on in your homeschool, if needed.

There are more ideas for writing assignments in the "Writer's Workshop" sidebars.

☺ ☺ Coloring or Narration Page

For this activity, you will need:

- "Oceans" printable from the Printable Pack
- Writing or drawing utensils

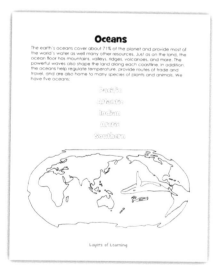

1. Depending on the age and ability of the child, choose either the "Oceans" coloring sheet or the "Oceans" narration page from the Printable Pack.

2. Younger kids can color the coloring sheet as you review some of the things you learned about during this unit. On the bottom of the coloring page, kids can write a sentence about what they learned. Very young children can explain their ideas orally while a parent writes for them.

3. Older kids can write about some of the concepts you learned on the narration page and color the picture as well.

4. Add this to the Geography section of your Layers of Learning Notebook.

Writer's Workshop

Create your own "undiscovered" marine animal. Where does it live? What features does it have to help it survive in its environment? What does it eat?

Name it, draw a picture, write a story, and describe what it's like.

Additional Layer

Place some shells out on a table and have everyone try to draw each of them, paying close attention to each detail.

Famous Folks

Sylvia Earle was the first female chief scientist of the National Oceanic and Atmospheric Administration. She led the first all-female team of scientists to live underwater on the seafloor for several weeks. She also set the record for the deepest dive ever made by a human in 1979.

Unit Trivia Questions

1. How much of the earth's surface is covered by ocean?

   a) 50%

   b) 71%

   c) 79%

   d) 85%

2. Name all five oceans.

   Pacific, Atlantic, Indian, Arctic, Southern

3. Which ocean animal is the largest known mammal in the world?

   The blue whale

4. What is the name of the deepest point in the ocean?

   Challenger Deep (inside the Mariana Trench)

5. True or false - Volcanoes can't erupt underwater because the water cools them and puts out the fire.

   False - About 80% of the volcanic eruptions on Earth occur underwater.

6. Name at least five resources we get from the ocean.

   (Answers will vary)

7. True or false - A lighthouse is more likely to be found on a headland than in a valley.

   True - It would be more visible to ships atop a headland than it would be down low in a valley.

8. What is the number one cause of the rising and falling tides on the earth?

   The gravitational pull of the moon

☺ ☺ ☺ Ocean Lapbook

For this activity, you will need:

- "Ocean Lapbook" printables from the Printable Pack, 4 pages
- File folder or card stock
- Scissors
- Glue stick
- Markers, crayons, or colored pencils

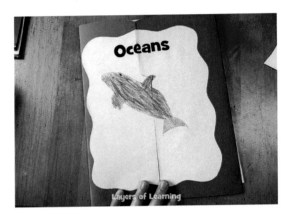

1. Fold a file folder or two pieces of card stock to create a tri-fold booklet. Color the cover printable and then cut it in half, hot dog-style, and glue each half on to the front panels of your file folder.

2. Cut apart the remaining lapbook printables on the solid or heavy lines.

3. Label the ocean zones from memory. Then, color the zones, raw pictures of life found in the zones, or write facts about the zones.

4. Create a mini-book on something about the oceans or coast you learned during this unit. Each little page should have its own fact. Fold the booklet accordion-style.

5. Write and draw a different fact about oceans on each of the square cards. Then, cut them apart. Cut out the pocket on the solid lines and fold on the dashed lines. The fact cards will fit inside the pocket.

6. Create three flap books on "Plants of the Ocean", "Animals of the Ocean," and "The Ocean Floor." One inside page is provided, but you can cut paper to size and add many more pages if you'd like.

7. Make "An Ocean Food Chain" by creating a link of who eats who in the ocean. Start with plankton or algae.

8. Arrange all the parts of your lapbook in the inside pages of the file folder any way you'd like.

9. Finally, choose one of the maps of the ocean you created earlier in this unit to glue to the back of your

lapbook.

10. Present your completed lapbook to an audience. Be prepared to take questions at the end of your presentation.

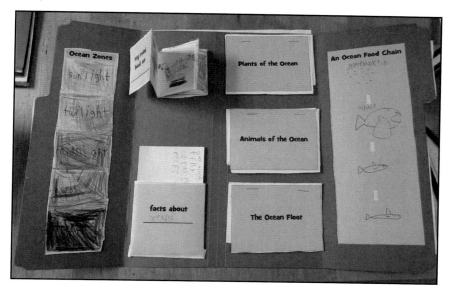

☺ ☺ ☺Big Book of Knowledge

For this activity, you will need:

- "Big Book of Knowledge: Oceans" printable from the Printable Pack, printed on card stock
- Writing or drawing utensils
- Big Book of Knowledge

1. Color, draw on, or write on the Big Book of Knowledge page. Record concepts, definitions, and facts you learned during this unit. It's a record of the things you learned and hope to remember. Add the page to your Big Book of Knowledge.

2. Use your Big Book of Knowledge regularly to help you review, quiz, or create games that will help you commit the things you've learned to memory.

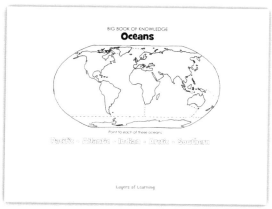

Big Book of Knowledge

The Big Book of Knowledge is a book for you, the mentor, to use as a constant review of all of the things you're learning about. You can use it to quiz your kids or prepare tests or review games. Whenever you learn something in Layers of Learning that you want your kids to remember, add it to your Big Book of Knowledge.

Assemble your Big Book of Knowledge in a binder or with binder rings. Divide it into sections for each subject.

In the Printable Pack for this unit you will find a "Big Book of Knowledge" sheet. You can add this sheet to others you collect or create yourself as you progress through the Layers of Learning curriculum. Customize the Big Book of Knowledge to your family by adding facts and topics that you enjoyed exploring as you were learning.

Visit Layers of Learning online to find more information on how to assemble and use your own Big Book of Knowledge.

You will also find cover and section pages to print along with creative games to play with your Big Book of Knowledge to keep school, even the tests, fun!

Glossary

Aquatic: relating to water   215

Archipelago: a group or chain of islands that occur in a cluster   135

Arch: natural bridge made of stone that is created when water wears away the underside of a rock   249

Assimilation: rejecting all or part of a native culture and adopting the culture of the host in order to fit in   170

Atoll: a ring-shaped island formed of coral on the top of a sunken undersea mountain   129

Basin: a depression or dip in the earth's surface with sides higher than the middle, sometimes basins are filled with water   169

Beach: a pebbly or sandy shore   249

Biodiversity hotspot: a place where many species are threatened by human activity   125

Biomes: geographical regions with dominant plant and animal populations due to the climate   209

Blowhole: when a sea cave grows into a vertical shaft leading to the land above   249

Boreal forest: (taiga) a region of mostly coniferous trees in the high latitudes or in mountains with very cold winters and warm or hot summers   74, 211

Cardinal directions: the four main compass points - north, south, east, and west   26

Climate: the average temperature and precipitation a place receives over a 30-year period   153

Compass rose: a circle that is printed on a map that shows the points of a compass, or cardinal directions, in relation to the map   26

Continental climate: cold, snowy winters, warm to hot summers   154

Continental island: lies on the continental shelf and is completely surrounded by water   135

Continental shelf: the area of seabed around a large landmass where the sea is relatively shallow compared with the open ocean   247

Continent: large masses of land, mostly surrounded by water   32

Coral island: built of coral reef that has emerged from the sea   135

Craton: ancient continental rock from the Precambrian Period. These are the core of the continents   95

Deciduous forest: a forest with trees that lose their foliage at the end of the growing season   74

Demi-: means less (or almost, but not quite); demigod means almost a god   18

Desert climate: cold to warm winters and hot summers, very little rain   154

Desert: land with sparse vegetation that gets less than 10 inches (25 cm) of rain per year   50, 103, 211

Drought: a prolonged period of low rainfall that leads to a water shortage   68

Elevation: distance above sea level   158

Endemic: a species that is native and only lives in one place on earth   49, 126

Equator: an imaginary line around the earth that divides it into northern and southern hemispheres, equally distant from both poles   17

Erosion: when earthen materials are worn away and transported by natural forces like wind or water   41

Ethnic group: a large group of people who identify with one another because they have a common language, culture, and history   170

Fault: a crack in the earth between two rocks   249

Floe: frozen block of saltwater that is floating freely on the surface   225

Flood: a large amount of overflowing water that travels beyond its normal confines   68

Flow resource: a resource that will always exist but that moves because of the natural

People

About the Authors

Michelle and Karen are sisters from Idaho, USA. They grew up playing in the woods and on the lakes of the northern Rockies. Karen is married with four children, two boys and two girls. Michelle is married with six kids, all boys.

Michelle has a BS in biology and Karen has a BA in education. Since the early 2000s, they have been homeschooling their kids and taking them to the lake as often as possible.

In 2008, at a family reunion (at the lake, of course), they were opining about all the things they wished they could have in a homeschool curriculum. Their mom suggested they write their own curriculum. They looked at each other in doubt, then thought, "Why not?" And Layers of Learning was born. Thanks, Mom.

Visit **Layers-of-Learning.com** for more family-style curriculum, planners, and resources to add to every unit.